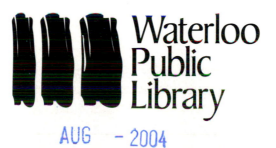

How It Works®

Science and Technology

Third Edition

Marshall Cavendish
99 White Plains Road
Tarrytown, NY 10591

Website: www.marshallcavendish.com

Third edition updated by Brown Reference Group plc.

Library of Congress Cataloging-in-Publication Data
How it works: science and technology.—3rd ed.
p. cm.
Includes index.
ISBN 0-7614-7314-9 (set)   ISBN 0-7614-7332-7 (Vol. 18)
1. Technology—Encyclopedias. 2. Science—Encyclopedias.
[1. Technology—Encyclopedias. 2. Science—Encyclopedias.]
T9 .H738 2003
603—dc21   2001028771

Consultant: Donald R. Franceschetti, Ph.D., University of Memphis

Brown Reference Group
Editor: Wendy Horobin
Associate Editors: Paul Thompson, Martin Clowes, Lis Stedman, Dawn Titmus
Managing Editor: Tim Cooke
Design: Alison Gardner
Picture Research: Becky Cox
Illustrations: Mark Walker, Darren Awuah

Marshall Cavendish
Project Editor: Peter Mavrikis
Production Manager: Alan Tsai
Editorial Director: Paul Bernabeo

Printed in Malaysia
Bound in the United States of America
08 07 06 05 04   6 5 4 3 2

Title picture: Surgeons transplanting a liver, see *Transplant*

How It Works®

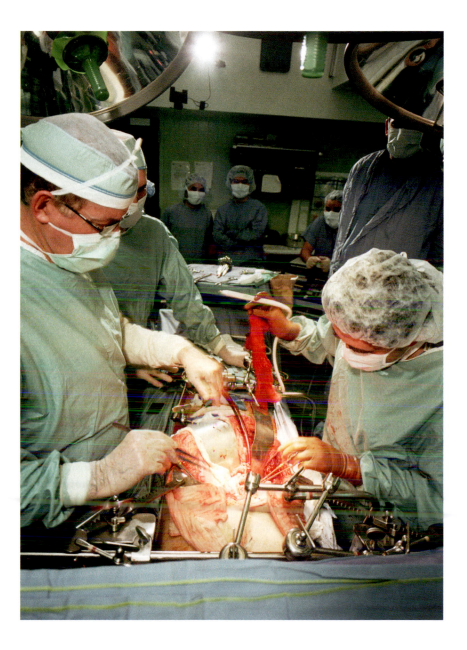

Science and Technology

Volume 18

Tire

Video Camera

Marshall Cavendish

New York • London • Toronto • Sydney

Contents

Volume 18

Tire

The pneumatic tire was invented by a Scot, R. W. Thomson, and first patented by him in 1845. A set of tires made according to Thomson's design was fitted to a horse-drawn carriage and covered more than 1,000 miles (1,600 km) before it needed replacing. It was not until nearly 50 years later, however, that the tire industry was founded by J. B. Dunlop, an Irishman from Belfast.

A vehicle tire consists of an inner layer of fabric plies that are wrapped around bead wires at their inner edges. The bead wires hold the tire in position on the wheel rim. The fabric plies are coated with rubber, which is molded to form the sidewalls and the tread of the tire. There are two main types of tires. In the cross-ply, or bias, tire, the plies run diagonally from bead to bead, making an angle of around 40 degrees to the beads. Successive plies run in opposite directions to give a crisscross pattern. With the radial-ply tire, the plies run directly from bead to bead at 90 degrees to the tire circumference. Tread-bracing layers, or belts, are fitted around the circumference of the tire between the radial plies and the tread. The radial-ply design offers significantly better cornering and wear characteristics than the bias tire and is rapidly replacing it for automotive use. Some of the advantages of the radial-ply tire are offered by the bias-belted tire that has cross plies with a tread belt.

Making a tire involves three separate stages: preparation of the components, assembly into the shape of a tire, and heating with sulfur in a suit-

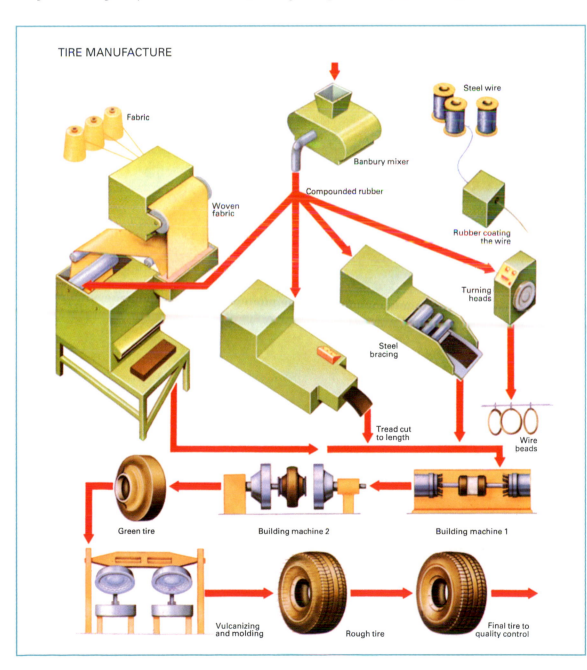

TIRE MANUFACTURE

Fabric

Steel wire

Banbury mixer

Compounded rubber

Woven fabric

Rubber coating the wire

Turning heads

Steel bracing

Tread cut to length

Wire beads

Green tire

Building machine 2

Building machine 1

Vulcanizing and molding

Rough tire

Final tire to quality control

◄ Tire production involves three separate stages: fabric preparation, preparation of the rubber mixes, and the actual building of the tire. The mixes are made first, and then the compounded rubber is braced with steel and fabric before moving on to the building, molding, and completion stages.

◄ Treadless slicks give the best grip for high-speed motor racing in dry conditions. When rain makes the track greasy, drivers have to enter the pits to have the tires changed for ones with a tread pattern.

able mold to vulcanize the rubber. During vulcanization, the rubber in the tire structure combines with the sulfur, a process that sets it in its final pattern and gives the rubber components the required physical properties.

The main materials in tire construction are steel wire for the inextensible beads, textile fabric or steel for the casing and reinforcing breakers, and rubber mixed with various additives to give the required strength and resistance to wear and fatigue. For tire casings, rayon, nylon, Kevlar, and polyester are the most commonly used materials, although thin steel cable is often used in truck tires. The tread belt is usually made of steel in truck tires and car tires, but rayon and other materials, such as glass fiber, are also used in car tires. The rubber mixes are made from synthetic rubbers for car tires; heavier truck tires are made of natural rubber, which runs cooler than synthetic rubbers.

Rubber mixes

The first operation is to prepare the rubber mixes by working the rubber into a plastic state in an internal mixer and milling into it sulfur for vulcanization and other ingredients for the different types of rubber mixes needed in the various parts of the tire. In the tread, a high loading of finely powdered carbon black is used to give resistance to tread wear, with the tread mix being chosen to give the required combination of wear characteristics and wet and dry grip. These conflicting requirements result in a compromise. An alternative solution tried by some manufacturers uses a

▲ High-performance tires are made to strict safety standards. In many countries, drivers are legally required to change their tires when the tread has worn down to a specified minimum.

combination of rubbers for the tread area. With tubeless tires, the inner surface of the tire and the bead are covered with a soft rubber mix to give good sealing between the bead and the wheel and to provide sealing around any object that punctures the tire, thus reducing the risk of sudden deflation and loss of control of the vehicle.

The casing rubbers are mixed to give strength in the thin layers that bond the casing cords together and to give resistance to fatigue under repeated flexings and continuous tension. For use on the bead wires, a hard mix with a high sulfur content is prepared that will set into a solid mass on molding under heat and pressure.

The bead wires are prepared from high-tensile steel wire assembled as a ribbon of five or six strands, side by side, and enclosed in the hard rubber mix to form a tape. A number of runs of this tape are wound up on a former of the correct size, and on vulcanization, the bead is set in a solid and virtually unstretchable form.

As well as holding the tire on the rim, the bead wires provide structural strength, so their breaking force must never be exceeded.

Fabric preparation

Cotton, which was originally used, has been replaced in tire casings by synthetic textiles, which are made of long, continuous filaments and have much greater strength for a given thickness than the old cotton thread spun from a collection of short, hairlike fibers.

The material for the plies and for the breakers consists of a practically weftless fabric, with the strength all in the warp and with the sheet held together only by a system of fine, widely spaced weft threads. This construction is used to eliminate the knuckles that occur in a normal cross-woven fabric (where warp and weft threads cross) and to reduce the sawing and chafing that take place when such a fabric is flexed under load. The sheet of weftless fabric is made into a sandwich, between two films of rubber, in a calendering operation (pressing between rollers). The rubber-coated fabric is then cut into strips, with the threads running in one direction, for use in building up the casings of the different types of tires.

Tire building

Both radial- and cross-ply tires are built up on collapsible steel formers. The layers of fabric plies are secured by turning the edges around the coil of bead wire. The structure is then enclosed in suitable reinforcing and packing strips.

The process of adding the smooth strip of extruded rubber compound that will form the tread differs in the two types of tires. The cross-ply receives its tread while still on the almost-flat building drum. Afterward the complete cylindrical tire is shaped into the usual doughnut (toroidal) form as it is introduced into the mold. The radial-ply tire requires different treatment. Here the casing must be taken from the nearly flat cylindrical building drum and shaped into the required toroidal form before the unstretchable rigid bracing bands are added. The tread is then fitted on top of these bands.

The final stage in tire manufacture consists of molding the built-up raw tire in a suitably designed steel shell mold. The mold is either engraved with the tread and wall pattern or has die castings riveted inside it to make up the complicated pattern of ribs, blocks, grooves, and fine slots that give the final tire its all-important road grip and even-wear characteristics.

The mold is in a press containing a cylindrical rubber diaphragm that is inflated under high pressure inside the tire as the mold closes. This operation forces the raw plastic tire into the pattern on the inside of the mold. Heat is then applied, in the form of steam, both from cavities in the press through the outer mold and from the inside of the diaphragm within the tire. This heating causes the chemical combination of the rubber with the sulfur that has been included in the various rubber mixes in the components of the tire. The result, when the molding is finished, is a tire of permanent shape and of specific physical properties for its intended use.

Provided that the main body, or carcass, of the tire is not damaged, a worn tire can be retreaded for further use. In this process, the tread and wall rubber is stripped from the tire body and a new tread and wall layer bonded on. With heavy-duty truck tires, the tread rubber is often made thick enough to allow the tread pattern to be recut when the top layer has become worn.

Safety tires

The outstanding weakness of the pneumatic tire has always been the risk of puncture. The sudden deflation of tires, as when a blowout occurs, can cause loss of control to the vehicle. Various safety tires have been developed. Most rely on the use of locking devices to keep the tire on the wheel rim when it has deflated, giving a measure of stability and steering control. Some designs allow the tire to be run at low speeds in a flat state for some distance to reach a service station. Recently, self-sealing tires that prevent air from escaping if a puncture or leak occurs have been developed.

Faithfully holding the road

It is not only the automobile tire that strains the abilities of tire manufacturers. The tires of ordinary motorcycles are even more violently stressed than those of high-powered automobiles. It is in Formula 1 racing cars, however, that tires are pushed to the limit of their capabilities. Paradoxically, these tires are made by traditional methods, but their outstanding performance depends much on the conditions of track racing.

Carefully smoothed track surfaces allow modern racing cars to be so aerodynamically designed that a downforce of as much as twice the weight of the car may be generated at top speeds of about 185 mph (300 km/h). This force greatly increases the rate of heat input (roughly proportional to load and exactly proportional to speed) but yields a huge increase in cornering power.

In a slow corner, a car may sustain a lateral force equal to perhaps one and a half times its own weight, which may be expressed as a lateral acceleration of 1.5 g. In a fast bend, the force may exceed 2.5 g. Curiously, the tremendous heat generated actually makes tire design easy.

The tread compound, or mixture, can be formulated to suit the expected high temperatures, and the driver can warm the tires quickly to the designed operating temperature. Today inflation pressures have to be high, and the tire carcass has to be tremendously strong to withstand the forces.

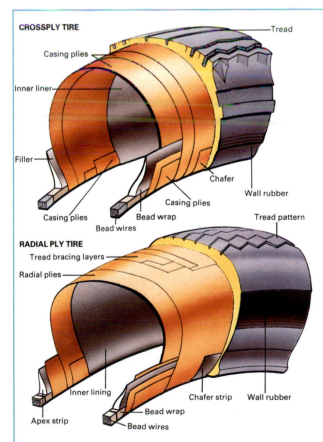

CROSSPLY TIRE — Tread — Casing plies — Inner liner — Filler — Casing plies — Bead wrap — Bead wires — Chafer — Wall rubber — Casing plies — Tread pattern

RADIAL PLY TIRE — Tread bracing layers — Radial plies — Inner lining — Apex strip — Bead wrap — Bead wires — Chafer strip — Wall rubber

CROSS-PLY AND RADIAL TIRES

Radial-ply tires (bottom) differ from cross-ply tires (top) in that they have very flexible sidewalls and a stiff, braced tread. Both are built up on steel formers and layers of fabric. The rubber is laid onto cross-ply tires before it is bent into a circular shape; the radial tires are coated after shaping and bracing with rigid bands across the width of the tire.

In these circumstances, radial-ply tires might appear the obvious choice, but many racing cars are fitted with bias-ply tires that, although older in concept, are more suitable to retain the wide, specialized profile. In single-seater racing, however, radial-ply tires are coming to the fore, and they are now the rule for every kind of road-going production car.

Before radials could become the rule, much research was necessary to overcome the shortcomings inherent in the original concept. It had always been a handicap that the belt cords of a radial had to be angled away from the circumferential cords, usually by 18 to 22 degrees. Inclined in successive layers (eventually reduced to two in belts made of steel cords), these angled cords gave the tire strength by completing a triangulation with the radial cords of the body plies running across the tire from bead to bead.

In theory, the belt should be inextensible and laterally stiff, a beam capable of distortion only in radial flexure. The angled set of the cords, nevertheless, allowed some of the distortion that a bias-ply tire suffers, so the simple radial cords of the sidewall had to be modified by additional stiffening. Thus, the compromise between ride comfort and grip remained in force: the road-holding and handling properties of a radial could easily be improved by making the tire wider in relation to its height (by giving it a lower aspect ratio), but the ride would be harsh.

Manufacturers sought to develop a carcass that was as nearly as possible evenly stressed throughout. Goodyear produced the neutral contour tire (NCT), with an elliptical cross section allowing easy flexure for ride comfort despite high inflation pressures for stability and fuel economy. Michelin's design stipulated a special wheel rim with a bead flange sloping outward. To keep the tire's shape under control, a laterally stiff belt was needed. Both edges of the lower belt ply were folded up (very difficult in steel) over the cut edges of the upper belt. Varying the widths of the overlaps, or hems, and the angles of the cords gave the desired control. Michelin's development led to the TRX, in which only the narrower cut belt is steel. The wider one with upfolded edges is made of the much more manageable aramid fiber Kevlar, which is light and flexible yet tremendously strong in tension.

It was in another synthetic fiber, the more familiar nylon, that the real answer lay. By devising a method of prestressing nylon cords so that they were always in tension and running them as a bandage around the outside of the belt, the Pirelli company was eventually able to bring belt distortion under control.

The nylon bandage prevented longitudinal stretch, leaving the steel belt plies to do their basic job as a laterally stiff girder beam because they were restrained to maintain their flat (or other chosen) profile. With the tread so stabilized, the sidewalls could at last function with true independence and were redesigned to become the ultimate in radially pliant and laterally stiff sidewalls, flexing much as bellows do.

Pirelli has also used the same nylon bandage construction to make an energy-efficient tire—the P8. The P8 absorbs less energy, so it gives lower fuel consumption. This low-impact tire achieves this economy at no cost to performance, safety, or durability.

Recent developments

Some tire manufacturers have developed a new technique to make tires that skips many of the intermediate steps. Certain Goodyear factories, for example, use a hot former that applies 12 of the 23 components of a truck tire in one continuous strip of rubber.

Apart from self-sealing tires, mentioned above, new technologies include computer software to optimize tread design, casing shape, materials, and construction based on performance needs; tires that use a single, continuous strand of bead wire (instead of several strands or one with an overlapping joint) to improve control and steering response; and tires that contain a higher-structure carbon than the carbon black used to reinforce conventional tires—it resists wear better and thus extends the tire's life.

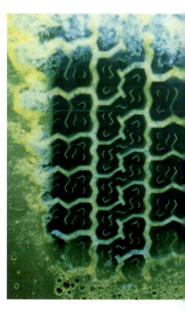

◀ A DC-10 jet airplane tire being tested under wet weather conditions. Airplane tires are built to withstand heavy impacts at high landing speeds.

▼ Tire manufacturers thoroughly test prototypes of new tires before going into full production. These photographs of the footprints of two tires reveal the relative effectiveness of the tread patterns at dispersing water in wet conditions.

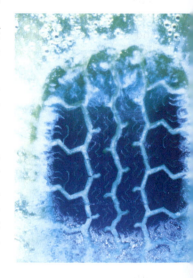

 SEE ALSO: AUTOMOBILE • FIBER, SYNTHETIC • RACING CAR AND DRAGSTER • RUBBER, NATURAL • STEERING SYSTEM • TRUCK

Toilet

◀ Even the bathroom is becoming a high-tech zone, complete with toilets that have heated seats and automated cleansing functions. The Japanese are the leaders in developing advanced toilet technology—the Toto company has a model that can check the user's health on site. Instead of urine immediately being flushed away, it is analyzed for a variety of medical conditions.

The toilet, consisting of a bowl and flush mechanism, has a long but not well-documented history. Generally, attempts to dispose of wastes through the flushing action of water have been associated with plans to supply water and to carry away sewage. Neolithic people appear to have used latrines recessed in the walls of stone huts (in the Orkneys, Britain), and crude disposal ditches have been discovered. Comparatively advanced latrines have been discovered in Crete, Greece, in the Palace of Knossos, dating from Minoan times, and one of them seems to have been a cistern and flushing device. Water-flushed latrines have been discovered in ancient (2500–1500 B.C.E.) cities in the Indus Valley, and Rome had such devices in the fourth century C.E. The presence of such toilets required a prodigious water supply—360 gallons (1,360 l) per person per day.

Relatively sophisticated systems of this sort generally fell into disuse as the civilizations that produced them failed. Early replacements included the garderobe (or wardrobe), which was built into the thick walls of a medieval house or castle and consisted of a seat over a vertical shaft. Where possible, the shaft was arranged to drop into a stream or moat; otherwise there might be a pit, which would be cleaned out at infrequent intervals. Later various types of water-flushing systems were introduced, and drainage networks were gradually introduced in larger towns. Often wastes were accumulated in a cesspit that had to be emptied when it eventually became full.

Flushing systems

Early designs of flush closets were the type with a valve between the pan and the waste pipe that opened for disposal of the contents with a water flush. The widespread use of such systems, however, was dependent on the availability of suitable sewerage systems, which started to become widespread only in the middle of the 19th century. By 1870, the future of the modern flush toilet was assured when inventors and engineers took up the competition to fulfill public sanitation requirements. Strange creations came on the market, for example, Twyford's earthenware device, which had a shallow bowl that held about an inch of water. The syphonic toilet with fast and slow flush, also patented in 1870, superseded Twyford's model. The Reverend Henry Moule had already invented an earth toilet in 1860: a wooden seat led to a bucket beneath, and there was a hopper above and behind the seat. Pulling the handle made a layer of fine earth, cinder, or ashes fall down into the bucket.

The valve-controlled tank toilet eventually won the day, however, and the technology of most toilets starts here. The operation of the flush

◀ A 19th-century earthenware toilet. A hand lever opens the valve at the pan base.

▼ A cross section of a typical airplane toilet. The tank is flushed and cleaned by a pump situated on top of a filter. Out in space, NASA engineers had more trouble developing a zero-gravity toilet than any other piece of equipment on board the space shuttle. The version installed in *Endeavour* cost $23.4 million to develop.

after each flushing action, and the float, which rises with the water level, cuts off the water supply at the correct level so the tank does not overflow.

Modern toilets, based on the principles of the siphon, have replaced the old units in most countries. A siphon is an arrangement of airtight tubing that permits water to be transferred from a high position to a low position over a separating obstacle. The system normally consists of a short rising length of tubing that reaches a crown and then turns down into a longer leg. Water forced to the crown through the short leg falls down the long leg, leaving a low-pressure area in the long leg, and thus, more water is forced up the short leg by atmospheric pressure.

Today's flush toilets incorporate siphon tanks, which are described as valveless discharging apparatus. The tank contains a siphon with a short leg of tubing leading from a barrel to the crown and into the long leg, which descends to the flush pipe. The barrel is a closed-off chamber fitted with a sealing disk at the bottom and leading at the top to the short leg of the siphon. The disk is attached to an operating lever. When the lever is operated, the disk rises to the top of the barrel and forces water into the short leg of the siphon,

mechanism is simple in that a plug (valve) is drawn from the opening at the bottom of the tank to release about 2 gallons (7.5 l) of water into the bowl. Waste is sent into the disposal pipe. The valve is weighted and pivoted so that, when it is released, it drops back into the opening in the pipe and prevents more water from leaving the tank. The tank is automatically filled with water

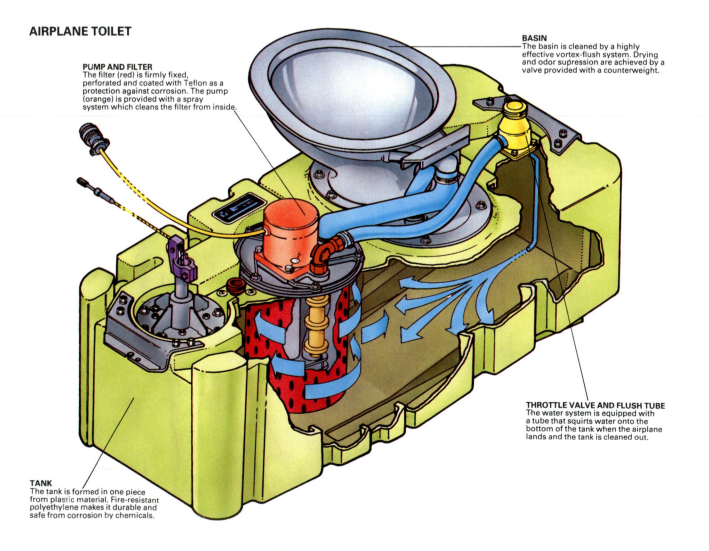

AIRPLANE TOILET

PUMP AND FILTER
The filter (red) is firmly fixed, perforated and coated with Teflon as a protection against corrosion. The pump (orange) is provided with a spray system which cleans the filter from inside.

BASIN
The basin is cleaned by a highly effective vortex-flush system. Drying and odor suppression are achieved by a valve provided with a counterweight.

THROTTLE VALVE AND FLUSH TUBE
The water system is equipped with a tube that squirts water onto the bottom of the tank when the airplane lands and the tank is cleaned out.

TANK
The tank is formed in one piece from plastic material. Fire-resistant polyethylene makes it durable and safe from corrosion by chemicals.

FLUSHING MECHANISMS

There are two main mechanisms used in flushing a toilet, and the method used is influenced by the water regulations of a particular country.

The wash-down bowl depends on equal atmospheric pressure on both sides of the trap. Water flowing into the bowl causes its contents to be flushed past the trap and down the soil pipe. The double-trap siphonic type uses the venturi effect of the air in the tube to create a partial vacuum, which in turn causes the siphoning action into the lower trap.

Efforts to conserve water have led to research into more efficient cisterns that use less water. Another alternative is to reuse "grey" water from baths and rain guttering that has been collected and undergone primary treatment on site. It is delivered to the toilet by a separate pipe system.

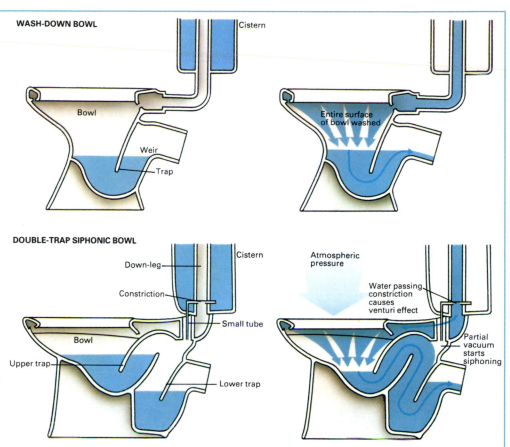

WASH-DOWN BOWL — Cistern, Bowl, Weir, Trap, Entire surface of bowl washed

DOUBLE-TRAP SIPHONIC BOWL — Down-leg, Cistern, Constriction, Bowl, Small tube, Upper trap, Lower trap, Atmospheric pressure, Water passing constriction causes venturi effect, Partial vacuum starts siphoning

setting off the action. Water is forced by atmospheric pressure from the tank through one-way flaps in the disk into the siphon until the water level drops sufficiently for air to enter the barrel.

Siphons are made of copper, high-density polyethylene, or ceramic ware. The materials and design of all soil appliances must conform to national or international standards. The parts of a toilet must be durable, impervious to water, and resistant to corrosion. The design must include a smooth surface to facilitate cleaning and self-cleaning by flushing and simplicity so that there are no dirt-catching crannies. The two main types of bowls are the wash-down pedestal and the siphonic pedestal. In the wash-down design, water from the flush pipe is distributed around the bowl by a flushing rim, and the water flow washes the bowl contents through the water trap and down the soil pipe. In the siphonic design, the down leg beyond the water trap is made so that, at the start of the flush, it is filled with water, giving a siphon action that assists the wash down.

An alternative arrangement uses a double-trap system to provide the siphon effect. With both designs, the trap remains full of water to provide a seal from the soil pipe, so preventing the entry of foul air. Ventilation pipes may be provided to maintain the trap against siphonage effects in systems with long soil pipes. Where direct connection to normal soil systems is impracticable,

special toilets fitted with an electric macerating unit can be used. This design reduces solid wastes to a fine slurry that can be carried along narrow pipework before connection to the soil pipe.

Alternative designs

Although the pedestal toilet with a seat has been widely adopted, the alternative squat toilet—in its simplest form consisting of raised foot positions in a shallow bowl with a central drain—is still preferred in some countries.

Toilets with minimal flush and a simple drop evacuation mechanism, assisted by vacuum, are used in airplanes to conserve scarce water. The amount of water used can be as low as 0.5 gallons (2 l). Modern regulations tend to require lower flushes even on domestic toilets, with 1.5 gallons (6 l) rapidly becoming standard.

Computerized toilets of great sophistication are popular in Japan, with some manufacturers now exporting to the United States. A water-spray cleansing cycle is built in, as is a heated air dryer, heated seat, and deodorizer. The water pressure and temperature can be regulated using a control pad. Some models have remote controls, and the lid can be automatically opened and closed.

SEE ALSO: DRAINAGE • SIPHON • WASTEWATER TREATMENT

Tool Manufacture

People have been making tools for half a million years, and the general shape and application of modern hand tools were formulated as long ago as Roman times. Most ancient tools are instantly recognizable for what they are by today's craftspeople. Hand tools are an excellent example of ergonomic design—the worker knows better than anyone what type of tool is easiest to use, and craftspeople often made their own tools until the Industrial Revolution in the 19th century.

The earliest manufactured tool was probably the ax, made of flint or stone in Neolithic times (4000–5000 B.C.E.). An early example of the specialization of tools was the development of the adze, a primitive type of chisel. In comparison with the ax blade, which was securely mounted to a handle with the cutting edge parallel to it, the adze was more lightly bound, with the cutting edge at a right angle to the handle. The ax was designed to split wood, and the adze was invented to remove strips of wood in order to shape it.

The saw and the bow drill were developed in ancient Egypt. Saws were made of copper or bronze, and the teeth were sharpened on the back edge so that the cutting took place as the worker pulled the saw inward, to avoid buckling the soft metal. An early advance in technology was the setting of the saw teeth in alternate directions; this type of blade, in carrying away the sawdust and leaving a kerf (saw-slot) slightly wider than the saw blade, reduced friction. Early carpenters, having no screws or nails, secured their constructions with wooden dowels (round pegs). The bow drill was used as long ago as 3000 B.C.E. for carrying out various drilling operations.

Planes

In the first century C.E., Roman craftspeople already possessed a range of carpenter's planes not much different from those of today—with a wedged cutting iron and a cleared-away holding stock to allow the unrestricted escape of shavings. About 1860 in Boston, Massachusetts, an American toolmaker, Leonard Bailey, filed the first of several patents for bench planes. His name can still be found on many factory-made planes as an acknowledgment of his contribution.

The modern bench plane is made up of a steel cutting blade set into a triangular casting, called a frog, which in turn is mounted on the plane base.

The blade is pressed from carbon–chrome steel, is surface ground to a precise thickness, and has a beveled cutting edge, hardened and tempered. The edge must be honed by the user, the factory edge being unsuitable for fine work. The frog and the base are cast from gray iron and machined on the appropriate surfaces to provide accurate seating of the frog and to provide smoothness on the bottom of the plane, the sole, which comes into contact with the wood. In some designs, the cutting edge is presharpened, and a disposable blade is clamped in place on the frog. With wooden planes, the frog is cut into the body (stock) of the plane. Molding planes have profiled cutters, ground to shape for cutting various standard sections.

Hammers

A hammer is a striking tool used to drive nails into wood and to work metals and other materials. It comprises a shaft, which acts as a lever-extension of the user's arm, and a hardened and tempered steel head. The shaft is usually made of straight-grained ash or hickory wood—these timbers have high cross-sectional strength with a degree of resilience to absorb shock. Hardened metal tubing and glass-fiber-reinforced plastics are also used.

Hammerheads are made by drop forging using carbon tool steel; forging the steel while it is in a hot state of plasticity improves the molecular structure, causing the grain flow to redistribute itself for best mechanical properties. Heat treatment of the hammer face prevents it from breaking up or chipping when it is struck against other metal objects. The hammerhead is usually fastened to the shaft by means of three wedges: a large wooden wedge and two smaller ones made of malleable metal, which act to spread the wood in the eye section of the head.

There are many types of hammers, but the most common are the carpenter's claw hammer and the peen hammer. The carpenter's hammer has a split claw opposite the face, specially designed to pull out nails. Straight and cross peen hammers have wedge-shaped blades opposite the striking face, and the ball peen is rounded. A softer action is provided with hammers that have heads made of rubber, rawhide, or plastic. The carpenter's mallet has a wooden head on a wooden shaft.

Files

Flat files for woodworking were made of copper in Egypt as long ago as 1500 B.C.E. Modern files for removing stock from wooden or metal surfaces are pressed from strip steel. The specialized pressing operation results in a corrugated surface, and the high spots are sharpened by grinding; the blade is then hardened and tempered. Some files are produced with tangs (prongs) on the end for wooden handles, and others with holes in each end for fastening to wooden or diecast frames.

The diversity of files is enormous. The cross-section of the blade and the shape of the teeth are determined by the intended use of the tool. Single-cut files have a series of parallel teeth set at an angle of about 75 degrees to the file axis. With double-cut files, a second set of teeth is cut at an angle of about 45 degrees to the first to give a series of small, pointed teeth. Rasps have a large number of individual rounded teeth formed by a punching action. Mill or saw files are used to sharpen teeth on saw blades, for lathe work, and for smooth filing in general. Knife files have a cross section like a knife blade and are used by tool-and-die makers in corners and for cleaning worn screw threads. Bastard files, rasps, and wood files have coarse teeth for rapid removal of stock. Curved tooth files come in several varieties— when moved across the work toward one edge, they remove stock rapidly; in the other diagonal

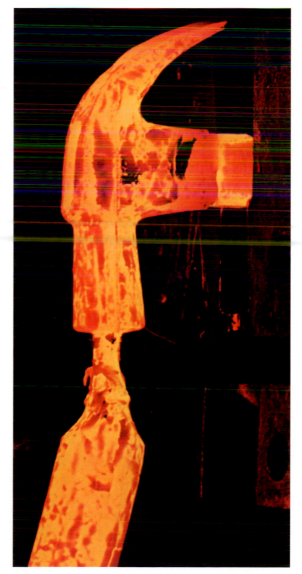

◀ Forging a hammerhead from a bar of steel that has been heated to a state of plasticity.

direction, they leave a smoother finish. Special-purpose files are made in many cross-sectional shapes, including square, triangular, half-round, round, and rat-tail (round and tapered). In the shaping tool, the teeth take the form of a large number of small cutting edges with an action similar to that of a plane blade.

Wrenches

Wrenches come in various sizes and are used for turning nuts and bolts. They are always forged of high-quality steel for strength. One-piece wrenches are either open ended or box ended (enclosed), for more gripping power where there is room to fit the box shape over the nut. A combination wrench has one end open and a box of the same size at the other end. The open end on a wrench is usually offset at an angle to the body for more versatility when the nut or bolt is hard to reach. As the name suggests, the adjustable wrench has parallel jaws that can be adjusted relative to each other by a screw action to fit a range of bolt sizes. The pipe wrench has hardened adjustable jaws that can tilt under the application of force, with the tilting action increasing the grip.

An Allen wrench, or Allen key, is a hardened and tempered piece of hexagonal tool steel that fits into a matching hexagonal recess in the head of an Allen screw.

Saws

Saw blades are stamped out of high-quality steel strip, and teeth are cut into the edge. Lower-price handsaws are of uniform thickness, but better-quality saws have blades that taper away from the

▲ Automatic pointing and parting of a bar during the manufacture of Pozidriv screwdrivers.

◀ Heat treating the heads of sledgehammers to give them extra hardness. The process of heating and cooling—also called tempering—modifies the microstructure of the metal.

tooth edge to give better clearance in the saw cut. Backsaws have the back edge of the blade stiffened with a brass or steel strip. Saw blades are often coated with Teflon to prevent rusting. Without a Teflon coat, the blade has to be protected with a coat of grease or oil when not in use.

The main types of carpenter's saws are the rip saw and the cross-cut saw. Rip saws are designed for sawing wood along the grain and have coarse teeth—around five per inch (per 2.5 cm)—filed to a chisel edge and set with their tips bent over in alternate directions. Cross-cut saws have finer teeth—around seven per inch—sloped on their leading edges at an angle to the blade and set. Other types of handsaws meant for finer work have smaller teeth. In some designs, such as the bow saw, fretsaw, and coping saw, a narrow blade is carried by a separate frame.

Hacksaws are used for cutting metal. The blades have holes in each end by means of which they are held under tension in a steel frame. The American National Standard for hacksaw blades, for example, specifies that blades having 24 or 32 teeth per inch shall be set wavy, and other types shall be alternate set or raker set (every third tooth unset).

A welded composite blade is made of two or more pieces of steel joined together, with a high-speed steel cutting edge welded to a flexible alloy steel backing that is less likely to break. According to the standard, a standard steel blade must contain not more than 1.25 percent tungsten or an equivalent alloy, and a high-speed steel blade must retain its hardness at temperatures up to 1000°F (537°C). For general work, where the blade is not changed for each job, a blade of 18 teeth per in. (7 per cm) is recommended.

Screwdrivers

A screwdriver is a hardened and tempered steel blade, usually made from chrome–vanadium tool steel. The working end is formed by forging or grinding and has a narrow rectangular section made in various sizes to match the slots of screw heads. The handle end of the screwdriver has localized projections called wings formed on the bar. The traditional wooden ball handle is still widely fitted, but injection-molded plastic handles are more common.

Crosshead screwdrivers, such as the Phillips and Pozidriv designs, are variations on the conventional screwdriver in which a winged point has been substituted for the rectangular blade tip. The winged point is formed by milling and driving the point into a sizing die, followed by heat treatment. It complements an equivalent female form in the screw head, giving more positive contact between screw and driver. These designs were developed to allow more torque for high-speed assembly, especially using power-driven tools.

Pliers and cutters

Pliers can be divided into two categories: one for gripping and twisting and one for cutting. Combination pliers can be used for both functions. Pliers have a simple scissor action—the force applied to the handles is magnified to grip the workpiece in the jaws, which may have hardened cutting edges built in. Locking-grip pliers have a cam action that maintains the grip until they are released.

Quality pliers are made of well-forged steel and have a firm joint that does not wobble. Traditionally, there were three types of joints: box joints, lay-on joints, and slip joints.

Box joints, which are seldom made today, are formed by one handle being forged around the other. This joint is traditionally considered to be the firmest. Lay-on, or lap, joints are made by one handle being laid onto the other and riveted. Recent models are considered to be of the same high standard as box-joint pliers. Slip joints are forged in the same way as lay-on joints except that the rivet hole is lengthened and the rivet is not tightened. This enables the two halves to be opened further to give a wider jaw opening.

The geometry of the cutting edge is important, too. The bigger the angle, the stronger the

▼ A batch of heated hacksaw blades is lowered by robot into the quenching vat at a highly automated tool manufacturing plant. Made of high-quality steel, the blades are tempered in the vat to give them additional hardness. The robot, hardening furnaces, quench facility, and conveyor system are constantly monitored by an advanced, computerized program controller, which ensures that high quality and uninterrupted production are maintained at all stages of the process.

◄ A computer-controlled finishing and plating line, which can be programmed to apply platings of nickel, nickel and chrome, or zinc to tools. The tools are slung on the transporter, which moves along a series of baths, dipping the tools into the appropriate baths according to the type of finish required.

cutting edge, but the narrower the angle, the easier it is to cut. With diagonal cutting pliers, for cutting wire, the cutting edge is at a slight angle to the handles, allowing the cut to be made close to a flat surface. In end cutting pliers, also for cutting wire, the cutting edge is at 90 degrees to the handle to allow a very close cropping of the wire.

Utility knives, levels, and punches

Utility knives have a separate hardened and tempered blade of high-carbon steel with a precision-ground cutting edge. The blade is hardened in an electric furnace in an inert atmosphere to prevent surface contamination and then tempered—the cutting edge has the characteristics of a razor blade, but the blade is made of thicker material and is more durable. Blade handles are traditionally diecast with provision for positive location of the blade; some are designed to allow full retraction of the blade when not in use, both for safety and to prevent accidental damage to the blade.

The spirit level assists in achieving true vertical and horizontal planes during construction processes. Adjustable models can be set to check any prescribed angle. The vial, a sealed plastic or glass tube, contains a dyed liquid such as kerosene. The volume of liquid is controlled at the filling

stage to allow an air bubble; the tube is barrel-shaped or formed in a radius to allow the bubble to take a position at the tangent of the radius when level. The vial is securely set and precisely

◄ Replacing six old machines, this CNC (computer numerical control) machining center makes 40 ratchets at a time.

located in a parallel extruded aluminum frame under known level conditions.

Punches are used with a hammer to remove pins, drive out pins through parallel holes, mark out or line up holes, and drive nails below the surface of wood. A rivet set is a combined tool with a long hole, which ensures that the material to be joined is in good contact with the head of the rivet, and a hemispherical dome, which is used to finish off the domed head after the shank of the rivet has been formed. Belt punches are used for making holes in leather, and wad punches are for making larger holes or for cutting out circles in leather or similar materials. Pin pushes are used for driving thin pins without a hammer.

Chisels, braces, and drills

Wood chisels are made of high-carbon tool steel and are forged, hardened, and tempered. A beveled cutting tip is provided, but like that of the blade in the bench plane, it must be honed by the user to his or her requirements. Cold chisels are used for cutting hard materials, such as metal or brickwork, and are made from alloy steel.

A brace is a drilling device made up of a steel body that is bent from bar stock into a crank shape, with a center handle and a bearing-assisted thrust pad on the opposite end from the drill for applying pressure. The crank throw varies from about 6 to 14 in. (15.2–35.5 cm)—the wider the throw, the more torque can be applied.

A hand drill has, instead of a crank, gears that are driven by a cranked handle. The gears are made of annealed (tempered) cast iron or sintered iron (bonded iron particles that have been shaped and partially fused). Both devices have self-centering chucks with jaws held in place by springs.

The part of a drill that makes the holes is called the bit. A greater variety of bits—as well as attachments such as sanders and wire brushes—is made for power drills.

Auger bits for drilling in wood are used in a brace and have a central feed screw that pulls the bit into the wood; cutting edges and spurs remove the wood as chips, which are carried clear by the screw action of the twisted body.

Twist drills generally have two cutting edges formed to a point, with spiral flutes to carry the cut chips away from the cutting edges. High-speed and alloy steel drills can withstand the heating caused by the cutting action better than carbon steels and are generally used in power drills. Hard-alloy cutting tips are used in masonry drills.

Machine cutters

Cutters for use in machine tools are normally made from tool steels that are formed to the required shape, hardened, and ground to give the required cutting edge or edges. Improved performance is given by the use of carbide and ceramic tips that can withstand higher working temperatures and pressures. Such tips are brazed or clamped to the main body of the cutting tool. Diamond tips are used in a similar manner.

▲ A CNC lathe, which is used to manufacture a range of products, including torque wrench components. Because the lathe is so versatile and quick to set up, design changes and new product lines can be arranged very easily.

SEE ALSO: ALLOY • DRILL • LATHE • METALWORKING • SURFACE TREATMENTS • WOODWORKING

Toothpaste

Compositions for cleaning teeth have been known for a long time—Hippocrates (430–377 B.C.E.) recognized the value of powdered marble (calcium carbonate) for cleaning teeth, and this compound in various forms has been used ever since. In the Middle Ages, various strange mixtures, often with names such as Magistery of Pearls, Dragon's Blood, and Powdered Crab's Eyes, were rubbed onto the teeth to make them look cleaner and sweeten the breath.

Prophylactic toothpastes

The latter half of the 20th century saw the function of toothpaste change from being purely cosmetic to prophylactic—disease-preventing. Modern toothpastes have three functions: they remove plaque, the sticky film that harbors decay-causing bacteria; they strengthen tooth enamel against acid attack; and they contain components that enable teeth to repair themselves by a process of remineralization.

Compositions

Toothpastes neither bleach nor alter the natural color of the teeth; they clean by removing the accumulated film from the surface and may also heighten the luster by polishing.

The most important cleaning and polishing agent in toothpastes is an insoluble mineral powder. Often this is calcium carbonate, which is mildly abrasive as well as being an antacid, or it may be a phosphate salt, a hydrated aluminum oxide, or especially in the clear-gel types of toothpastes, a silicate or silica gel. The precise shape and size distribution of the particles are carefully controlled by the manufacturer both to get the best cleaning effect when the particles are brushed over the surface of the tooth and to make sure that the teeth will not be damaged. The part of the tooth normally above the gum margin, the crown, is covered with a hard layer of enamel. Beneath the enamel of the tooth crown is a softer tissue called dentine. Particularly in older people, the dentine of the tooth root may sometimes be exposed along the margins of the gums, and so toothpaste must be able to clean this soft dentine as well as the harder crown enamel without damaging either. A good polish on the teeth is important not merely for appearance but also because it will reduce the ease with which bacteria can anchor themselves to the tooth surface.

In addition to the cleaning and polishing constituents, toothpastes today usually contain a water-binding material (humectant), such as glyc-

◄ Toothpastes have a number of ingredients, the most important of which is a polishing agent. It is usually a mild abrasive, such as hydrated silica particles, that will help to remove stains and plaque without damaging the tooth surface. Detergents are used to loosen food debris, and therapeutic agents, such as fluoride, are added to keep the teeth and gums healthy.

erine or sorbitol, to help keep the paste moist in the tube. A detergent, such as sodium lauryl sulfate, might be included to help loosen bacterial plaque and food debris. Thickening agents such as natural gums, celluloses and alginates are added to prevent the liquid and solid phases in the toothpaste from separating by acting as hydrophilic colloids, and saccharin and flavoring make the paste taste pleasant.

Because toothpaste is intended to be used regularly, it provides a simple method of treating teeth with beneficial, biologically active compounds. Fluoride in various forms is widely used in toothpaste to give protection against dental decay.

Fluorides

The fluoride in toothpaste makes the tooth enamel more resistant to acid attack. In laboratory tests, when extracted teeth are brushed for only one minute with fluoride toothpaste, then washed, their resistance to acid attack is increased by as much as 25 percent. Fluoride also depresses the activity of acid-forming bacteria on the tooth's surface, and this might be another reason why fluoride toothpaste helps reduce dental decay.

Fluoride is most commonly added to toothpaste in the form of sodium monofluorophosphate, sodium fluoride, stannous (tin) fluoride, or in some countries, an amine fluoride. Most manufacturers making fluoride toothpastes regularly test them in the laboratory to ensure that the type of fluoride they are using is not rendered ineffective by the other ingredients in the toothpaste.

 SEE ALSO: ABRASIVE • DENTISTRY • DETERGENT MANUFACTURE

Torpedo

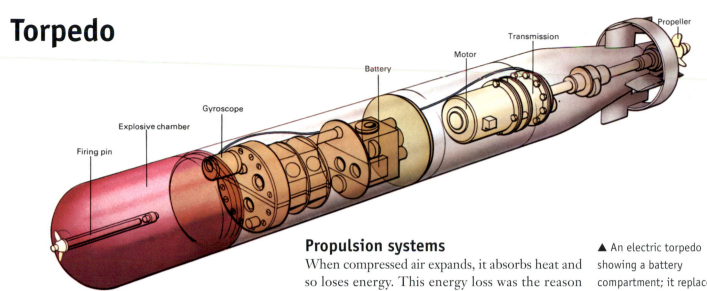

Firing pin

Explosive chamber

Gyroscope

Battery

Motor

Transmission

Propeller

Originally, a torpedo was any type of explosive device that would sink ships by damaging their most vulnerable area, below the waterline. It was named after a genus of fish that have organs in their head designed to give electric shocks. Various forms of mobile naval mine were tried in early-19th-century naval warfare but were unsuccessful. During the American Civil War, the spar torpedo was used by the Confederates with limited success, the weapon consisting of an explosive charge fixed to the end of a pole on the bows of a steamboat and designed to explode when rammed against the target. In theory, the length of the spar (pole) protected the steamboat from damage.

When the self-propelled torpedo appeared, it was called a fish, to indicate that it had a built-in propulsion system; from this name was derived tin fish, used loosely to describe weapons launched from submarines or surface warships. The first successful fish torpedo was developed by Robert Whitehead, a British engineer, working in Italy. He demonstrated the new weapon in 1867, and in 1872, the British government purchased the manufacturing rights.

By World War II, most countries had developed variants of the original Whitehead: they were about 20 ft. (6 m) long by 21 in. (54 cm) in diameter, weighed just over a ton, had a speed of 45 knots, a maximum range of 14,800 ft. (4,510 m) and delivered a 600 lb. (270 kg) payload of high explosive. Correctly placed, a single hit was enough to sink a medium-sized merchant ship or a small warship such as a destroyer. Torpedoes were fired from standard tubes 21 in. (54 cm) in diameter in trainable triple or quintuple mountings on surface ships: fixed tubes, built into the bow and stern structures, were used in the case of submarines. Weapon expulsion was by compressed air from submarine tubes and a small cordite charge in surface ships.

Propulsion systems

When compressed air expands, it absorbs heat and so loses energy. This energy loss was the reason for the Whitehead torpedo's limited performance, which was the power ceiling until the introduction of the Fiume heater system in 1909, which sprayed oil into a combustion chamber with compressed air and water. When ignited with a firing cartridge, the combination of hot gases and steam generated enough energy to drive a 350 horsepower (260 kW) piston engine. The density of seawater is such that large power increases are necessary for modest speed improvements, and the Fiume system was able to provide them.

Air contains 80 percent nitrogen, an inert gas that is insoluble in water, the expansion of which in the exhaust gases leaves a considerable trail of bubbles behind a running torpedo. This track can be readily recognized by alert lookouts aboard potential targets and gives sufficient warning for evasive action. This operational disadvantage was not eliminated until the introduction of battery-driven electric motors replaced the compressed-air-fuel thermal system.

Modern torpedoes have powerful propulsion systems to help them attain much greater speeds. As of 1989, the weapon used by U.S. attack submarines and Ohio class ballistic submarines was the Mk 48 ADCAP (advanced capability). It is propelled by an axial-flow pump jet driven by an

▲ An electric torpedo showing a battery compartment; it replaced the air-flask section of earlier torpedoes, which left a trail of bubbles.

▼ An Italian A-184 torpedo, now superseded by a new generation of heavyweight underwater weapons. Because of their mass, heavyweight torpedoes must be launched through the tubes of submarines.

◄ A computer-controlled Stingray torpedo launched from a British Royal Navy helicopter.

chase it. One of the most remarkable examples of a passive sonar is the U.S. Navy's Captor. Basically, it is a mine encapsulating a torpedo, which it will release to engage a target when its acoustic sensors recognize a hostile signature. The torpedo used in Captor is the lightweight Mk 46.

The active sonar carried by torpedoes has become extremely sophisticated to cope with the confusing environment of certain sea and seabed conditions. Britain's Stingray torpedo uses a multibeam sonar that feeds information to an onboard computer that can be programmed before firing to take account of the type of target and the difficulties presented by its environment. Both Stingray and the U.S. Navy's torpedoes are capable of turning to reengage the target if they miss on the first run. They also have built-in resistance to false targets and other countermeasures that may be employed by submarines under attack.

Lightweight torpedoes are totally dependent on their onboard systems for homing logic, but the heavier submarine- or ship-launched torpedoes, such as the U.S. Navy's Mk 48 ADCAP and the British Royal Navy's Spearfish, are wire guided for the initial portion of their journey and then switch to either active or passive sonar as they approach their target. The wire is a communications link with the shipboard computer, which generates instructions to direct the torpedo toward the target.

external combustion gas piston engine. The U.S. Navy has tried both solid and liquid fuels for its torpedo engines. The solid fuel has had limited use because the liquid Otto Fuel has proved to be more practical. With it, the Mk 48 ADCAP can attain 58 mph (93 km/h) and has a range of 29 miles (46 km).

Steering systems

Before firing, a torpedo is preprogrammed to steer an interception course so as to hit the target and to run at a depth selected as suitable for causing the maximum damage. Its course is controlled by a gyroscope that is run up to speed as part of the firing sequence and controls the vertical rudders via a small air motor. The depth mechanism, which is a combination of hydrostatic valve and pendulum, senses running depth variations and angles of rise or dive and corrects them by controlling a pair of horizontal rudders. For correct vertical and horizontal control while the torpedo is moving, it is important that the torpedo should remain level and not roll.

Modern torpedoes carry onboard guidance and homing devices, which are either active or passive sonar systems small enough to be contained in the torpedo's nose section. Passive sonar recognizes a target's acoustic signature and is programmed to

The warhead

In larger torpedoes, the warhead consists of 600 to 800 lbs. (270–370 kg) of high explosive, contained in the torpedo's bulbous head and triggered by an exploder mechanism. The explosives used, such as torpex or plastic-bonded explosive (PBX), are inert to shocks, vibration, and high temperatures. The exploder mechanism consists of a small spring-loaded inertia weight that fires a detonator. When the torpedo hits its target, the sudden deceleration causes the inertia weight to strike the detonator. This explosion sets off a larger 2 lb. (0.9 kg) charge called the primer, and it is the energy that this charge generates that detonates the warhead proper. The exploder mechanism is also fitted with safety devices that make it impossible for the warhead to explode until after the torpedo has been fired and has run for several hundred yards. The warheads of the lightweight torpedoes developed for use from aircraft platforms are considerably lighter, and the Mk 46, for instance, has only 100 lbs. (44 kg) of explosives.

SEE ALSO: Explosive • Missile • Sonar • Stealth technologies • Submarine • Warship

Tracked Vehicle

A tracked vehicle is a cross-country machine that lays its own road, runs along it, and picks it up behind. The track is made either of metal links pinned together by hinged joints or of continuous rubber belting. It spreads the weight of the vehicle over a wide area, so reducing sinkage on soft ground. In addition, tracked, or crawler, vehicles have a greater pulling or pushing power and are easier to handle in difficult conditions, such as on slopes, where there is less side slip than with wheeled vehicles. Some tracked vehicles are articulated, with the main body split into two parts linked by some form of joint. Single-bodied vehicles, such as tanks and crawler dozers, need to be short enough to do pivot turns.

Articulated vehicles are long in relation to their breadth and so have less rolling resistance on fertile soils, such as clay, or on snow—the track marks are narrower for a given sinkage compared with single vehicles. They range from small snow vehicles, much like a tracked scooter, to huge Arctic load carriers. In some, the two parts are not of equal size, having the relationship of an articulated truck tractor and trailer. The tracks in all parts of the articulated vehicle are driven.

Steering

Articulated tracked vehicles are steered by bending the vehicle at the joint, usually by hydraulic jacks. Single-bodied vehicles steer by slowing down the inside track and speeding up the outside one; this work is done by the transmission. For slow-moving vehicles, it is sufficient to disconnect the drive to the inside track with a clutch and then to apply a brake to hold it. This system is often used as supplementary steering for fast tracklayers. As it is steered, the track has to slew, or skid, over the ground surface, and on hard surfaces, tracklayers are generally less maneuverable than wheeled vehicles. On softer surfaces the necessary slipping action is easy and can allow high maneuverability, such as the ability to turn on the spot.

Suspension

The layout of wheels on which the vehicle runs on the track and any springing depend on the speed required. Slow-moving machines, such as crawler tractors and dozers,

traveling only about 6 mph (10 km/h) have no springing. The wheels are of steel and run on the track in a manner similar to railroads. For high speed, about 40 mph (65 km/h), such as the speed achieved by tanks, other armored fighting vehicles (AFV), and snow vehicles, springing systems are needed, and the wheels have rubber tires, solid for AFVs and pneumatic for snow vehicles. The most common springing system consists of steel torsion bars running across the floor of the

◄ Part of a dozer track. Each track shoe is bolted to a pair of track links, and the chain passes around the drive sprocket.

▼ Tracked vehicles that move at relatively high speeds need springing, which is achieved by using rubber wheels attached to the ends of trailing suspension arms, torsion bars, and large shock absorbers. Dozer tractors run on a track similar to that of a railroad. A shock-mounted front idler guides the track. Small roller wheels carry the tractor over its moving rail.

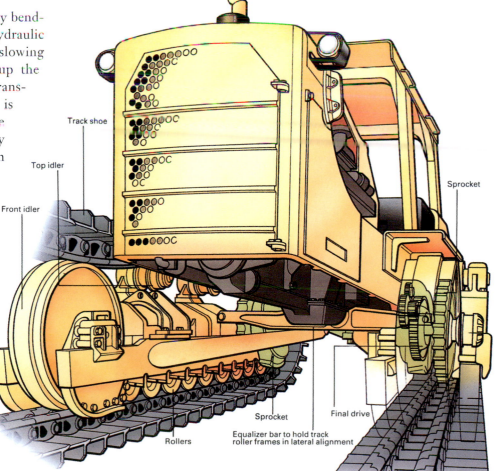

Track shoe

Top idler

Front idler

Sprocket

Sprocket

Final drive

Rollers

Equalizer bar to hold track roller frames in lateral alignment

◄ A diesel-driven German Leopard tank. Tracks are useful in battle conditions, as they enable the vehicle to travel over a wide variety of ground conditions that wheeled vehicles would find difficult.

vehicle, with the wheels mounted on the ends of trailing suspension arms. Large shock absorbers keep the vehicle from bouncing.

For low rolling resistance and good tire life, the wheels must be large, and in order to spread the load evenly along the track, there must be as many wheels as possible. The best compromise is five or six on each side, as large as can be fitted, although in fighting vehicles, this requirement often clashes with the need to keep the vehicle height as low as possible.

Most high-speed tracked vehicles have an idler wheel, which does not carry any weight and is adjustable to tension the track. Vehicles with small wheels, owing to some design constraint, may need small support rollers to hold the top run of the track. At the opposite end to the idler is the drive sprocket.

Transmission

The sprocket teeth engage the track to propel the vehicle. The transmission delivers the engine output to the sprocket at suitable speed and torque and provides steering speed differences for the inner and outer tracks. When steering, the power

available from slowing the inner track must be regenerated—that is, passed across to the outer track. The simplest layout would have the engine drive an electric generator or hydraulic pump, with motors at each sprocket, but this arrangement would have limited speed range and would need a complex control mechanism to be regenerative. Normally the main drive is by a conventional transmission system supplemented by the steering drive, the two fed together in differentials. All are usually housed in one unit, using mechanical gears, although recent designs split part of the power through hydraulics. Convenience in the overall layout of the vehicle design is the major influence on choice of front or rear drive.

Tracks

Slow vehicles, such as bulldozers, have steel tracks with steel pinned joints. The tread has a sharp grouser (projection) for grip. High-speed vehicles have various layouts with rubber-padded soles to limit damage to roads in peacetime—the pins joining them are sometimes made of plain steel but are more often rubber bushed. The links are normally steel, although aluminum can be used where weight saving is important. Noise levels can be reduced by an inner rubber lining on the track acting as a running surface for the rubber-tired wheels. Much of the noise comes from the contact between the track and the drive wheel, and it can be minimized by the use of a rubber (neoprene) liner on the wheel.

For snow and marsh vehicles, the tracks must be so wide that rubber belting is usually used. The belting is reinforced by steel cords and steel cross bars (acting as grousers for grip and for the sprocket to engage) and shaped to guide the wheels.

Half-track vehicles

There have been many successful vehicles that had wheels at the front and tracks at the rear. Pioneer work was led by a Frenchman, Adolphe Kegresse, who was a former garage manager for Czar Nicholas II of Russia before moving back to France. Kegresse had first developed the idea of a tracked vehicle in 1909 and produced a half-tracked touring car for the French company Citroën in 1921.

In the 1930s, the German army developed half-tracked armored troop carriers. Soon afterward, similar vehicles were developed in the United States. These vehicles were derived from trucks. The engine was at the front, with a conventional front axle whose wheels provided the steering. The Germans used a steel link track of high quality but complex design, the pins being sealed and lubricated.

The Americans used a rubber band track for their M3 half-track (which went into production in 1940 and was still in use in the Arab–Israeli War of 1973). Half-tracks were compromise designs without the clear advantage of either tracks or wheels. They were popular at a time when suitable designs for efficient tracked steering systems were not available, and they used existing truck production facilities. Today steering systems and other components for full-tracked vehicles are available commercially in a wide range of sizes.

Performance

Soft-ground ability used to be quoted by reference to nominal ground pressure, the relationship of weight to area of track on the ground. Now mean maximum pressure is used, applying to both wheeled and tracked vehicles and taking account of actual pressure owing to wheel size and spacing

▲ This large crawler is fitted with a ripper attachment, which is used to break up hard ground.

and track-link design. A tracked vehicle has a better soft-ground performance than a wheeled vehicle of similar size and payload. Tracks are usually more expensive and noisier than wheels and need more servicing. Wheeled AFVs are chosen for their cheapness and their ability to patrol long distances on roads.

Agricultural tracked tractors have developed into slow, unsprung vehicles that perform poorly on long hauls, such as earthmoving, or carting between field and farm, so they are used only in extreme cases.

Bulldozers are used where high traction is called for, as in dozers and in other heavy earthmoving equipment. Tracks are needed for working on sharp stones or rocky soil that would lacerate tires and for vehicles that cannot afford to fail on soft ground, such as tanks and snow or marsh vehicles.

FACT FILE

- Tracked crab submersibles are used to carry out deep-sea tasks such as heavy construction, rescue, and aircraft retrieval. Powered by umbilical cables, the remote-controlled crab submersibles can be programmed for self-rescue should the cables break. Seadog is a tracked submersible that lays submarine telephone cables, such as the transatlantic cable, by remote control from a mother ship.

- Wheelbarrow is a tracked robot vehicle used by bomb-disposal teams. Closed-circuit television built into Wheelbarrow enables the team to inspect suspected explosive devices from a distance. The tracked robot can also disable devices by firing a shotgun charge or a high-velocity jet of water that destroys the circuitry.

- Tortoise was the heaviest British tracked armored vehicle ever constructed, weighing in at around 79 tons (72 tonnes). The Tortoise's designed speed was a mere 12 mph (19 km/h), and it could carry a crew of seven. It never progressed beyond the prototype stage. Tortoise was almost 4 tons (3.6 tonnes) heavier than the heaviest-ever fully operational tank, the 13-person French Char de Rupture 2C bis of 1922, which had a maximum speed of 8 mph (12 km/h).

▶ A half-track vehicle crossing an ice field. Half-tracks are less common today because of improvements in the steering mechanisms of tracked vehicles.

SEE ALSO: AGRICULTURAL MACHINERY • ARMORED VEHICLE AND TANK • EARTHMOVING MACHINERY

Traction Engine

◄ A fairground traction engine dating from the start of the 20th century. These engines were used both for moving caravans and for generating electricity to power the sideshows. The generator, at the front of the engine, was driven by a belt coupled to the flywheel. One major drawback of steam traction engines was the large quantity of water they needed—usually from 10 to 20 gallons per mile (24–27 l/km).

A traction engine may be defined as a steam-driven road locomotive for hauling trailers and for use as a power source. Steam rollers and steam trucks are now also included in the definition, but steam automobiles are not.

Several forms of road locomotive, beginning with that of a British engineer, Richard Trevithick, in 1801, appeared in the first half of the 19th century, but none was widely used. Portable steam engines were not self-propelled; they were moved from place to place by teams of horses and were used in agriculture from about 1840 onward. One maker alone built more than 2,200 of these machines between 1845 and 1856. They were designed to drive threshing machines, saw benches, plows, and moles for cutting drainage channels.

In 1859, Thomas Aveling of Rochester, England, later famous for his steam rollers, made some of these machines self-propelling by fitting a chain drive between the crankshaft and the rear wheels. The front wheels were steered by a horse harnessed in shafts hinged to the axle. Aveling soon had many imitators, and traction engines derived from the farmers' portable engines dominated the field throughout the 70 years in which they were important commercial vehicles.

Traction engines have had a distinctive type of steering gear from a very early stage. The front axle is arranged to pivot like that of a four-wheeled farm wagon. The ends of a loop of chain are fastened to the ends of the axle, and several turns of the middle part of the loop are wrapped around a spiral groove cut in a cross shaft. When this shaft is turned, the chain winds on at one side and pays out at the other, so pulling the front axle around. The cross shaft is rotated by a worm drive from a hand wheel on the footplate; the drive needs many rotations to turn to its maximum.

Construction

Unlike typical steam vehicle design, the boiler and fire box form the main frame of a traction engine. Of the locomotive type, they are made for steam pressures of up to 200 psi (13.8 bar). The power is developed by a horizontal steam engine and transmitted by a belt from the flywheel for driving machinery or through dog clutches and gearing for traveling. A simple single-cylinder engine is used for boiler pressures up to 120 psi (8.3 bar); higher pressures need a two-cylinder compound engine that came into general use in the 1860s. In a simple steam engine, the steam expands in only one cylinder. In the compound engine, two or more cylinders of increasing size permit greater steam expansion and efficiency. The first, smallest piston is operated by the initial high-pressure steam, the second by the lower-pressure steam exhausted from the first.

As in the earlier portable steam engine, having the engine mounted on top of the boiler leaves little room for the steam dome, regulator, and safety valve to be arranged as in a locomotive. The cylinders, slide valve chest, and regulator are combined in a single unit, usually positioned at the smoke-box end. The outer part of this combined unit forms the steam dome, and the safety valves are set on top of it. The regulator is controlled by the driver when the traction engine is on the move and by a belt-driven governor when it is driving machinery.

The slide valves are operated by a Stephenson link motion for forward and reverse working, but provision for varying the cutoff (the point in the operating cycle at which the steam valve closes), important in railroad locomotives, is seldom made. The fixed cutoff makes it necessary to have a two- or three-speed gear change for traveling, a problem solved simply by sliding pinions in and out of mesh while the engine is stopped.

Although in many traction engines the rear wheels are driven through a differential gear, some are fitted with cruder devices—even, in some steam rollers, a pin that has to be removed from the hub of one driving wheel before turning a sharp corner. The axles of traction engines are often unsprung to avoid having to compensate the gearing for axle movements. The brakes are also crude, often only friction bands around the rear hubs and a block pressing on the flywheel, all applied slowly by screws and liable to overheating.

Like all noncondensing steam engines, traction engines need large quantities of feed water, usually from 10 to 20 gallons per mile (24–47 l/km). Extra water is needed on hills to avoid uncovering the fire-box crown or the front ends of the boiler tubes. Water is supplied from tanks on the engine by a feed pump driven from the crankshaft, supplemented by an injector of the type found on locomotives. The tanks were replenished from any convenient source at intervals of about 10 miles (16 km), and a further injector, called a water lifter, with a flexible suction hose was carried for this specific purpose.

Steam trucks

Steam trucks were built for carrying goods and occasionally to haul a trailer; they were not intended to be used as mobile power sources or to work away from roads. In a steam truck, the boiler does not form part of the main frame; it is mounted with the engine and the goods platform on a steel chassis. Carrying capacities usually range between 4 and 8 tons (3.6–7.25 tonnes), although a few with six wheels can carry 12 tons (10.8 tonnes). Only the early types, of which few survive, have chain steering; Ackermann steering gear, also used in heavy trucks, is now the norm. This feature, along with the provision of automatic water feed, regulators, and internal expanding brakes, allows steam trucks to be driven by a single driver, but a traction engine needs two—one to drive and one to steer.

Engines

One type of steam truck, the over type, has its mechanism on top of a compact boiler resembling a locomotive boiler. The engine is usually compound and mechanically lubricated to allow high speeds. In the other type of steam truck, the under type, the engine is set under the body toward the rear and is completely enclosed. Two or four simple cylinders are arranged to work in parallel with poppet valves operated by cams, instead of slide valves operated by a link motion. Steam trucks of this sort usually have vertical water-tube boilers made for higher steam pressures and fitted with superheaters.

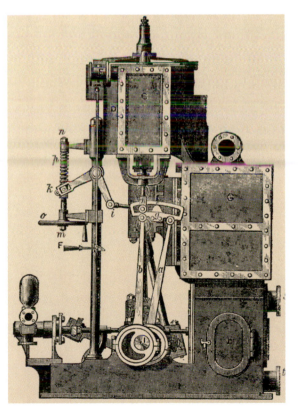

◄ A compound marine steam engine. The valve gears are operated from levers on the crankshaft.

SEE ALSO: Cam • Chain drive • Flywheel • Gear • Governor • Locomotive and power car • Marine propulsion • Steam engine • Valve, mechanical

Transducer and Sensor

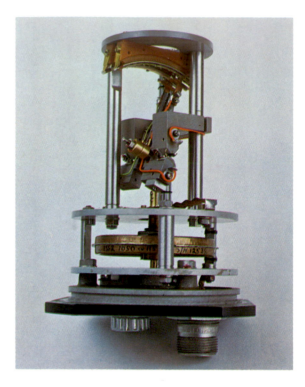

◀ A general-purpose pressure transducer for use in aircraft. It can be incorporated into instruments for measuring altitude, cabin pressure, or engine pressure.

A transducer is a device for converting energy from one form into another. A microphone, for example, is a transducer that converts sound energy into electric energy. The need for a transducer in instrumentation arises when a measurement of some inaccessible quantity, or parameter, is required or when data is required from this parameter for further analysis or computation. Common transducer systems are the oil-pressure gauges and fuel gauges used in many motor vehicles—they provide purely visual output. In other cases, it is often convenient or even necessary to have the data in electric-signal form. Most present-day transducers provide a measurement of the parameter in the form of an electric signal whose value is proportional to the quantity measured.

The automobile fuel gauge is a good example of an electric transducer. Although in the early days mechanical means were devised for measuring the fuel level, it is much more convenient and efficient to transmit this data from the fuel tank to the gauge by electric means.

The transducer itself is mounted on the fuel tank and consists of two main elements: a float that moves up and down with the fuel level, so providing a mechanical displacement, and a potentiometer element linked to the float, which converts this displacement into an electric signal. This signal is then transmitted by wire to the gauge on the dashboard.

The salient point about this example is that it illustrates the common transducer design practice of having two stages of transducing, first from parameter to displacement and then from displacement to electric output. The displacement transducer is one of the basic types of transducers.

The name given to a particular transducer usually indicates its operation. The fuel gauge, for example, is a potentiometric transducer, measuring fuel level by displacement and then providing an electric output by means of potentiometer. Similarly, a piezoelectric pressure transducer may sense pressure by means of a diaphragm or capsule mechanism and produce its electric output from a piezoelectric crystal.

Inductive transducers

Although the potentiometer is widely used, it is frequently necessary to use other types of transducers to avoid certain inherent disadvantages of the potentiometer. These occur mainly because of the necessary use of a sliding contact in a potentiometer, and arise from intermittent contact between the slider and the resistive element due to vibration, friction, or the ingress of dirt.

To overcome these problems, a number of noncontact designs have been developed, among the most common being the inductive transducers. These transducers take many physical forms, but all work on the same basic principle of having a moving armature and a stator of magnetic material and a system of coils that are coupled magnetically, the coupling being altered by any displacement of the armature.

An inductive system must be polarized by an AC voltage or current, and this necessity is a complication compared with the potentiometer, which basically requires only a DC battery type of supply for polarization. In industry, however, it is convenient to use the local power supply (transformed down to a suitable voltage), and for aircraft, to use their 400 Hz supply.

Typical examples of this type of transducer are the synchro, the AC pick-off and the linear variable differential transformer (LVDT). The LVDT is a good example of an inductive transducer, and it works on the E and I core principle with zero displacement arranged to give zero voltage output.

The fixed element is an E-shaped magnetic core with a coil of wire wound on each of the three limbs of the E. The two outer coils are connected in series and to the polarizing AC supply. The middle coil produces the output voltage. The I-section armature, a single magnetic bar, is mounted near the face of the three poles of the E and may be arranged to either rotate or move linearly with displacement.

Under zero displacement conditions, the magnetic fluxes generated by the two outer coils couple through the I core and into the center limb of the E, canceling each other out so that there is no output from the center coil. When displacement of the I core takes place, the flux balance is upset and greater coupling takes place from one outer coil than from the other, and so cancellation no longer exists, and the resulting flux in the center limb creates a voltage output.

This output varies in magnitude with respect to displacement. There is also a phase relationship that depends on the direction of the displacement. Frictional and dirt problems are minimal, and apart from its use within transducers, this principle is widely used in industry to measure the movement of parts of machinery, often as part of a servo control system.

Capacitive transducers

The capacitive transducer is extremely simple mechanically, consisting of two electrically conductive plates suitably spaced to form the two plates of a capacitor. The capacitive value depends on the dielectric material used, the distance between the two plates, and the area of the plates. Any of these may be altered to produce a change in the capacitance, which can be detected by the appropriate circuitry.

Although capacitive transducers are mechanically simple, they are prone to electric difficulties,

so their use is restricted to occasions where they have a particular advantage, for example, in detecting the minimal mechanical loading on the capsule of an altimeter, or where electric safety is of paramount importance, such as in aircraft fuel gauging.

Strain gauges

As the name implies, strain gauges are designed for measuring strain in structures and materials, but they may also be used in conjunction with mechanical systems for measuring displacement. In an electric weigh station, for example, where the displacement takes the form of a bending beam, a strain gauge can measure the deflection by measuring the strain on the beam.

A strain gauge is basically a conductive element, such as a piece of wire that has electric resistance. If this element is mechanically stretched, it will become longer and thinner—as a result the resistance will increase by a small amount proportional to the strain. A measurement of the resistance will give an indication of the value of the strain force.

Such a free wire system is known as an unbonded strain gauge. Because of its fragility, it is usually designed as an integral part of a transducer. Strain measurement of bridges or concrete structures would normally be achieved with the bonded strain gauge, which usually takes the form of a grid of conductive material, either wire or foil, that is physically attached to the structure being measured; hence, deformation of the surface of the structure also deforms the grid and creates a change in its electric resistance.

Semiconductor strain gauges rely on a piezoresistive effect and are more sensitive than the wire type, but they also have the disadvantage of being extremely temperature sensitive, so they are confined to applications where suitable compensation can be provided.

Other resistive devices include the photoresistor (or photoconductive cell) and the elements used for sensing temperature, such as nickel or platinum wire, and the thermistor frequently used to measure automobile engine temperatures.

Electret foil transducers

Electret foil transducers are made of insulating materials called electrets that are capable of retaining an electric charge for many years. These materials are usually in the form of a foil or film with one surface negatively charged and the other positively charged. Deformation of the film caused by sound waves or mechanical pressure, for example, can be used to induce a current. Electret foil transducers are used in a wide variety of applications, such as seismic detectors, hearing

▼ In gas pumps, a flowmeter measures the rate at which fuel is dispensed; a transducer converts it into an electric signal, and the measurement is displayed in digital form.

aids, ultrasonic detectors, earphones, and micro-phones, as well as cellular phones, voice-controlled toys, and modems. Telephones and electronic calculators use electret foil transducers in their push-button keys to convert mechanical energy into electrical energy.

Other transducers

In addition to the types already mentioned, many other transducers are available, including flowmeters, anemometers, accelerometers, thermocouples, ultrasonic transducers, and loudspeakers. Gyroscope-based transducers are widely used in aircraft instruments and inertial guidance and navigation systems.

A free gyro measures displacement, and a spring added to the gimbal assembly changes the free gyro into a rate gyro, which gives a measure of the rotational velocity. If the gimbal motion of a rate gyro is measured with a velocity transducer, the gyro will measure rotational acceleration. A velocity transducer is a displacement transducer, which, when it is in motion, generates electric signals in proportion to the velocity of movement. The signals are in fact proportional to displacement, the rate of change of which equals velocity.

A number of transducers produce data in terms of frequency, for instance, induction tachometers and resonance transducers. These transducers are often termed digital transducers, but in fact, the only true digital transducers are a range of instruments known as digitizers, or encoders, that generate a unique digital word for a given position. Frequency data may be conveniently digitized but are fundamentally of analog form, the advantages of digitizing being that much of the accuracy is preserved and that digital readout devices reduce the likelihood of human error in recording the readings.

Force balance, or feedback, transducers, derive the electric data signals without the limitations of mechanical displacement. In the force balance transducer, the parameter is first detected by displacement, but by servo action, this displacement is forced back to zero, and the electric power required to do so is then a measurement of the input parameter.

This is a principle that may be applied to almost any type of transducer and has been available for the hot-wire anemometer for many years, but in the case of the more mechanical transducers, only the accelerometer is readily available in this form.

Transducers in accelerometers

An accelerometer is an instrument that uses a transducer for measuring acceleration. There are two types, one for measuring linear (straight line)

accelerations, the other for measuring angular (twisting) accelerations.

Accelerometers may also be used to measure deceleration, such as the braking of a car. They are much used in the motor industry both to measure the forward acceleration and deceleration of a car and to measure the sideways and up-and-down accelerations caused by cornering and bumpy roads.

Other uses include testing the strength of safety belts (by measuring the deceleration force at which they break when carrying a known load) and studying vibrations in the hulls of ships and the wingtips of aircraft. They are also important components of inertial guidance systems.

The linear accelerometer usually contains a body of known mass attached to a coil spring and free to move only along the axis of the spring, which is a straight line down the middle of the coil. This line is called the sensitive axis of the accelerometer. In order to measure the acceleration of any moving object, the axis must be placed in line with the direction of movement.

The tension of the spring and the weight of the body on its end are adjusted so that when a known force is applied to the accelerometer along the sensitive axis, the body moves a known distance along the spring. Either the body is connected to a dial or its movement is detected electronically using, for example, a piezoelectric transducer.

The dial is calibrated by placing the accelerometer on a body of known acceleration and marking the position of the indicator. If this is repeated with various known accelerations, the marks will provide enough information to allow the rest of the scale to be filled in.

SEE ALSO: ANEMOMETER • AUTOMOBILE • ELECTRET • FLOWMETER • GYROCOMPASS • INERTIAL GUIDANCE • LOUDSPEAKER • MICROPHONE • PIEZOELECTRIC MATERIAL • WEIGH STATION

Transformer

A transformer is used to transfer electric power between two electric circuits that operate with alternating currents at different voltages.

In its simplest form, it consists of two electric windings linked by a common magnetic circuit. When an alternating voltage is applied to the primary winding, an alternating current flows, limited in value by the inductance of the winding—the size of the voltage induced in the winding compared with the rate of change of current in the winding. This magnetizing current produces an alternating magnetomotive force (mmf), which creates an alternating magnetic flux. The flux is constrained within the magnetic circuit and induces a voltage in the linked secondary winding, which, if it is connected to an electric load, produces an alternating current. This secondary load current in turn produces its own mmf and creates a further alternating flux that links back with the primary winding. A load current then flows in the primary winding of sufficient magnitude to balance the mmf produced by the secondary load current. So the primary winding carries both magnetizing and load current, the secondary winding carries load current, and the magnetic circuit carries only the flux produced by the magnetizing current. In an autotransformer—often used to convert a local power line voltage to another voltage—part of the winding is common to both the primary and secondary circuits. The desired voltage is obtained by tapping the coil at a particular point.

The relative voltages across each winding and the current flowing in them are related by the ratio of turns in the two windings. If the primary winding has N_1 turns and the secondary winding has N_2 turns, the primary and secondary voltages are related by $V_1/V_2 = N_1/N_2$, and the currents by $I_1/I_2 = N_2/N_1$.

When a transformer is used to transfer power between two electric circuits operating at different voltages, the current flowing in each winding is in inverse ratio to the voltage.

Design

The magnetic circuit, or core, is made from steel to reduce the reluctance—the magnetic equivalent of resistance—of the flux path and give a low magnetizing current. If a solid core were used, it would act as a shorted turn enclosing the flux path, permitting eddy currents to flow and producing a high energy loss. To reduce this loss, the core is made up of thin steel laminations insulated from each other.

▲ A consignment of 100 kVA panel radiator-type distribution transformers is checked in the assembly plant before shipment to a customer.

◄ Autotransformers use a continuous-spiral low-voltage winding, which is tapped at a particular point along the coil to obtain the voltage required.

in a transformer is therefore usually a silicon–iron alloy that has been cold reduced to increase the degree of grain orientation within the laminations. This property produces a hysteresis loop with a smaller area and thus results in a lower hysteresis loss. The core cross-sectional area is chosen to maintain the core flux density below a saturation point. Above this point, the core becomes less effective as a low-reluctance path, and the magnetizing current rises dramatically.

The windings are made from a low-resistivity material such as copper or aluminum in strip or foil form. The cross-sectional area of the conductor must be sufficient to reduce the loss, caused by resistive heating of the windings when carrying load current, to an acceptable level. The actual current density allowable depends upon the cooling system used; a transformer immersed in oil can work at an appreciably higher conductor current density than an air-cooled transformer. If a conductor has to carry a heavy current, it may be necessary to break the area up into several smaller parallel connected conductors insulated from each other, to reduce the conductor eddy current loss.

The winding conductors must also be large enough to withstand any mechanical forces that the transformer may be subjected to in service, and they should be able to withstand the surge due to a short circuit, where the fault currents may be several times the normal full-load current. The currents in primary and secondary windings flow in opposite directions around the core, so

Energy in transformers is also lost through a process called hysteresis. It occurs as a lagging of the magnetization of the ferromagnetic material behind the change in the magnetizing field. When plotted as a graph of field strength against flux density, a closed loop is produced, and the area contained within this loop is proportional to the amount of energy lost as heat. The steel used

TRANSFORMERS

In a transformer, the ratio between the primary and secondary voltages is the same as the ratio between the numbers of turns of wire in the primary and secondary windings. The ratio between the primary and secondary currents, however, is the inverse of this winding ratio. The two main winding layouts for power transformers are also shown, as well as the way a laminated core, made of alternating layers of steel and an insulating material, reduces the induced circulating eddy currents and thus lowers the amount of energy lost from the transformer as heat.

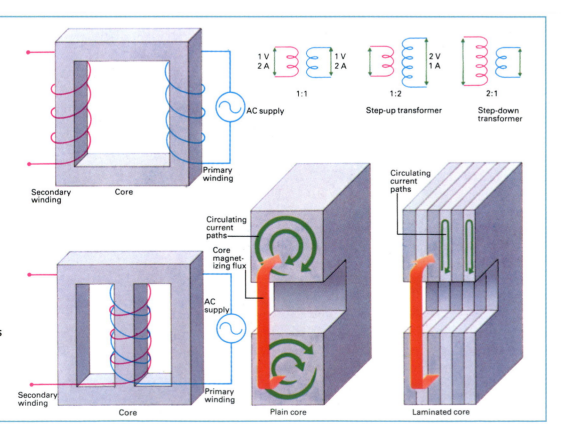

the windings will repel each other magnetically, causing the conductors to bend in an inadequately designed winding and the transformer to fail.

The electric insulation of windings is of great importance. Not only must the conductor turns be insulated from each other, but there must be adequate insulation strength between windings and from each winding to ground. The insulation must withstand not only the normal service voltage but also overvoltages that may occur in service owing to lightning strikes and switching operations. The usual insulating materials used in large transformers are paper, wood, and mineral oil—considerable attention is paid to ensure that the materials are all free from water contamination, which would drastically reduce the insulation strength. Air-cooled transformers are usually made with high-temperature inorganic insulating materials, which may be impregnated with resin or silicone varnish to avoid moisture contamination.

Transformers operate with a high efficiency (98 to 99 percent), the only losses arising from hysteresis and eddy current loss in the core, resistive loss in the windings, and circulating current loss in structural parts owing to the proximity of heavy current leads or (in the case of nonlaminated cores) eddy currents generated by load currents in the windings. Although the total loss may be only 1 percent of the power transmitted, the loss may be equivalent to 10 MW on a large transformer; careful design is needed to avoid overheating of the windings, which would cause premature aging of the insulation and lead to an electric breakdown in the windings. An oil-filled transformer can be cooled by tubular radiators mounted on the tank or by a separate radiator bank. An oil pump may be fitted to circulate oil through ducts in the winding for more effective conductor cooling, and an air fan may be used to increase the efficiency of a radiator bank; their use can extend a transformer's life by many years.

Power transformers

Transformers for transferring power between subcircuits of an electric power supply system are known as power transformers. A generator transformer is a step-up transformer used to transfer power supplied by an alternator at about 20 kV into a higher voltage network operating at a voltage up to, say, 750 kV to reduce losses for long-distance power transmission. Transmission transformers are step-down transformers for reducing the voltage back down to a level more convenient for supply to a town at, say 110 kV, or down to an even lower voltage of, say, 11 kV for distribution in a neighborhood. Distribution transformers are the final step-down transformer to the

◄ A transformer at a power plant in Venezuela. Transformers are used to step-up the current that has been generated to a level suitable for transmission over a long distance network.

consumer at 110 volts. Power transformers may be single-phase or three-phase transformers, depending upon size and transportation difficulties.

Instrument transformers

Instrument transformers are used to make accurate measurements of heavy current or high voltage, using low-current, low-voltage instruments. They may also be used in protection schemes in a transmission or distribution network. The power transmitted is low (only a few watts), but high accuracy may be required not only in magnitude but also in phase angle of the currents or voltages to be measured. Because there is very little power involved, and so no problem with cooling, it is possible to use a compressed gas, such as sulfur hexafluoride, as the major insulation to ground.

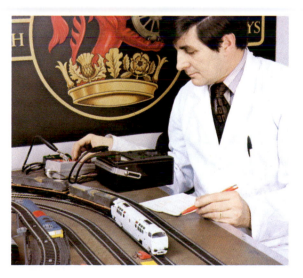

◄ This model railway's controls incorporate a step-down transformer and an AC to DC converter.

SEE ALSO: Electricity • Electromagnetism • Induction • Power supply • Tesla coil

Transistor

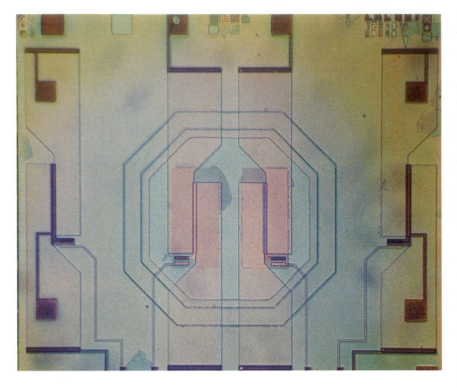

The term *transistor* derives from the words "*trans-fer*" and "*resistor*" in reference to the ability of a transistor to transfer (conduct) current or resist current flow according to circumstances. Given this ability, transistors can act as switches that are on when conducting and off when resisting. Furthermore, certain transistors conduct current only in one direction when they are in the "on" condition, so they can rectify an alternating current. That is, they conduct the parts of a signal where current flows in the allowed direction while blocking the rest of the signal.

Transistors can also act as modulators, their resistances changing in response to changes in an input signal. A modulating transistor also acts as an amplifier if the amplitude of the variations in the current that passes through it is greater than the amplitude of the input signal.

Vacuum tubes and relays

The invention of radio at the end of the 19th century created a need for circuit components that could rectify and amplify signals. Rectification is part of the detection process that separates the sound signal from the carrier wave of a received signal, and amplification is the process that creates a signal strong enough to drive a speaker from a weak detected signal.

For the first half of the 20th century, the tasks of rectification and amplification were performed by vacuum tubes. Rectification was done by use of a diode—a vacuum tube with a heated emitter

▲ This picture is a close-up of an ion-sensitive field-effect transistor, or ISFET. The gate of such a transistor consists of a material that attracts a specific type of ion. If the appropriate ions are present near the ISFET, they will accumulate on the gate in a number that corresponds to their concentration. The resulting change in the gate potential translates into an electrical signal whose amplitude reflects the concentration of the ion. Arrays of ISFETs sensitive to different ions can analyze blood for electrolyte concentrations and screen water samples for inorganic pollutants.

electrode that could release electrons into the vacuum and a cold collector electrode that could receive electrons only from the vacuum.

Signals were amplified by use of a triode—essentially the same device as a diode but with a grid electrode between the emitter and collector electrodes. In an amplifier circuit, the emitter and collector of a triode connect to the negative and positive terminals, respectively, of a direct-current supply. The strength of the current between the emitter and collector of a triode depends on the voltage of the grid relative to the emitter, so triodes are classed as voltage amplifiers.

While vacuum tubes performed the functions of amplification and rectification, some switching was done by electromechanical relays. A relay is a device in which a contact arm swings between "on" and "off" positions under the influence of an electromagnet that acts in opposition to a spring. When no current passes through the electromagnet, the spring holds the contact in one position, either "on" or "off," and when the electromagnet is energized, the contact swings to the other position. By including them in appropriate circuits, relays can act as logic gates for computing or as line connectors for telephone exchanges.

Vacuum tubes and relays are not without drawbacks, however. Vacuum tubes are quite large—from around the size of a small electric lamp—and the glass envelope that holds the vacuum makes them prone to breakage. Furthermore, the operation of a vacuum tube depends on a filament that heats the emitter electrode. The filament takes a while to warm up, uses energy to remain hot, and can be broken by vibrations; furthermore, the whole tube must be replaced if the filament burns out. Also, a machine that uses several tubes can be prone to overheating. Relays are somewhat unreliable, and they are slow and noisy in operation.

In contrast to these vacuum-tube and relay devices, transistors are extremely small, energy efficient, and reliable. Their introduction and subsequent integration on silicon chips led to the introduction of numerous portable devices, such as the transistor radio, and made microprocessors and powerful computers possible to build.

The first transistors

It was while seeking a more efficient replacement for relays in telephony that a team of U.S. physicists at the Bell Telephone Laboratories invented the first transistors. In 1940, Russell Ohl demonstrated the potential of semiconductors to act as switches. He had a cracked rod of silicon whose conductivity increased significantly when exposed to light. It turned out that the levels of impurities in the silicon on either side of the crack were different, and light enabled electrons to jump from one material to the other. He had inadvertently discovered the *p-n* junction that would later be used in transistors and photoelectric cells.

Research into the properties of semiconductors continued at Bell under the leadership of William Shockley. In 1947, Shockley set two of his team members—John Bardeen and Walter Brattain—the task of determining why a silicon amplifier he had devised failed to work.

Working first with silicon and then with germanium—an element in the same group of the periodic table as silicon—the team set about creating an amplifier that would work. Using his knowledge of the electronic structures of semiconductors and his own theories, Bardeen calculated that it would be possible to control current flow through germanium. He placed the sample on a metal plate that would act as one terminal of the power supply and attached two closely spaced contacts elsewhere on the sample—one connected to the other terminal of the power supply, the other to provide a controlling signal.

The practical problem was that the wires available at the time were too thick for the tolerances required—a spacing of around 0.02 in. (0.5 mm). Brattain solved this problem by fixing a sheet of gold foil to a triangular plastic wedge and cutting the foil at the point of the wedge using a razor. The razor cut provided the necessary separation between the two halves of the foil, which would act as contacts. The whole assembly was held against the germanium by a spring. When connected to a circuit, a weak signal to one of the gold contacts opened the gateway for a much stronger signal to flow between the metal plate and the second gold contact. Having produced the first semiconductor amplifier, the point-contact transistor, the team of Shockley, Brattain, and Bardeen demonstrated the device on 23 December 1947 and filed for a patent in 1948.

One drawback of the point-contact transistor was that it used only a thin surface layer of the germanium to control current flow and was therefore much bulkier and less efficient in use of materials than if the whole of a much smaller sample of semiconductor were to be used. Also, imperfect contact between the electrodes and the semiconductor made the point-contact transistor unreliable and added noise to the signal.

Later in 1948, Shockley had the idea of producing a transistor by forming a sandwich of two layers of one form of impure semiconductor on either side of a third layer with a different type of impurity. He envisaged that current flow between the outer layers could be controlled by feeding an electrical signal to the middle layer. By April 1950, together with two coworkers, Gordon Teal and Morgan Sparks, Shockley had devised a way of producing a thin sliver of germanium crystal that was a three-layer sandwich as required.

The sandwich amplified signals as predicted, but the thickness of the middle layer scrambled the current passing between the outer layers when rapidly varying signals were used. The problem was resolved by reducing the thickness of the middle layer, and Bell announced the first effective junction transistor in July 1951.

Semiconductor diode

To understand the action of components such as junction transistors, it is necessary to know about the electrical properties of junctions between regions of semiconductor materials that have different types of impurities. The two types of impure semiconductor materials are labeled *p* (for positive) and *n* (for negative).

A pure semiconductor, such as silicon or germanium, forms covalently bonded crystals in which each bond has exactly two electrons. These electrons are essentially fixed in place, so conductivity is low. An *n*-type semiconductor contains traces of an element that has five electrons in its outer shell, rather than the four of silicon or germanium. Suitable impurities, called dopants, include phosphorus and arsenic, and their extra electrons move through the structure with relative ease. Under the influence of an electrical field, these movements constitute a current, and electrons are therefore classed as the majority charge carriers of the *n*-type region.

▼ The metal cases of these transistor components contain silicon junction transistors. The three wires connect to electrodes attached to the transistor chips and can be soldered at the appropriate points in a printed circuit.

A *p*-type semiconductor contains traces of dopants such as boron or gallium, which have three electrons in their outer shells. The result is a structure in which some bonds have one rather than two electrons, and these electron-deficient sites are called holes. Electrons can jump from a doubly occupied bond to a hole with relative ease; this action is the equivalent of the hole moving through the structure. Hence, the majority charge carriers in a *p*-type semiconductor exposed to an electrical field are positive holes.

When the *n* region is biased negatively with respect to the *p* region (when an operating voltage is applied across it), free electrons cross the junction from the *n* to the *p* region in great numbers. Similarly, holes cross the junction from the *p* to the *n* region. They are the majority charge carriers of their respective regions, and their movement is equivalent to a considerable current crossing the junction. This conducting state is referred to as forward bias.

If the *n* region is biased positively (with the voltage applied in the opposite direction) with respect to the *p* region electrons are withdrawn from the *n* region and holes are withdrawn from the *p* region. The result is a depletion layer at the junction, where there are no majority charge carriers and the flow of current is therefore blocked. This condition is called reverse bias.

By reversing the bias, a *p-n* junction can be switched between conducting and nonconducting states. This behavior resembles that of a vacuum-tube diode, and *p-n* junctions have applications in rectification and detection. An important point is that doped semiconductors also have minority carriers—holes in *n*-type regions and electrons in *p*-type regions. Reverse bias favors conduction by minority carriers, and a small leakage current occurs, unlike what happens in diodes.

Junction transistor

A junction transistor is a crystal of semiconductor doped to have either an *n* region sandwiched between two *p* regions (a *p-n-p* transistor) or a *p* region between two *n* regions (an *n-p-n* transistor). Connections made to the outer layers are designated the emitter and collector electrodes, while the connection to the middle layer is the base electrodes. An essential feature of the construction is that the central (base) region is very thin. The device can be regarded as two semiconductor diodes connected back-to-back in series.

Working mechanism. In normal operation of the transistor, the base–emitter junction is forward biased. Thus, in a *p-n-p* transistor, the emitter would be wired to the positive terminal of a direct-current supply. The collector is wired to the opposite pole, so the base–collector junction is reverse biased.

When no current is fed to the base electrode, the flow of current between the emitter and collector is limited to the leakage current at the reverse-biased base–collector junction. Current can be made to flow by reducing the number of majority carriers in the base layer—by feeding electrons into the holes of the base of an *n-p-n*

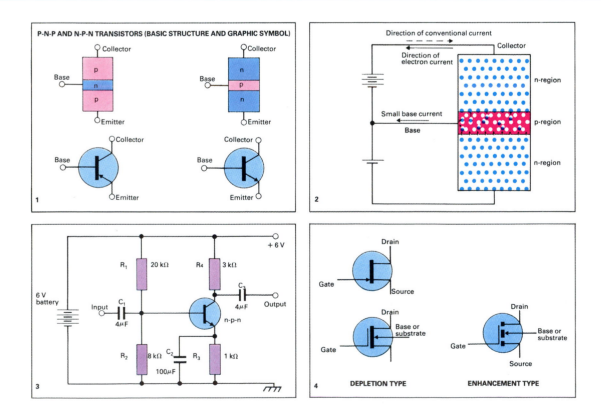

◄ Graphic symbols and basic structures for *p-n-p* and *n-p-n* transistors (1). Action of an *n-p-n* junction transistor biased for amplification (2). The resistors, R_1, R_2, R_3, R_4, establish the optimum voltage and current conditions for the transistor to function satisfactorily and reliably (3). Graphic symbols for various types of *n*-channel field-effect transistors (4).

sandwich or by draining the electrons from the base of a *p-n-p* sandwich. In this process, the reverse-biased *p-n* junction presents a less severe barrier to current flow, since the base current temporarily adjusts the character of the base layer to be more like the collector layer.

Up to a certain threshold, the amount of current that flows between the emitter and collector of a junction transistor varies in proportion to the current through the electrode attached to the base layer and is often 100 times as great. Consequently, a junction transistor is a current amplifier under these conditions: its output current varies in proportion to a weaker base current. By contrast, in the vacuum-tube triode, the emitter–collector current varies in proportion to the voltage (rather than current) at the grid. Junction transistors are described as active when they behave in this way, and they are used as modulators in amplification circuits.

Electrons move somewhat faster than holes. Consequently, *n-p-n* junction transistors, whose majority charge carriers are electrons, tend to be favored for amplifying high-frequency signals where current oscillations are rapid.

Above a certain value of base current, the emitter–collector current is limited by the concentration of majority charge carriers in those layers and will not increase if the current through the base increases. This condition is called saturation, and it is used as the "on" state when junction transistors are used as switches.

Phototransistors. A phototransistor is a three-layer junction transistor in which current flow is determined by the action of light rather than an electrical signal. This phenomenon occurs because electrons at the reverse-biased junction can absorb photons and use their energy to jump the energy barrier that impedes their flow. Thus, current flow in a phototransistor varies in proportion to the number of photons absorbed.

Field-effect transistors

There are two basic types of field-effect transistors, or FETs: junction-gate FETs (JFETs or JUGFETs) and metal-oxide-semiconductor FETs (MOSFETS), also called insulated-gate FETs (IGFETs). In both types, the main current flow is through a channel of one type of semiconductor (*n* or *p*) that connects two electrodes: the source electrode and the drain electrode. Current flow is controlled by a gate electrode.

JFET. In the case of an *n*-type junction-gate FET, the gate is a collar of *p*-type semiconductor that impinges on the *n*-type channel. Its influence is to restrict current flow, rather as pinching a garden hose cuts the flow of water through it. If

the potential (voltage) is equal to the source potential, current flows well through the channel. If the gate is at a negative potential relative to the source, the holes in the *p*-type semiconductor become filled by electrons, and the negative field repels electrons from the *n*-type semiconductor near the gate. This action creates a depletion zone—a volume of semiconductor devoid of charge carriers—in the part of the channel near the gate. The reduction in the cross section of the conducting channel increases the resistance of the channel and reduces the source–drain current.

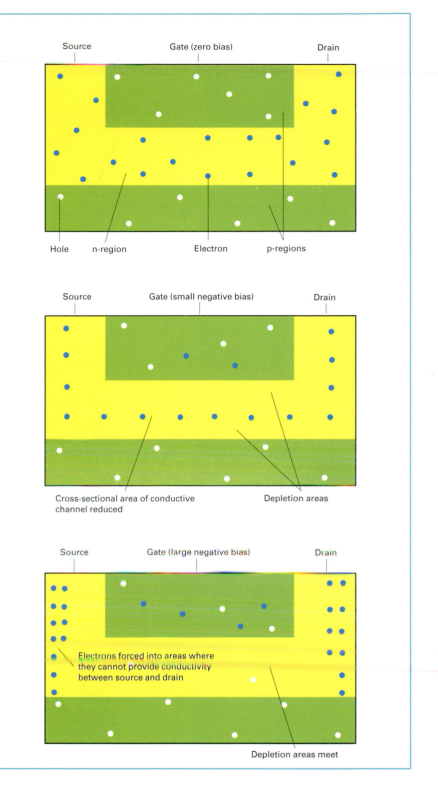

▲ Operation of a junction-gate FET. With zero gate bias, electrons are distributed throughout the *n*-region, forming a conductive path. Applying a negative voltage to the gate confines the electrons to a smaller area. With a large gate voltage the depletion areas meet and there is no conduction.

Source · Gate (zero bias) · Drain

Hole · n-region · Electron · p-regions

Source · Gate (small negative bias) · Drain

Cross-sectional area of conductive channel reduced · Depletion areas

Source · Gate (large negative bias) · Drain

Electrons forced into areas where they cannot provide conductivity between source and drain

Depletion areas meet

If the negative bias on the gate is increased sufficiently, the depletion areas can be made large enough to meet at the center of the channel. In such a condition, there is no conducting path between source and drain, and the drain current is zero. This is known as the pinch-off condition, and the minimum negative bias necessary to achieve it is known as the pinch-off voltage.

In normal operation, a bias voltage equal to about half the pinch-off value is used, and the signal to be amplified is connected in series with the gate terminal so that the effective width of the channel is modulated by the signal and varies the drain current in sympathy. The gate is always negative with respect to the source, so the gate–channel junction is reverse biased. Hence, no current flows between gate and source, and the FET takes no current from the input signal. A FET is a voltage-controlled resistance and is in this respect similar to a vacuum-tube triode.

In complementary JFETs, the channel is a *p*-type semiconductor, and the polarities of all the electrodes are reversed. The source is therefore positive with respect to the drain, and a positive potential applied to an *n*-type gate attracts electrons that fill holes and form a depletion zone.

MOSFET. In contrast to JFETs, not all MOSFETs have a permanent channel between the source and drain. In one type of MOSFET, which operates in the so-called enhancement mode, a temporary conducting channel is created when the gate potential attracts appropriate charge carriers from neutral semiconductor. The source and drain are attached to separate regions of similarly doped semiconductor, say, *n*-type silicon. The gate is a metallic layer positioned adjacent to the region of semiconductor between the source and drain electrodes but isolated from it by a layer of insulating silicon dioxide. A positive potential at the gate will attract electrons from the silicon substrate to create a temporary channel of *n*-type material; as a result, current will flow between the *n*-type regions at source and drain. The magnitude of the current depends on the gate potential, and no current flows when the gate is at zero potential relative to the source.

In another type of MOSFET, which is manufactured to operate in the so-called depletion mode, the region of semiconductor between the source and drain is of the same type as the material at those electrodes, so there is a conducting channel even in the absence of a gate potential. In this type of MOSFET, current is controlled by applying a gate potential that repels the necessary charge carriers from the channel, creating a depletion zone near the gate electrode. This type of operation is similar to that of a JFET. An *n*-

◄ An airplane fuel-level sensing control, which employs both integrated circuits and discrete transistors. Transistors are the most significant development in electronics since World War II. In electronic chips, transistors make possible the reduction in size of electronic equipment.

type depletion MOSFET uses negative gate potential to restrict the flow of electrons through an *n*-type region from a negative source electrode to a positive drain. In contrast, a *p*-type MOSFET uses a positive gate potential to restrict the flow of holes from a positive source through a *p*-type region to a negative drain.

MOSFETs are readily created on the surfaces of silicon chips by the appropriate deposition and etching sequences. They are isolated from surrounding components by using a channel of opposite dopant polarity to the base material of the chip, so the junction between the channel and surrounding chip is always reverse biased. MOSFETs can perform both modulation for amplification purposes and switching for logic circuits. Modified MOSFETs with two or three independent gates exist, and these have characteristics similar to those of tetrode and pentode vacuum tubes for radio-frequency amplification.

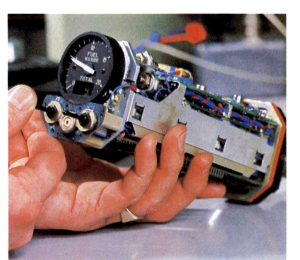

◄ A combined indicator-processor for an airplane's fuel-quantity-indicating system, which incorporates thousands of transistors—as well as capacitors, diodes, and resistors—in its minute, wafer-thin, integrated circuit.

SEE ALSO: AMPLIFIER • CONDENSED-MATTER PHYSICS • DIODE • ELECTRONICS • INTEGRATED CIRCUIT • MICROPROCESSOR • RADIO • SEMICONDUCTOR • SILICON • VACUUM TUBE

Transition Element

The term *transition element* applies to the metallic elements that bridge the gap between the highly reactive alkali and alkaline earth metals at the left of the periodic table and the nonmetals and metalloids at the right. It was coined by Dmitry Mendeleyev, the Russian chemist who devised the periodic table, before the electronic structures of atoms were understood. He used the term to refer to a group of nine elements that share similar chemical properties: iron, cobalt, and nickel in the fourth period of the periodic table; ruthenium, rhodium, and palladium in the fifth period; and osmium, iridium, and platinum in the sixth period. The last six of these elements are collectively known as the platinum metals.

Definitions

More recent definitions of transition elements include many more elements, and they usually refer to electronic structure—the main factor in determining chemical and physical properties. The broadest definition describes transition elements as being those elements that participate in chemical bonding using electrons from more than one type of orbital. The lightest transition element by this definition is scandium (Sc), which has two 4s electrons and one 3d electron that can participate in bonding. This configuration is sometimes written $[Ar]3d^14s^2$, which indicates the presence of the three valence electrons around a core that has the same structure as the electron configuration of argon. By this definition, the first transition series extends as far as copper (Cu; $[Ar]3d^{10}4s^1$), which loses a 3d electron and a 4s electron to form the Cu^{2+} ion. Another definition classifies as a transition element only those elements that have partially filled d orbitals, and this definition ends the series one element earlier, at nickel (Ni; $[Ar]3d^84s^2$).

In a similar way, the second transition series starts at yttrium (Y; $[Kr]4d^15s^2$—this time the core is that of krypton) and continues to palladium (Pd; $[Kr]4d^{10}$) or silver (Ag; $[Kr]4d^{10}5s^1$), depending on the choice of definition. Palladium and silver are members of the groups of nickel and copper, respectively. In fact, the definition that requires partially filled d orbitals should exclude palladium, since its configuration has each of the five 4d orbitals occupied by an electron pair. However, the properties of palladium are so similar to those of the other members of its group, which do have d-orbital vacancies, that palladium is included with the transition elements as an exception to the more general rule.

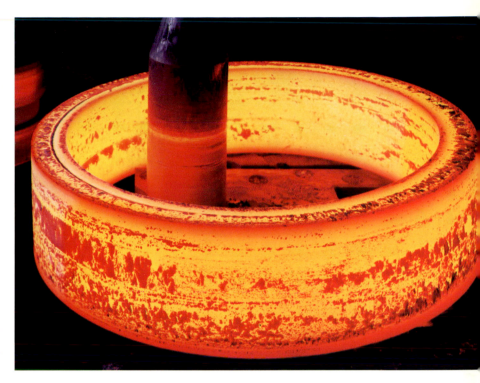

▲ The red-hot ring is an aircraft component made of an alloy of titanium, a transition metal. The low relative density of the alloy—4.43 compared with 7.87 for iron—makes it ideal for use in aircraft construction. Tensile strengths as great as 200,000 psi (13.8 MPa) can be achieved.

The third transition series includes lanthanum (La; $[Xe]5d^16s^2$), hafnium (Hf; $[Xe]4f^{14}5d^26s^2$), and the following elements as far as platinum (Pt; $[Xe]4f^{14}5d^96s^2$) or gold (Au; $[Xe]4f^{14}5d^{10}6s^2$). The properties of these elements are strikingly similar to the corresponding elements in the previous series, and this similarity is greater even than the similarity between the first and second transition series. In this series, there is a leap of 15 units of atomic number between lanthanum and hafnium, where the series resumes with full 4f orbitals.

The interruption in the third transition occurs because of a reversal in the relative energies of the 5d and 4f orbitals after lanthanum, so electrons start to occupy the lower-energy 4f orbitals. This arrangement is seen in the configurations of the elements that follow lanthanum: cerium (Ce; $[Xe]4f^15d^16s^2$) and praseodymium (Pr; $[Xe]4f^36s^2$). Since the 14 elements in this series have valence electrons in two or three types of orbitals, they all qualify as transition elements by the broadest definition. To avoid confusion with the d-block transition elements, these elements are more commonly classified as lanthanides; this name reflects their position after lanthanum in the periodic table.

A similar reversal in orbital energies occurs at actinium (Ac; $[Rn]6d^17s^2$), which is followed by 14 elements, the actinides, whose 5f orbitals are gradually occupied by electrons. The success of the periodic table in predicting similarities in chemical properties for elements in adjacent rows would suggest the resumption of a fourth transition series after the actinides, but the instability with respect to radioactive decay of the heavier elements prevents their full analysis.

Physical properties

All the transition elements are metals, as is evident from their luster and conductivity. They differ significantly from the main-block metals, such as potassium and calcium, however. Transition metals are much harder and have higher melting points. Titanium melts at 3038°F (1670°C) and chromium at 3326°F (1830°C), for example, whereas calcium melts at 1542°F (839°C). These differences stem from the contribution of d-orbital electrons to the interatomic bonding of transition elements, whereas main-block metals are held together by metallic bonds based on s-orbital electrons. The stronger the bonds, the greater is the thermal energy—and therefore temperature—required to break them so that the atoms can flow as a liquid. Melting points increase down the periods—a consequence of the d orbitals becoming more accessible for bonding—and also with the number of unpaired electrons. These two trends culminate at tungsten (symbol W, from the German *Wolfram*), which has six valence electrons in six valence orbitals—five 5d orbitals and one 6s orbital. Tungsten melts at 6120°F (3382°C), a property that makes it ideal for its use in the filaments of electric lamps.

Metals that bond with equal strength in all directions pack together as if they were spheres so as to give the most tightly packed structure, which is either a face-centered cubic (f.c.c.) or a hexagonal close-packed (h.c.p.) crystal structure. Both these structures are are equally efficient in terms of the ratio of occupied space to unoccupied space, and they are adopted by metals that bond through s electrons alone or through s electrons and certain combinations of d orbitals.

Unlike s orbitals, which are spherically symmetrical, d orbitals each have four lobes that represent the space an electron in that orbital is most likely to occupy. For four of the orbitals, these lobes form an X-shaped distribution centered on the nucleus; the fifth has two lobes that point out from the nucleus in opposite directions and a ring that surrounds the point where they meet. For some transition metals—iron, chromium, and vanadium, for example—the participation of the d orbitals in bonding favors the body-centered cubic (b.c.c.) structure, in which adjacent atoms lie on the axes of the d-orbital lobes.

The influence of crystal structure on mechanical properties is twofold. First, metals that occupy b.c.c. structures are more brittle than those with close-packed structures, since the directional nature of the bonds inhibits relative motion of adjacent layers. Second, the larger interstices (gaps) in the b.c.c. structure can be occupied by small nonmetal atoms, which provide a further impediment to the relative motion of layers and consequently increase hardness. In the case of iron, which is comparatively soft as a pure metal, the addition of only 0.03 percent (by weight) carbon causes a considerable increase in hardness.

Magnetic properties

The magnetic properties of materials stem from the intrinsic magnetism that electrons possess owing to their spin. When a pair of electrons occupy a single orbital, their spins are opposed so that they have no net magnetic moment. If an external field is applied, it distorts the orbitals slightly, and a slight repulsion occurs. This property is diamagnetism; it is the most common magnetic property.

If a single electron occupies an orbital, however, its magnetic moment can align with an external magnetic field, and an attraction results that is much stronger than the repulsive force caused by paired electrons. This effect, called paramagnetism, is characteristic of transition metals whose d or f orbitals are partially filled; it is strongest for elements with half-full d or f subshells, since they have most unpaired electrons.

A third type of magnetism, called ferromagnetism, is much stronger than either diamagnetism or paramagnetism. This is the familiar magnetic effect exhibited by iron and also by cobalt and nickel. Of the rare earths, gadolinium is ferromagnetic up to 68°F (20°C) and terbium up to −58°F (−50°C), and dysprosium, holmium, and erbium exhibit ferromagnetism at temperatures close to absolute zero (−460°F, −273°C).

▼ All these objects are made from transition metals. Clockwise from bottom, the collection comprises gold jack plugs, tungsten drill bits, a mercury thermometer, a chromium-plated Newton's cradle, silver cutlery, a titanium camera body, copper piping, a vanadium spanner, and a platinum ring. At the center are an iron magnet and some steel nails (steel is an alloy of iron with carbon).

LANTHANIDES AND ACTINIDES

Lanthanides and actinides are two series of metallic transition elements whose f subshells gradually fill through the series. The lanthanides—also called the rare earths—are the sequence of 15 elements starting at lanthanum and increasing by one atomic number for each element to lutetium, which has a full f subshell. Similarly, the actinides—also called the transuranic elements—are the series of 15 elements from actinium to lawrencium. Scandium and yttrium are often classified with the lanthanides, since they have many chemical properties in common with the elements of that series.

Despite the name "rare earth," the lanthanides are not particularly scarce elements; yet the complexity of their extraction and purification limits the scope of their practical applications. Lanthanide-bearing ores typically contain compounds of several lanthanides, often with compounds of thorium (an actinide), and the uniform chemical properties of those elements make their separation by chemical means inefficient.

The most common lanthanide ore is monazite, a mixed phosphate of cerium, lanthanum, neodymium, and praseodymium (in order of decreasing concentration) with thorium phosphate and traces of other lanthanide phosphates. Digestion with sodium hydroxide (NaOH) solution forms the hydroxides of the metals, which yield a mixture of chlorides when treated with hot hydrochloric acid (HCl). At this point, thorium forms an insoluble oxide (ThO_2), which separates as a slurry from the solution of lanthanide chlorides.

After drying, electrolysis converts the chlorides into a lanthanide alloy called misch metal, which is often used without separation of its component metals. Misch metal sparks when struck, and its alloys are used to make lighter flints and tracer bullets. The addition of misch metal to steel improves its malleability by aiding the formation of graphite nodules from its carbon content, so reducing brittleness.

Some applications of lanthanides call for the separation of individual elements; one such application is the manufacture of phosphors—rare earth oxides—for use in

the colored dots of television screens and computer monitors. In such cases, the separation process starts with a solution of lanthanide (III) nitrates in water. This solution is brought into contact with tri-*n*-butyl phosphate, $(C_4H_9O)_3PO$, a solvent that is immiscible with water. The relative solubility of the nitrates in this solvent increases with the atomic number of the lanthanide, so the lighter lanthanide nitrates become concentrated in the water, while the heavier nitrates concentrate in the solvent. Repeated solvent extractions of this type result in separate solutions of the individual nitrates, and the process can be automated for efficiency on a large scale. The nitrates are then converted into the required oxides by chemical methods.

The actinides are much rarer than the lanthanides. In fact, only two actinides occur in significant amounts in natural deposits: thorium and uranium. The rarity of actinides is explained by radioactivity. The repulsive forces between protons in such heavy nuclei exceed the binding forces that keep lighter nuclei together. For this reason, all actinides undergo radioactive decay to form other elements, and thorium and uranium are the only actinides that have isotopes whose decay is slow enough for them to have survived from the formation of the Universe. Traces of actinium, protactinium, plutonium, and neptunium occur in uranium deposits, but

▲ A technician examines a crystal of synthetic yttrium–aluminum garnet (YAG). YAG is used as a synthetic gemstone, and variants of YAG are used as lasing materials in some types of solid-state lasers.

they are the results of sequences of nuclear reactions that start with the decay of radioactive uranium isotopes.

Thorium oxide from the extraction of misch metal is still used in small amounts for the manufacture of incandescent gas mantles, but its significance is dwarfed by the extraction of uranium for nuclear fuel. This process takes uranium ores, such as pitchblende (U_3O_8), and produces sulfate salts of a complex cation (UO_2^{2+}) by treatment with sulfuric acid. The reaction of this salt with concentrated nitric acid forms a nitrate, $UO_2(NO_3)_2$, that can be purified by solvent extraction into tri-*n*-butyl phosphate. Heat and subsequent reduction by hydrogen form a pure oxide (UO_2), which forms the basis of fuel.

The chemistries of the lanthanides and actinides resemble those of the d-block transition metals in that they are metals that form compounds and complexes in various oxidation states. However, the 3+ oxidation state dominates the compounds of lanthanides, and little is known of the properties of actinides beyond uranium owing to their radioactive instability and the effect of radiation on chemical bonds.

Ferromagnetism arises from a phenomenon called exchange interaction, which exists independent of any external field and is a property of collections of atoms that have unpaired electrons. Exchange interaction occurs only when the distance between neighboring atoms in a crystal lattice falls within a certain range. In the case of manganese, the spacing is just below the critical value, and the addition of a small amount of an element such as nitrogen can induce ferromagnetism.

Chemical properties

The compounds of main-group metals are almost exclusively ionic, containing metal ions in which all s electrons have been lost. Transition metals also form some simple ionic salts, such as nitrates and sulfates, but their chemistry is dominated by the formation and reactions of compounds and complex ions in which atoms or molecules, called ligands, attach to transition metals by covalent bonds—a process called coordination.

Even in apparently simple salts, there is a tendency to form compounds in more than one oxidation state, because the energy required to remove d-orbital electrons is often well matched by the energy released when the more highly oxidized metal forms compounds. In the case of iron, for example, oxidizing and reducing agents quite easily interconvert the +2 and +3 oxidation states, and thus, both iron (II) chloride ($FeCl_2$) and iron (III) chloride ($FeCl_3$) exist.

The existence of alternative oxidation states in complex ions is demonstrated by the hexacyanoferrate ions. In these species, six cyanide (CN) ligands coordinate around an iron atom through covalent bonds between their carbon atoms and the iron atom. The oxidation state of the iron atom determines which complex ion is formed—hexacyanoferrate (III), $Fe(CN)_6^{3-}$, or hexacyanoferrate (II), $Fe(CN)_6^{4-}$. Although the iron "ion" has a nominal charge of +3 or +2, respectively, and the cyanide a charge of –1, these species are better thought of as covalently bonded molecules in which the charge spreads over many atoms.

One of the most unusual properties of transition metals is their ability to form compounds in which their oxidation state is apparently zero. One example of this type of compound is nickel carbonyl, $Ni(CO)_4$, formed by exposing powdered nickel to carbon monoxide (CO) at 122°F (50°C). This compound boils at 109°F (43°C), and its distillation is an important step in the manufacture of pure nickel. Bonding is possible despite the zero oxidation state because each carbonyl group donates an electron pair to form one bond, while the metal back-donates another pair to form a second bond. Manganese carbonyl, $Mn_2(CO)_{10}$, is particularly interesting in that each metal atom bonds to five carbonyl ligands while also bonding to the other metal atom.

A phenomenon that is of vast importance for industrial catalysis is the ability of transition metals to form bonds with the electron pairs that constitute the bonds of organic molecules. In one example, nickel acts as a hydrogenation catalyst by forming bonds with the double carbon–carbon bonds in unsaturated molecules. This weakens the double bond and makes it more susceptible to hydrogenation. In another process, titanium (III) chloride catalyzes the polymerization of ethene (ethylene, $CH_2=CH_2$) by first forming an ethyl complex, $TiCl_3(C_2H_5)$, in a reaction with tetraethyl aluminum, $Al(C_2H_5)_4$, and then accepting the electron pair from an ethene double bond to form $TiCl_3(C_2H_5)(CH_2=CH_2)$. The ethyl radical attaches to one end of the ethene ligand to form a butyl group attached to the metal atom in $TiCl_3(C_4H_9)$. Successive insertions of ethene molecules into the growing alkyl chain then form the basis of the polymerization.

The variable oxidation states of transition metals make them useful as oxidation and reduction catalysts, as in the case of the air oxidation of sulfur dioxide in the presence of vanadium pentoxide (V_2O_5)—a key stage in the production of sulfuric acid. In biology, the ability of iron atoms in hemoglobin to form loose complexes with oxygen molecules helps it carry oxygen through the body. The toxicity of carbon monoxide to animal life stems from its ability to latch onto the hemoglobin molecules in place of oxygen.

Color

Compounds of both transition and rare earth elements are noted for their intense colors, which vary according to oxidation state. These colors are due to the absorption of specific wavelengths of light as electrons move from lower to higher energy states in incomplete d or f subshells.

Colored compounds of iron (red), cobalt (blue), and chromium (green) provide the hues of stained glass, paint pigments, and natural minerals. In some cases, the color caused by one impurity can be overcome by the addition of another, so that a yellow tint due to iron impurities can be counteracted by adding neodymium. Glassworkers' goggles, which offer protection by absorbing the intense yellow light from sodium-colored flames, are tinted with praseodymium.

SEE ALSO: ALLOY • ATOMIC STRUCTURE • CATALYST • CHEMISTRY, ORGANOMETALLIC • ELEMENT, CHEMICAL • IRON AND STEEL • MAGNETISM • METAL • PERIODIC TABLE

Transmission, Automobile

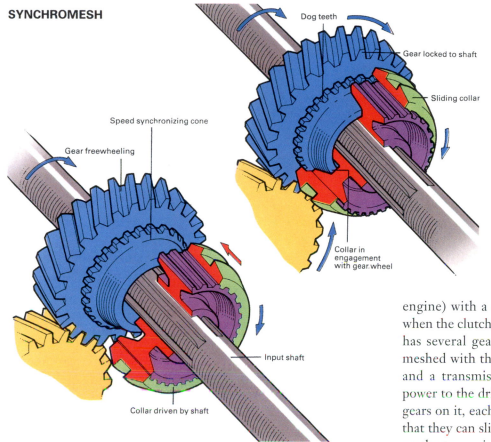

Speed synchronizing cone

Gear freewheeling

Dog teeth

Gear locked to shaft

Sliding collar

Collar in engagement with gear.wheel

Input shaft

Collar driven by shaft

Internal combustion engines are the most common power source for vehicles, such as automobiles and trucks, but they have the disadvantage that they work only over a limited speed range and have a limited torque output. It is impossible to run an internal combustion engine smoothly below 500 rpm, and it would be unwise to run it at above 7,000 rpm. These characteristics are such that the engine cannot be connected directly to the drive wheels, because such an arrangement would give poor starting and hill-climbing ability together with a limited speed range. The solution is to use a transmission, or gearbox, to match the engine characteristics to the driving force required to move the vehicle. Manual transmissions usually have four or five ratios. Top, or high, gear (four or five) is usually about 1:1, or direct. In practical terms, then, most automobiles cannot run smoothly in high gear at below 20 mph (32 km/h). The lower gears allow the automobile to run smoothly at lower speeds and enable it to start up from rest.

For starting from rest, the requirement is for high torque at low speed. The initial match between the engine and the stationary drive system is achieved by slipping the clutch. Once

▲ To avoid grating gears, cars are fitted with synchromesh. A conical ring on the gearwheel in front of the dog teeth engages gradually with a matching conical hole in the collar. Friction quickly slows down or speeds up the gear wheel to match the speed of the collar. A spring-loaded outer sleeve on the collar slides forward over the dog on the gearwheel. Both halves of the dog clutch are locked together, so drive is transmitted smoothly and evenly.

the vehicle is moving, the torque has to overcome the vehicle's rolling resistance, together with providing a sufficient margin for acceleration or hill climbing. At cruising speed, the main resistance to motion comes from air and rolling resistances. Here the lower torque levels required are applied at higher speeds.

A manual transmission has a clutch shaft (driven from the engine) with a clutch gear on it that is turning when the clutch is engaged; a countershaft, which has several gears on it, one of which is always meshed with the clutch gear and is turned by it; and a transmission shaft, which transmits the power to the drive shaft and which has a series of gears on it, each larger than the other, splined so that they can slide on the shaft. Each of the gears on the transmission shaft is fitted with a shifting yoke, a bracket for pushing it back and forth on the shaft. The shifting yokes are selected and shifted by the driver by means of the shifting lever, which pivots between the driver's compartment and the top of the case containing the gears.

When the driver selects first gear, or low gear, the largest of the gears on the transmission shaft is pushed along the shaft until it meshes with the smallest gear on the countershaft. Then the clutch is engaged, allowing power to be transmitted from the engine through the transmission to the wheels. The gear ratio between the transmission shaft and the countershaft is 3:1, and the effective ratio between the crankshaft and the wheels is about 12:1 (because of further reduction gearing in the differential, another set of gears that transmits power between the drive shaft and the drive wheels).

When the vehicle is moving fast enough, about 10 mph (16 km/h), the driver shifts to second gear, engaging the next largest transmission gear with the large countershaft gear. The gear ratio is now 2:1, and the ratio between the crankshaft and the wheels about 8:1. For cruising speed, as the driver shifts through the intermediate gears to high gear, the smallest transmission gear is forced axially (lengthwise) against the

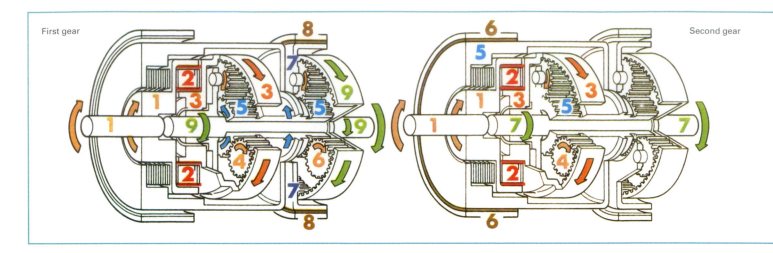

clutch gear. Teeth on the sides of these gears engage, and the gear ratio is now 1:1; the transmission shaft and the clutch shaft (hence the crankshaft) are turning at the same speed. The ratio between the crankshaft and the wheels is now about 4:1. Thus, the speed of the engine is always within the range of efficiency for the engine while the vehicle builds up speed.

The reverse gear is positioned at the back end of the countershaft, and turns a small idler gear that meshes with the large transmission gear when the driver selects reverse. When two gears mesh, they turn in opposite directions; the inclusion of an idler gear between them enables them to turn in the same direction so that the vehicle reverses its direction.

In a gear system, speed reduction means an increase in torque. So the transmission, when first gear is selected, transmits less speed from the small countershaft gear to the large transmission gear (because, when two gears turn together the larger gear turns more slowly) but transmits more torque from the crankshaft to twist the drive shaft and overcome the inertia of the vehicle to get it moving.

For automobiles with large powerful engines, a three-speed transmission can be satisfactory, but with smaller engines or where maximum performance is required, four- and five-speed transmissions are generally used. Often the fifth speed is an overdrive designed to give comfortable high-speed cruising at relatively low engine speeds. On a large truck, the transmission may have 16 or more forward gears to match the engine power output to the heavy starting and running loads. In some truck transmissions, the large number of ratios needed are obtained by the use of duals, or two-gear units in series, which double the range of selectable gears.

In the early days of automobiles, transmissions were simple devices such as described above, and it took muscle power and skill to shift the gears smoothly. The edges of the gear teeth were chamfered (rounded) so that they meshed as smoothly as possible. Downshifting was particularly complicated, requiring double-clutching: disengaging the clutch, engaging neutral, letting the clutch in, revving the engine to increase the speed of the countershaft gears so they matched the speed of the output gears, disengaging the clutch, engaging the required gear (possible because the speeds have been matched), and then reengaging the clutch. Apart from being noisy, these early transmission systems were susceptible to damage.

Constant-mesh transmissions

Today transmissions are of the constant-mesh type: all gearwheels remain constantly in contact with each other. Dog clutches—simple square teeth placed on the shaft next to the gearwheels—are used for gear ratio selection. The gearwheels themselves use teeth that are helical in pattern and produce far less noise than straight-cut gearwheels, because more than one tooth on the wheel is engaged at any one time.

A transmission in a rear-wheel drive automobile usually has three main shafts. The input shaft, driven by the engine via the clutch, is usually known as the primary, or first-motion, shaft. Gearwheels engage with the lay shaft, or second-motion, shaft. The gears on the lay shaft, in turn, drive the output shaft, which turns two final drive gears. Sliding one set of gearwheels on the first-motion shaft engages the dog clutches of another set of gearwheels. The effect is to couple the drive to the output shaft—the ratio has been selected. When a particular set of gears is engaged, the other sets idle, transmitting no power.

Synchromesh

Before a gear can be selected, the speeds of rotation of both halves of the pair of gearwheels (and their dog clutches) have to be closely matched. At the time of gear change, the two speeds of rota-

▲ An automatic transmission. (Above left) First gear: input shaft (1) turns; forward clutch (2) is locked, driving the first annulus (3) and the first planet wheels (4), which turn the sun wheel (5) backward. Sun wheel drives the second planet wheels (6) forward; the second planet carrier (7) is stopped by a band brake (8), so the second annulus (9) turns very slowly, driving the car's wheels. (Above right) Second gear: input shaft (1) turns; the forward clutch (2) is locked, driving the first annulus (3) and the first planet wheels (4). The common sun wheel (5) is locked by a band brake (6); therefore the first planet carrier (7) turns slowly forward, driving wheels through the output shaft that is linked to it, as well as driving the second annulus, which freewheels.

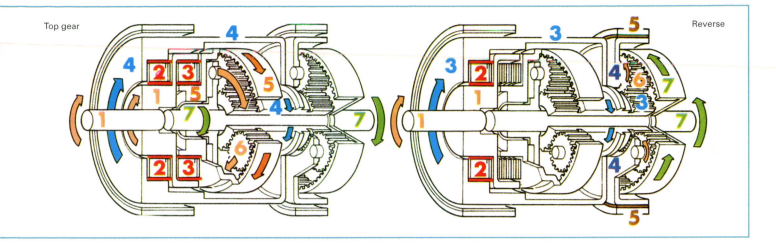

Top gear

Reverse

▲ (Above left) Top gear: input shaft (1) turns; both clutches (2) and (3) are locked, so (1) drives both common sun wheel (4) and first annulus (5). Planet wheels (6) lie between the two and are carried around without themselves revolving, taking with them first the planet carrier (7) and output shaft linked to it and so driving the car's wheels.

(Above right) Reverse: input shaft (1) turns; reverse-high clutch (2) is locked, so common sun wheel (3) is driven directly. The second planet carrier (4) is locked by the band brake (5), so the sun wheel turns the planet wheels (6) against the second annulus (7), turning the second annulus, and the car's wheels linked to it slowly backward. The first planet carrier freewheels.

tion are not the same. Typically, an upward change from third to fourth will involve pushing together one set of dog clutches turning at 6,000 rpm with another set turning at 4,000 rpm.

Part of the solution is to slow the engine and with it the input shaft and lay shaft. Good driving instructors will train their pupils to release the accelerator during manual upward gear change. The effect should be to slow the shafts' rotation. In practice, the shafts do not slow sufficiently because of the combined inertia of the input shaft, the lay shaft, and the attached clutch plate. Conversely, on a down change, the input shaft, lay shaft, and clutch plate need to be accelerated. Again, the recommended push on the throttle will fail to accelerate the three components sufficiently to match the rotational rates of the two sets of dog clutches.

To solve this problem, automobile engineers came up with synchromesh devices. They are incorporated into each dog clutch unit to match the gearwheels' rotational speed. The gears that are to be engaged need to be modified so that they have cone friction surfaces. A cone clutch rubs against these friction surfaces so that the two gears are turning at the same rate. With the rotational rates matched, the two sets of dog clutches can be safely brought together without damaging each other. The dog clutches are usually part of a separate sleeve linked to the shaft by a set of tiny ball bearings, which are spring-loaded into detents, or depressions.

During a gear change, the first-gear-lever movement forces the two halves of the cone clutch together, matching their speeds. As the gear lever is moved further, the spring-loaded balls lose their grip and the dog clutches engage.

The design is not perfect, because rapid gear changes can push the two sets of dog clutches together before their rotational speeds are matched; wear and transmission noise result. To cure this problem, most transmissions incorpo-

rate balk rings, additional rings on the outer face of the cone clutch. The balk rings have their own set of dog clutches that must engage before those on the gearwheel are engaged.

Differential

The differential is a transmission assembly in a motor vehicle that allows the propeller shaft, or drive shaft, to turn the drive wheels at different speeds when the vehicle is going around a curve. When a vehicle goes around a curve, the wheel on the inside of the curve travels less distance than the other and so must turn more slowly, for safety in handling and to keep tire wear to a minimum.

For maximum traction, a four-wheel-drive vehicle can have three differentials, separating the left from the right wheels and the front from the rear so that each wheel turns at its own speed.

The differential is encased in a casting, which is located between the driven wheels. Thus, a front-wheel-drive automobile has its differential between the front wheels, and a rear-wheel-drive automobile between the rear wheels. The power from the engine goes first to the transmission and then to the differential. Each driven wheel is connected to the differential by a driveshaft. A pinion gear, which is splined to the end of the driveshaft from the transmission, turns a beveled crown gear, which is fastened onto the differential cage. An assembly of four small beveled gears (two pinions and two star gears) is bolted to the cage and turns with it. Each axle is connected to one of the star gears. The assembly drives both axles at the same speed when the vehicle is being driven in a straight line but allows the axle opposite the crown gear to turn slower or faster as the vehicle turns.

Some units are designed to give a limited-slip, or slip-lock, differential, to equalize power between the wheels on a slippery or a soft road surface; this feature provides safer handling and minimizes the likelihood of an automobile's becoming stuck in snow or soft earth.

The gear ratio (ratio of the number of teeth on one gear to the number of teeth on the other) between the crown gear and the pinion gear on the driveshaft is one of the factors that determines the performance characteristics of the automobile, such as acceleration and top speed.

Early automobiles had pinion and crown gears with straight teeth on them. They produced noisy operation of the differential and allowed play in the gear teeth, causing undue wear. Modern pinion and crown gears are helical, that is, the toothed surfaces are beveled, and the teeth themselves are curved. This design eliminates play between the teeth, because as the gears spin together, one tooth is in full contact before the previous tooth leaves. A properly constructed differential should last the life of the automobile without maintenance.

In order to produce a particularly quiet differential, the pinion and crown gears are lapped together in a lapping machine, which duplicates the operating conditions of the completed differential. After lapping, the two gears are kept together as a set. They are inspected together in a machine in a quiet room to determine the exact thickness of shims (sheet metal disks used to ensure a close fit) required in the assembly to provide quiet operation; then they go to the differential assembly line. All the gears in the system are installed against roller bearings, the proper shimming is installed, and then the unit is test run, filled with a heavy oil and sealed.

Transmission arrangements

With the conventional front engine, rear-wheel-drive automobile, the transmission is normally fitted to the engine and transmits power to the rear axle through a driveshaft. An alternative arrangement, sometimes used to give a better weight distribution, has a driveshaft running directly from the engine to a transmission unit coupled to the final drive at the rear. Both front engine, front-wheel-drive and rear engine, rear-wheel-drive automobiles generally have the transmission and final-drive system combined in a single unit. With four-wheel-drive vehicles, the drive is normally split by a mid differential after the transmission unit.

In the United States, most automobiles have automatic transmission, whereby ratio changes are made according to the road and engine speeds and the acceleration required by the driver. Thus, this system does not require the driver to operate a clutch pedal. Typically, such systems have epicyclic gear systems engaged by hydraulic clutches, with a fluid flywheel or torque converter providing the coupling to the engine.

A DIFFERENTIAL

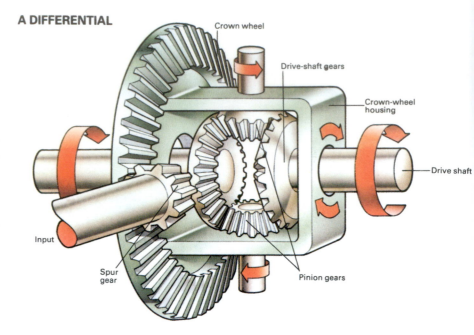

Crown wheel

Drive-shaft gears

Crown-wheel housing

Drive shaft

Input

Spur gear

Pinion gears

Other types of transmissions

Although direct-gear devices are used for most road vehicles, a number of other types of transmissions are in use for more specialized applications. Most electric transmissions are used with battery-powered vehicles, but coupled systems consisting of an engine-driven generator powering individual wheel motors are also in use. Hydrostatic drives have an engine-driven pump that supplies high-pressure hydraulic fluid to individual motors at the wheels.

An internal combustion engine has an optimum rate of revolutions at which it can run. Ideally, an engine should be made to operate at this optimum level, but to do so would require many more gears than are currently used. One way of achieving an optimum rate is through a continuously variable transmission (CVT), which allows the small changes in gear ratio that enable the engine to run most efficiently. The goal is achieved through the use of a drive belt running around pulleys that have adjustable V-shaped grooves in which the band sits. By altering the depth of this groove, the belt is made to ride higher or lower; the result is a continuous range of different gear ratios. In the past, these systems tended to be expensive and less reliable than conventional transmission and so were rarely used in automobiles. Recently, however, improvements in materials, hydraulics, and the introduction of high-speed sensors have enabled practical automobile CVTs to be developed, and they are now used in cars produced by Honda and Toyota.

▲ The function of the differential is to divide the torque and feed it to the road wheels so that each driven wheel turns at different rates when rounding corners. In a curve, one wheel has farther to travel than the wheel opposite, so it must turn faster.

 SEE ALSO: AUTOMOBILE • BATTERY • CAM • CLUTCH • GEAR • INTERNAL COMBUSTION ENGINE • LUBRICATION • TRUCK

Transmission, Broadcasting

It is more than 100 years since the real birth of broadcasting. Before that, every form of communication had required some kind of physical link—cables were used for telephones and electric telegraphs, for example. In 1887, a German physicist, Heinrich Rudolph Hertz, first demonstrated the physical existence of radio waves and in 1894 came the first public demonstration, by Sir Oliver Lodge, a British physicist, in England, that radio waves were able to carry messages over a few hundred yards.

In 1895 the Italian inventor Guglielmo Marconi carried out similar experiments, and during 1896 he demonstrated radio communications first on the roof of the General Post Office's headquarters in London and then over 1.25 miles (2 km) on Salisbury Plain in southwest England.

His most exciting demonstration took place in 1901 when he showed that radio messages could be sent across the Atlantic between Cornwall in England and Newfoundland, a distance of about 2,000 miles (3,200 km).

Regular broadcasting

The first American radio program was broadcast from the experimental station at Brant Rock in Massachusetts on Christmas Eve 1906. Many experimental stations started operating when restrictions necessary for wartime purposes on the use of wavelengths were lifted at the end of World War I in 1918.

Some consider that the birth of modern broadcasting was on the evening of November 2, 1920, when station KDKA went on the air reporting returns of the presidential election that was won by Warren Harding who was opposed by James Cox. Eight stations were operating by the end of 1921, and one year later, there were 564 already crowding the wavelengths.

In 1921 Marconi himself started transmissions from Marconi House in London, using the call-sign 2LO, which soon became famous.

The number of broadcasting stations throughout the world increased from about 600 at the end of 1925 to 1,300 in 1935, and there were at least 10,000 by the early 1960s. As had been predicted, overcrowding and overlapping of wavelengths in use soon became a problem.

The first international agreements involving large numbers of countries were reached in 1932 by the International Telecommunications Union, set up for that purpose. In spite of failures to agree on the allocation of wavelengths between communist and noncommunist areas, further

▲ These journalists are in an outside broadcasting unit watching a press conference as it happens. The pictures they see can be taped for editing into a report later in the day or beamed live to a studio for simultaneous transmission.

In 1929 the British Broadcasting Corporation (BBC) began its first experimental television transmissions, followed in 1936 by a regular public high-definition television service, using at first 240 lines and later 405 lines. Early transmissions were broadcast live during the evening from Alexandra Palace in north London.

During the 1930s, about 12 experimental television stations began transmissions in the United States, broadcasting drama, sporting events, and even politics, though no commercial receivers were yet available. In 1945, 12 VHF channels were allocated to television in the United States (from 54 to 88 MHz and from 174 to 216 MHz). By 1948, 20 television stations were on the air, 80 more were partly completed and soon due to start broadcasting, and 300 were applying for licenses. Eventually, 70 more channels were allocated for television, using the UHF (ultra-high frequencies) band, the number of channels in cities varying in proportion with the population.

A major advance in broadcasting technology came in 1962 when the second communication satellite to be launched, Telstar 2, enabled television pictures to be transmitted between Europe and America. Today satellites play a large part in international communications and broadcasting.

The transistor radio

The development of the cheap, portable transistor radio set brought listening—to broadcasts from all over the world—within the reach of poorer pockets. At the end of World War II in 1945, there were about 150 million radio sets in the world; by 1972 there were at least 820 million, the vast majority of which were cheap, portable transistor radios. But whereas there were about 85 or 90 radio receiving sets per every 100 people in North America, the ratio in Africa was between two and three per hundred. The problem of local languages and dialects remained very substantial; for example, All-India Radio broadcasts in about 24 different languages and 146 local dialects.

Modern broadcasting

In a typical television studio, the visual sources come from four to six studio cameras, and there may be more outside broadcast units contributing to the program. Videotape recordings, made earlier from television cameras or ordinary film (with or without soundtrack), can be prepared on special machines called telecine machines and may replace live television camera pictures several times in a single program. News reporters in the field can also use satellite links and videophones, either live or prerecorded, for transmission on a news program.

agreements in the 1940s and 1950s broadly assigned domestic broadcasting to two sets of wavelengths, 150 to 550 kHz on the long wave and 550 to 1,660 kHz on the medium wave. External broadcasting on short wave was assigned the region between 2,200 and 30,000 kHz.

As wavelengths became more overcrowded, European countries and American stations particularly turned more and more to the use of very high frequencies (VHF), allocated for domestic broadcasting in the frequency range between 87.5 and 100 MHz.

▲ Satellite dishes have become a common sight since the introduction of cable television. Cable systems can carry hundreds of channels on one bandwidth and offer a range of other services, such as telephone connections and fast-access Internet provision.

Television broadcasting

The year 1926 saw the birth of television when John Logie Baird, a Scottish inventor, managed to transmit a crude black-and-white 30-line image of a human face onto a small screen. Although Baird was the first person to achieve a television picture in this way, he was actually using a patent taken out as long ago as 1884.

In the most modern studios in the United States and Europe, sophisticated electronic editing facilities are available that can combine elements from a number of different pictures to produce a composite. The simplest of these techniques is the traveling matte—a device borrowed from film studios. This device can produce fixed boundaries within the picture area and switch from one scene to another on those boundaries.

Chromakey is a system that relies on the use of brilliant blue or green backgrounds to generate movable boundaries around objects and actors in front of the background; this system allows alternative backgrounds to be switched into the picture. Such technology allows actors to appear to fly or to be filmed in precarious situations and broadcasters to deliver weather bulletins.

Even more advanced are the latest computer-based digital editing facilities. They can produce virtually any required combination of pictures, no matter how fantastic. If a historical documentary is being set in a town that now has a power station dominating the skyline, it takes only a few minutes to have the power station deleted and the space filled with sky that is a perfect match for the surrounding area, or at the director's whim, an imaginary castle can be placed on the site. This technology allows the production of effects that would otherwise have been dangerous, expensive, or even impossible.

The sound sources in a studio include up to 60 microphones, four record turntables, two tape machines, and access to three echo rooms to obtain echo effects. In a sound radio studio, there are usually fewer microphones but more machines for playing records, tapes, and compact discs (CDs).

Radio and television studios are usually arranged as part of a suite that is acoustically separate from the control room. In the control room, the studio manager has direct control over the recording levels and, in a television studio, camera directions and moving or still back projections. When a whole program is to be recorded before broadcasting, great skill is required to introduce prerecorded material at the correct time. Also, with the final editing of the recorded session, there must be no loss of sense or essential content where a reduction in program time is required to fit the predetermined program schedule.

Next the programs are coordinated in the continuity suite, which, as its name implies, provides a continuous stream of broadcasting. The continuity announcer works from a preplanned schedule and ensures that, as far as is possible, all programs run on time. He or she is provided with written material advertising future programs plus extra sound and visual material that can fill in any spare time.

From the continuity suite, the sound and vision signals pass through at least one switching

▼ A mobile broadcasting unit from Radio Clare, a local radio station in the west of Ireland. Units like these enable outdoor events to be broadcast, something that was impossible in the studio-based days of early radio.

center and then, via cable or short-wave radio link, to the regional transmitter stations. From here, the signals are transmitted at the standard radio and television frequencies to radio or television receivers in the home.

Cable television

Cable technology provided a new way of broadcasting television signals. At first, cable systems had a reputation for being unreliable and for not producing the best-quality picture. A series of amplifiers boosted the signal along the cable, and if one of these broke down, the picture was lost. In the 1950s, cable systems started using microwave transmitting and receiving towers that could receive signals from distant stations. This technology made television available to people who were outside the range of standard broadcasts and also allowed some people to receive several broadcast stations of the same network.

As interest in cable systems—or community antenna television (CATV)—grew, television manufacturers added a switch to new sets that could tune the sets either to channels based on the Federal Communications Commission (FCC) frequency allocation or to the cable systems. Because cable systems used cable and did not have to rely on antennas, they did not have to concern themselves with the FCC's broadcast plan—they could broadcast on the unused frequencies.

As the number of cable channels increased, so did the bandwidth of cable systems. Early systems operated at 220 MHz, while today they operate at 550 MHz. The development of fiber optics and analog-to-digital conversion improved the broadcast quality and increased the number of channels available. Because signals carried on fiber-optic cable required fewer amplifiers than the old coaxial cable, signal quality and the reliability of the service improved. By 1988, only one or two amplifiers were needed per household, down

▶ The control room of a television studio is where editors and production staff direct camera angles and cue lighting changes and sound effects. The bank of screens allows them to see what is happening in different areas of the studio and in outside links so that they can cut to another presenter at an appropriate point in the script.

▼ An AM radio signal is a combination of speech signals with a carrier wave. At the receiver, the speech is recorded and amplified.

from 30 or 40. Fiber-optic cable also allowed cable providers to target individual neighborhoods, and in the 1990s, they created local-area networks (LANs) and Internet access. By 1989, analog-to-digital technology had been developed, which allowed an analog signal to be converted to digital and transmitted using a standard 6 MHz

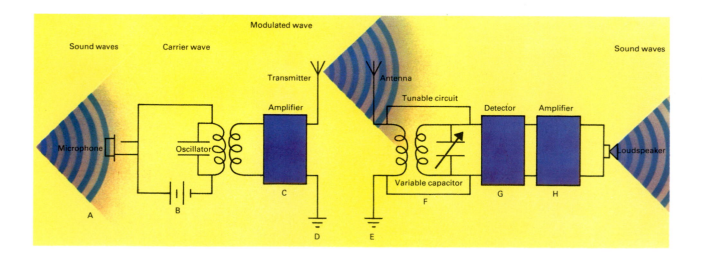

Small-dish satellites use digital signals. The programs are encoded in MPEG (moving pictures experts group) format before being transmitted to Earth and decoded by the set-top box. MPEG is a family of standards used for coding audiovisual information (such as movies) in a digital compressed format. The advantage of MPEG over other formats is that the files are much smaller for the same quality.

Digital television

Digital television, also known as DTV or HDTV (high-definition TV) uses MPEG encoding, as satellite television does. Digital cable and satellite systems are not true digital television, however. Although the set-top box receives a digital signal from cable or satellite, it converts this signal to analog and sends it to the analog television. True digital television, on the other hand, involves digital cameras, transmission, and display.

The main advantage of DTV is that it allows larger screen formats and produces a much-higher-resolution picture than analog systems do, as well as much better sound. The sharpness of a picture is determined by the number of pixels on the screen (or computer monitor). Pixels control color and intensity, and DTV allows ten times more pixels to appear on the screen than do analog television systems; the result is a picture with outstanding crispness and detail. Even the worst computer monitor displays a much-higher-resolution picture than does the best analog television set. DTV also allows broadcasters to send multiple programs on one channel.

The FCC has set deadlines in the United States for all broadcasters to convert to DTV. Commercial stations were scheduled to start simulcasting in digital by 2002, and public television stations by 2003. The FCC wanted all transmissions to be digital by 2006, but it is unlikely that these deadlines will be met because of the expense and complexity involved in the switch to digital. At the end of 2001, only 172 of approximately 1,250 commercial stations were transmitting DTV signals, and only 38 of 350 public stations had launched digital services.

Apart from improving what television broadcasting can do, another reason that the government is keen to replace the 50-year-old analog technology with digital is that it will free up transmission frequencies. It plans to sell these off to cellular phone companies, and the proceeds will go toward the federal budget.

TV channel. By 2001, CATV systems could transmit up to 10 channels of video in this bandwidth, and the combined bandwidth of 550 MHz allowed the possibility of 1,000 channels of video to be transmitted.

By the early 1990s, almost half the homes in the United States were receiving cable television. By 2001, about 60 million U.S. homes had access to cable systems, which not only deliver hundreds of channels but also provide high-speed Internet access and other services. However, digital cable signals are encrypted and must be decoded by a set-top box for the picture to appear on the television screen.

Satellite television

The other development in television broadcasting was the development of satellite communications. Satellite television uses either large or small dishes. Large-dish satellites receive analog signals from satellites orbiting Earth. The set-top box receives the signal and decodes it, if necessary, and sends it to the correct channel on the television set.

 SEE ALSO: Analog and digital systems • Cable network • Fiber optics • Radio • Television production

Transplant

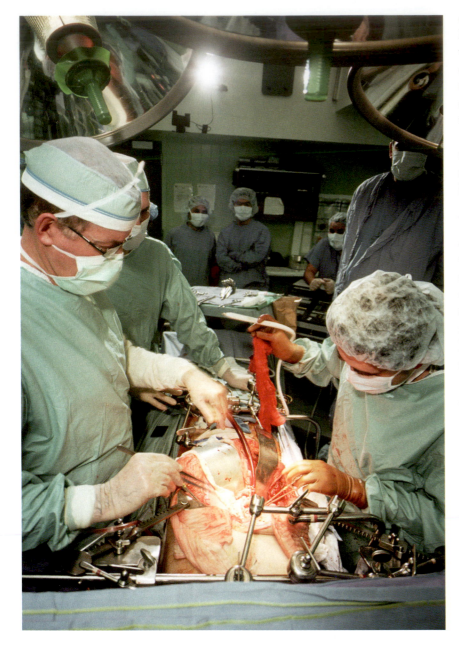

▲ Surgeons performing a liver transplant. The liver is an unusual organ in terms of its powers of regeneration. Sometimes surgeons need transplant only part of a liver, as the rest will grow back in time. All internal organs need to be transplanted as quickly as possible after removal from the donor as they begin to deteriorate after they have been disconnected from a circulating blood supply.

It is now possible to replace diseased parts of the human body, either with healthy parts removed from other people, with artificial parts made from plastics and metal, or, in the case of heart valves, with parts obtained from other species. Surgeons have developed their skills to the stage where they can replace almost any part of the human body. However, two major problems remain. When a healthy organ is used to replace a diseased organ, the body of the recipient must accept and not reject the new organ. Acceptance is effected by careful tissue typing and the use of drugs.

Transplanting live organs

When a diseased organ is to be replaced with a healthy living organ, as little time as possible must pass between removal of the organ from the donor and its placement into the recipient's body. Kidneys, after being removed from a donor whose tissues match the recipient's, are kept cooled on ice and have to be used within two days. Kidney transplantations are now common, and there would be many more if more people were willing to become donors.

Even more complicated are liver transplantations—there is a danger of the patient losing too much blood during the operation. Too little blood would then reach the new liver.

Tissue typing

All body cells carry certain chemicals that are part of the HLA (human leukocyte antigen) system of a particular person. If that person's white blood cells come in contact with cells that carry the same HLA molecules, nothing happens. However, if white blood cells come in contact with different HLA molecules, the "foreign" cells are rejected and destroyed as though they were an infection.

If a poorly matched organ is transplanted, the recipient's white blood cells will recognize foreign HLA molecules and fight off the organ. If the donor's and recipient's HLA molecules are only slightly different, the chances of rejection are reduced. Tissue typing involves very careful study of these HLA molecules, sometimes called cell fingerprints, to make sure that donors and recipients are as closely matched as possible.

Matching donors and recipients

Organs that are used for transplantation are usually taken from healthy people who have died as a result of an accident or brain damage caused by a ruptured blood vessel. The brain damage must be so extensive that there could be no possible chance of survival—it is essential to remove the heart while it is still beating. After much controversy and debate, the medical profession defined brain death as the lack of activity of the brain, along with other clinical observations. Death must be certified by a doctor who will not be involved in the transplant operation.

Once death has been certified, it is possible to remove the heart and lungs without needing to keep the donor on a life-support machine. If donors are kept on these machines for too long, the heart and kidneys are damaged.

Nowadays, a heart can be removed from a donor, perfused with a solution of electrolytes (magnesium and sodium salts), put in a sterile plastic bag that is then put in a freezer box and packed with crushed ice, and taken to the operating room where the recipient is waiting. The heart is also washed in a herapin solution (an anti-clotting agent) to remove the donor's blood.

The lungs are more delicate than the heart. A small, portable heart-lung machine can be taken to the donor. The heart and lungs can then be cooled by this machine—cooling the lungs with the salt solution could waterlog them.

Organs can be transported over long distances, but the shorter the transit time, the better the chances of survival. Kidneys have been flown across the Atlantic, but the maximum allowable time from removing a heart to reimplanting it is about five hours. Heart and lungs need to be reimplanted within two to three hours.

Computers play an important part in organ transplants, by storing information and matching donor with recipient. Countries in which transplant operations are performed have a network of transplant coordinators. The information on patients requiring an organ transplant is fed into a computer, and hospitals with potential donors feed in the information on tissue type and blood group to the coordinator. After donor and possible recipients are matched, the most compatible recipient is selected for the operation.

Diseased hearts are often enlarged, so a new healthy heart will comfortably fit into the chest cavity. Unless it is for small children, where size is important, the size of the new heart is immaterial. Lungs, however, must not be squeezed into the chest cavity. To ensure that the heart and lungs will fit, the chest measurements of donor and recipient must be known.

The survival rate for heart transplants is nearly as great as that for kidney transplants. With heart-and-lung transplants, the success rate about equals that of heart transplants, although the length of survival is difficult to forecast.

Drug control of rejection

Rejection of foreign material can also be lessened by using immunosuppressive drugs. The less closely matched the HLA fingerprints of donor and recipient, the more these drugs are needed.

A drug discovered in 1979 has been responsible for significantly improving the survival rate. Called cyclosporin, the drug has been in general use since 1982. It enables rejection to be controlled and allows lower dosages of steroids to be given. Steroids delay the healing process and increase the chances of infection. A drug called tacrolimus (FK506) was introduced in 1989 and is said to be 50 to 100 times more powerful than cyclosporin. Other immunosuppressive drugs include prednisone, a synthetic hormone similar to hydrocortisone, and azathioprine, which

has been prescribed for more than 25 years. In 1995 clinical trials were conducted on CellCept (mycophenolate mofetil).

The greatest problem in using immunosuppressive drugs is that they stop the rejection of all foreign material—including disease-causing bacteria. Patients lose much of their ability to fight infection, and there is the danger of death from what would normally be a simple infection.

The ability of the recipient to identify foreign bone marrow material and destroy it will be reduced but not completely removed by closely matching the antigenic properties. It is usually necessary to reduce the risks of rejection even further by temporarily paralyzing the patient's immune system. Immune paralysis can be achieved by sublethal irradiation of the whole body or by administration of drugs that destroy actively multiplying cells within the body. These cytotoxic drugs are not specific for the cells of the immune system and produce serious unwanted side effects on all the cells in the bone marrow.

Since the 1980s, the drug cyclosporin has been found to specifically inhibit the lymphocytes involved in the rejection process. This drug is now given preferably to recipients of allogeneic marrow, which carries important genetic dissimilarities from that of the recipient.

Spare-part surgery

Artificial parts that replace diseased or damaged organs of the body must be made of materials that will not cause physical or chemical changes in the body and will not be rejected by the recipient. A variety of compounds based on silicone, plastic, and nonstick PTFE are being used for softer tissues. Harder plastics and stainless steels have proven successful as bone and joint replacements.

There are many problems in designing these replacement parts. In most cases, they must be quite small, yet they must also be able to withstand the stresses and strains put on them by the body. Heart valves, for example, will open and shut more than 100,000 times every day.

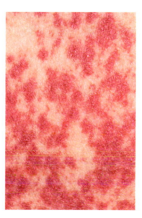

▲ A rash or blistering of the skin (bottom) are two of the symptoms of graft versus host disease (GVHD), which can affect unsuccessful recipients of bone marrow transplants. GVHD accounts for 10 to 20 percent of failures, with secondary infections following a course of immunosuppressant drugs causing another 20 percent.

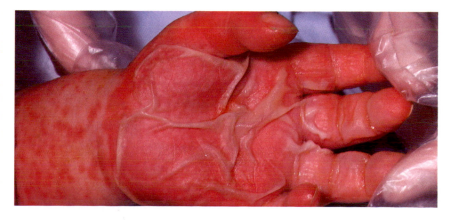

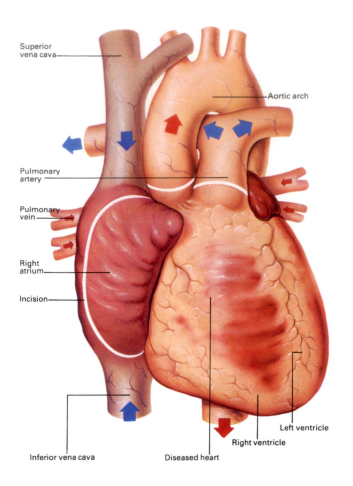

Superior
vena cava

Aortic arch

Pulmonary
artery

Pulmonary
vein

Right
atrium

Incision

Left ventricle

Right ventricle

Inferior vena cava

Diseased heart

Purely mechanical replacements, such as artificial hips and knees, have been used for many years. Softer tissues—artificial heart valves, for instance—have also been in use for some time. Valves from other species, usually pigs, have also been successfully transplanted into humans. These "bioprosthetic" valves, as they are known, are made biologically inert, functional, and durable by washing, denaturing, and tanning valves from other species.

Tissue engineering may be the future for replacement heart valves. Tissue from a lamb's artery has been successfully grown in an artificial culture medium to form valves, which then have been transplanted into a sheep. The perfect replacement would be produced from tissue from the patient, molded to the right shape.

Skin grafts

Artificial skin has also been developed for skin grafts. This artificial skin is not a permanent replacement but is used over serious burns so that new skin can grow underneath. Its bottom layer is a polymer that can be broken down by the body. It is gradually replaced by the new skin.

In 1998, the Food and Drug Administration (FDA) approved the use of a skin substitute called Apligraf for the treatment of leg ulcers that do not respond to conventional treatment. In 2000, Apligraf was also approved for treating diabetic

▲ One of the most commonly used methods of heart transplant surgery— the Shumway technique. This method involves removing the old heart, leaving behind the back wall of the two chambers (the right and left atriums), which collect blood from the lungs and from the rest of the body. The back of the donor heart is opened and trimmed to fit the recipient heart.

foot ulcers. Apligraf is the first mass-produced product to contain living human cells. It is similar to human skin in that it contains fibroblasts (connective tissue cells), keratinocytes (which form keratin), and collagen, but it does not have blood vessels, hair follicles, or sweat glands.

Heart transplant surgery

The first determined efforts to provide a replacement for the human heart were made in the late 1950s and early 1960s. Many scientists then believed that almost any aspect of technology could be conquered if enough money and effort were expended. In the medical field, this spirit of optimism led to a massive program of research aimed at producing an artificial heart that could be manufactured in a range of sizes. The hearts would be inserted in the vast number of people who could die of untreatable heart disease while they were otherwise fit.

The evidence, however, suggests that a mechanical heart is not a practical proposition. No materials so far discovered can resist the hostile environment of the body and be durable enough to pump several tons of blood every day—and beat 40 million times each year. No machine can compare with the product of millions of years of evolution.

The only possible way of replacing a failing human heart is by transplant surgery. A surgeon from the former Soviet Union, Vladimir Demikar, had successfully transplanted the heart and lungs of a dog as long ago as the early 1940s, and by the 1950s, many experiments aimed at transplanting the human heart—or heart and lungs—were under way. By 1962 a chimpanzee heart had been used in a human. In this way, the techniques of heart transplantation were established in the laboratory. No single step in the procedure was beyond the capability of a competent heart surgeon, but surgeons were still reluctant to perform the operations on humans because, in the early 1960s, the success rate of kidney transplants was less than 50 percent.

This impasse would have remained but for an apparently unrelated advance that came from immunologists and statisticians. Johannes J. van Rood in the Netherlands and Thomas E. Starzl in the United States showed that the closer the tissue type of the donor resembled that of the recipient in kidney transplants, the higher was the chance of success. Transplants from close relatives had a better chance of survival than those from unrelated donors. What is more, Van Rood discovered that there were genes on specific chromosomes that determined what kind of tissue type the patient might be.

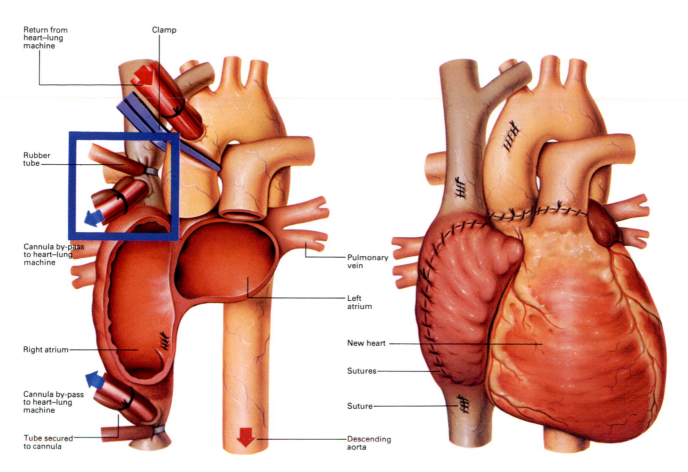

Return from heart–lung machine

Clamp

Rubber tube

Cannula by-pass to heart–lung machine

Right atrium

Cannula by-pass to heart–lung machine

Tube secured to cannula

Pulmonary vein

Left atrium

Descending aorta

New heart

Sutures

Suture

Transplantation technique

Dr. Christiaan Barnard, the South African pioneer of clinical heart transplantation, performed the first heart transplant in 1967, and a year later, Dr. Norman Shumway repeated the feat in the United States. Shumway's technique of heart transplantation is the one most commonly used today. It involves removing the heart but leaving behind the back wall of the two chambers that collect blood from the body and the lungs—the right atrium and the left atrium. Also left in the recipient are the pulmonary artery, to take blood from the donor heart to the lungs, and the aorta, to distribute blood around the body. The back of the donor heart has to be opened and trimmed to fit the atria of the recipient heart.

The septum (wall) between the two atria is the point where the sewing together of the two hearts starts. It forms a good landmark for siting the donor heart. The junction between the pulmonary artery of the donor heart and that of the recipient is done next. Great care is taken to exclude air from the right side of the heart at this stage—otherwise the pulmonary artery might become filled with froth that would damage the lung capillaries.

In the last part of the operation, the surgeon joins the aorta of the donor heart and the aorta of the recipient heart. Any air left in the cavity of the donor heart or in the stump of the recipient's aorta or adhering to the walls of the donor heart must be expelled and replaced by blood.

▲ A by-pass to the heart–lung machine is inserted before the old heart is cut away (left). The new heart is joined to the remaining parts of the old one; the septum is the point where the sewing together begins (right). This method of transplanting hearts is very successful, as it does not involve severing the main arteries and veins that enter the heart, which would be prone to rupture when the blood supply is reconnected.

▼ Two stages in the insertion of a cannulae tube. This tube connects the patient's circulatory system to a heart–lung machine, which pumps blood around the body while the transplant operation takes place.

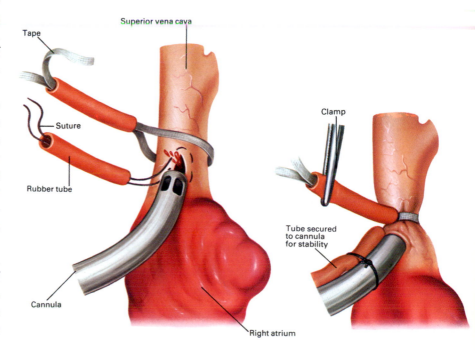

Superior vena cava

Tape

Suture

Rubber tube

Cannula

Clamp

Tube secured to cannula for stability

Right atrium

Once the patient's heart has been removed, the patient—and initially the donor heart—depend on the output of a heart–lung machine, which circulates and oxygenates the patient's blood, bypassing the heart that is out of action. When the recipient is connected to the heart–lung machine, the surgeon must ensure that the cannulae (tubes) that drain the upper and lower parts of the body are both large enough and sited so that they do not get in the way of the operation.

The operation itself takes between 30 minutes and an hour. During this time, the new heart has to be kept in good condition. Normally, the donor heart is removed from the donor as late as possible to minimize the time it has to be kept outside the body.

Other techniques

Another version of the heart transplant operation, practiced mainly by Barnard, is to place the donor heart in the right chest. It is then connected to the patient's own heart by plastic pipes or grafted human blood vessels. Again four connections have to be made.

The great advantage of this operation is that the patient's own heart is left virtually undisturbed. However, room has to be found in the right chest for the extra heart, and so lung tissue must be pushed aside; doing so leads to a risk of lung collapse and pneumonia. Another problem is the synchronization of heartbeats. Ideally, the two hearts will beat out of step with each other, but if the heartbeats coincide, the pressure in the aorta will be abnormally high, and the failure of either heart could result. This difficulty can be overcome by using suitably programmed pacemakers.

The biggest disadvantage of the extra-heart operation lies in the difficulty of diagnosing rejection. Shumway and his group have shown that after a conventional heart transplant, it is possible, under X-ray control, to pass a catheter into the donor heart through a neck vein. Using a special biopsy catheter, which has small controllable jaws at its tip, a tiny section from inside the new heart can be taken for examination.

Heart and lung transplants

Some patients with heart disease develop problems with other organs, especially the lungs. A disease known as pulmonary hypertension is caused by defects in the heart that result in raised blood pressure in the lungs. This complication makes the lungs more fibrous and impairs their ability to absorb oxygen, in turn putting more pressure on the heart, damaging it. A heart transplant would be ineffective, and it would be necessary to transplant both heart and lungs.

In transplanting heart and lungs, only three connections need to be made—the new organs are connected to the right atrium, the aorta, and the trachea. The lungs must be ventilated to maintain oxygenation and carbon dioxide elimination. If the pressure in the pulmonary artery is allowed to rise, the lung will lose its capacity to produce the agents that enable its millions of small air sacs to take up oxygen.

▼ In an autologous bone marrow transplant, the patient's own marrow is used. Drugs are first given to prevent resistance to the graft, and then the marrow is removed and deep-frozen, while the patient's body is treated with X rays to remove any residual leukemia. The marrow is then replaced.

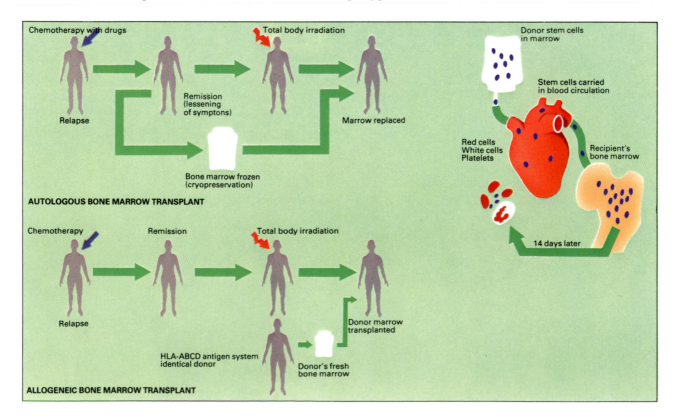

Bone marrow transplantation

A growing number of previously incurable blood diseases are now open to treatment with transplantation of bone marrow cells from a healthy donor to a recipient with the disease. The first successful transplantation was carried out in the United States in 1968, and considerable medical research has since led to expansion of the application of the new technique and to reducing the hazards associated with the procedure.

The problem of tissue matching is critical for bone marrow transplants, more so than for transplanting other organs. The success of the transplantation depends on the matching of nearly identical marrow between donor and recipient. Typing of bone marrow is the identification of specific antigens, by laboratory testing, that can then be matched with the antigenic characteristics of the recipient marrow cells. Ideally, there should be a perfect match of six antigens on donor and recipient blood cells. The closest matching is usually found within the immediate family of the recipient because they will share some of the same antigens.

Graft versus host disease

The first type of transplant performed was skin grafting, and the terms *graft* and *host* here become synonymous with *donor* and *recipient*. The major complication of bone marrow transplantation is not failure of the graft but damage to various body tissues of the recipient caused by lymphocytes in the donor marrow. This phenomenon of the graft rejecting the host is an immunological process affecting the lungs, liver, gut, and skin known as graft versus host disease—GVHD. As with marrow rejection, every attempt should be made to minimize GVHD by accurate matching of donor and recipient. GVHD occurs in as many as 70 percent of allogeneic marrow transplantations and can be fatal.

Specific groups of T lymphocytes, so called because of their embryological development within the thymus gland, are probably the mediators of GVHD. They are susceptible to interference by the drug cyclosporin that will prevent or delay the appearance of GVHD when given to the recipient.

In the United States, a more elaborate and ingenious approach has been developed by research workers in Minnesota. They remove the active T cells from donor marrow by poisoning them with ricin. To prevent the toxin from destroying all the marrow cells, it is coated with a monoclonal antibody that recognizes and binds only with T cells having the antigen specific to the antibody on the surface membrane of the cell.

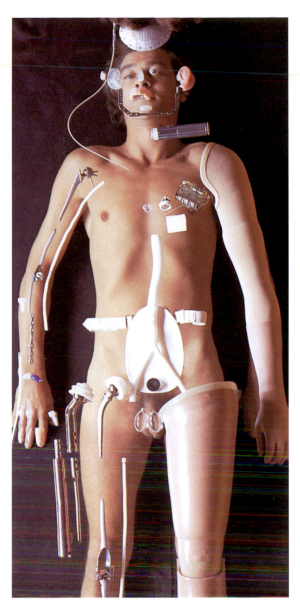

◄ A vast number and range of spare body parts are now available. They include fake ears, teeth, whole limb replacements, metal pins, plastic arteries, and heart pacemakers. Advances in stem cell technology may eventually lead to the ability to use the patient's own cells to grow new organs that will not be rejected in the body by the immune system.

This technique simultaneously improves survival of the transplant and reduces GVHD.

Other complications of marrow transplantation are infections, aplastic anemia, severe brain damage, and slowing of the heart. The risks constitute a formidable obstacle to progress and must be weighed against the risks of the natural disease and its alternative treatments.

The transplantation procedure

In contrast to the complexities of donor typing and preparation of the recipient, the procedure itself is relatively simple. A hollow steel needle attached to a syringe is pushed into the marrow bones of the donor at multiple sites and marrow cells are sucked out. The procedure is painful and requires an anaesthetic, but there are no risks for the donor, who soon replaces the cells that have been removed. The volume of marrow is not as important as the number of marrow cells obtained. Between 10^7 and 10^9 cells (10 million and 1 billion) are required for every 2 lbs.

FACT FILE

- Joint replacement techniques are now being refined to the point where they utilize transplant methods to combine mechanical with biological processes. Continuous passive motion—slow flexion and extension over many weeks—encourages the body to invade the computer-designed synthetic joint with fibrous tissue of its own.

- Severely damaged leg bones, which occur frequently after road accidents, can now be treated by replacing the damaged bone with one of the patient's own upper ribs, complete with its muscles and blood supply. The transplant is sandwiched between sections of cancellous (porous, or spongelike) bone from the end of the body's long bones, which is capable of continuous growth.

(1 kg) of the recipient's body weight. Blood is inevitably removed together with marrow, which is collected into anticoagulant to prevent clotting. Bone fragments and fatty clumps are filtered out, and the residual materials can be frozen in liquid nitrogen before being thawed and infused into the waiting recipient.

Donor material is injected by a drip into the recipient's circulation or occasionally into the abdominal cavity, though this route is less efficient than the intravenous infusion. Evidence of successful grafting does not appear until at least three weeks after transplantation. If the donor and recipient are of different sex, survival of the transplant can be detected by chromosome analysis of marrow cells that will contain a cell population with male and female sex chromosomes.

The recipient is extremely vulnerable to infection during the first few weeks after transplantation because of immunological paralysis produced by pretreatment with cytotoxic drugs and the effects of GVHD. The donor must be examined to ensure that blood-borne infection is not transmitted with the transplantation. The recipient may acquire a number of unusual infections despite treatment with antibiotic drugs and will have virtually no immunity to fight the infections. A germ-free environment is therefore preferable until the marrow shows signs of recovering. One way of achieving minimal exposure to germs is to enclose the patient in a plastic bubble into which filtered air is pumped.

Hand and arm transplants

In 1998, two microsurgeons Earl Owen of Australia and Jean-Michel Dubernard of France, along with a 50-member surgical team, performed the world's first successful hand transplant in France. Although the patient refused to take any postoperative drugs, he was able to maintain his new hand for the next two and a half years. In 2001, however, the same surgical team had to amputate the hand because of complications from transplant rejection.

Xenotransplants

Currently, research is underway into xenotransplant techniques. Derived from the Greek word *xeno*, meaning "foreign," xenotransplants involve the use of animal organs, which are usually genetically modified, in humans. In 1992 and 1993, Thomas Starzl transplanted baboon livers into two patients with hepatitis. Both the patients later died—not because of organ rejection, however, but because of runaway infections.

Pig organs appear to offer the best chance of successful xenotransplantation. Pig organs are the right size, the animals reproduce quickly and easily, and they can be raised in a sterile environment, so the likelihood of some pig diseases being transmitted to humans is reduced. The drawback, however, is that pig organs have molecular characteristics that cause the human immune system to go into attack mode.

Two different approaches to solving this problem are being explored. One is to remove specific pig genes and replace them with human genes to make pig cells seem less "piggish" and therefore less likely to be rejected by the human recipient.

Another way is to modify a sugar molecule that appears on cell surfaces in most mammals, except those of humans and their close primate relatives. It is this molecule that is attacked by the human immune system in xenotransplants. Researchers are attempting to insert a human gene to replace this molecule in pigs. It is not yet known whether these transgenic pigs will function normally or whether their organs will be accepted by the human immune system.

By the end of 1998, although there had not yet been any successful whole-organ transplants, more than 200 people in the United States had received xenografts of animal cells or tissues, such as the implantation of fetal pig neurons into the brains of people with Parkinson's disease.

SEE ALSO: BIOTECHNOLOGY • BLOOD • GENETIC ENGINEERING • HEART PACEMAKER • HEART SURGERY • IMMUNOLOGY • MICROSURGERY • OPERATING ROOM • PLASTIC SURGERY • SURGERY

Truck

A truck is a heavy-duty vehicle whose primary function is the transportation of heavy loads for commercial purposes. In Europe and the United States, they carry around two-thirds of the volume of overland cargo traffic; the rest goes by train.

Truck configurations

Different truck configurations cater for the various sizes and types of loads. In small trucks, the power plant, cab, and load-carrying space share a single rigid chassis. Larger trucks, called semitrailer rigs, consist of a tractor and a semitrailer that are united at an articulated joint called the fifth wheel. The fifth wheel provides vertical support and torsional stability for the semitrailer.

A semitrailer has stowable legs that support its front end when disconnected from the tractor. The typical carrying capacity of a semitrailer is around 40 tons (36 tonnes). Further capacity can be added by attaching full trailers to the rear of a semitrailer rig. The result is a road train. Both semitrailers and full trailers rely on the tractor unit to provide compressed air for braking and power for indicators and other lights.

Semitrailers and trailers offer benefits both to truck manufacturers and to the operators of haulage fleets. For the manufacturer, they make it possible to offer a variety of trailer types for each

tractor unit; for the hauler, the ability to unhitch semitrailer rigs improves productivity by leaving the tractor unit free to pull another load as soon as the trailer is unhitched from it.

Some tractors have movable third axles that make them more flexible in use. With the third axle raised, the tractor is effectively a 4 x 4 drive unit—all its four wheels are powered. This configuration is best suited to running with a light load. For heavier loads, the third axle is lowered to spread the load. This is the 6 x 4 configuration (six wheels, of which four are powered); it is less fuel efficient—the extra pair of wheels increases rolling resistance—but is often necessary to keep the load per axle within legal limits.

Trailers

The most basic trailers are flatbeds, to which large items such as tree trunks can be chained for safety during transport. Vertical side bars provide further protection against slippage. Modified standard-sized flatbeds are used to carry containers suitable for loading onto ships. Low loaders have load-carrying beds that dip between the fifth wheel and the trailing axles so as to allow additional headroom for tall loads; they also enable smaller vehicles to be driven onto them with ease. Another type of trailer consists of a compartment

▲ The front of this GMC General is dominated by a huge radiator grill that dissipates excess heat generated by its powerful engine. The aerodynamic dam behind the cab helps cut fuel consumption due to turbulence and drag by guiding the airflow around the trailer. Fuel economy is also assisted by the use of lightweight parts, such as aluminum fuel tanks.

with rear doors for loading and unloading, often with a hinged steel flap that drops to form a ramp to the ground or to a loading bay. Some trucks have sidewalls formed by flexible plastic sheets that can be lifted to provide access; after loading, the sheets are buckled tightly into place so as to provide a streamlined side profile.

More specialist trailers include tank trucks for carrying liquids, such as gasoline or drinking water. Refrigerated trailers have chilled compartments and integral refrigeration units to prolong the shelf life of fresh and frozen foods. Trucks for carrying livestock have slatted walls to allow air in for breathing and internal partitions that keep the livestock well distributed and prevent the animals from being thrown around in transit.

Engine

Practically all trucks run on diesel fuel rather than gasoline. There are two main reasons for this choice: first, diesel is cheaper and produces more useful energy per unit volume than does gasoline, so diesel engines are more economical; second, diesel engines require less maintenance and can operate under continuous heavy loads much longer than gasoline engines can, so diesel engines are better suited for powering trucks. Typical engine capacities range from 3 to 4.7 gallons (12–18 1), with power outputs in the 200 to 600 horsepower (150–450 kW) range. The range of power output options is wide because of the wide range of loads and the variety of terrains and road conditions that must be accommodated.

In modern diesel engines, electronically controlled fuel injection gives accurately metered charges of fuel that match the load at all times. This system ensures efficient operation and reduces pollution in the forms of soot and unburned fuel. Advanced diesel-fuel formulations also help to reduce harmful emissions.

The engine power of most heavy-duty trucks is boosted by a turbocharger. This device uses a turbine to harness the kinetic energy of exhaust gases. A centrifugal compressor on the same shaft as the turbine then pressurizes the intake air to 1.5 times atmospheric pressure. As a result, 50 percent more air enters the cylinders at each intake stroke. Simultaneously increasing the fuel supply by 50 percent results in the engine behaving as if its capacity were 50 percent greater, so there is an increase in power output. The net power boost is only around 30 to 40 percent, however, since the engine has to do work in forcing the exhaust through the turbocharger.

Turbocharger performance is improved by the use of an intercooler—a heat exchanger that cools the turbocharged air before it enters the engine.

Removing some of the heat generated by the compression process increases the amount of air forced into the cylinders for a given pressure, since air expands when heated. Hence, the intercooler, which resembles a small domestic radiator, improves turbocharger efficiency.

Transmission

The transmission and drivetrain are the systems that deliver power from the engine to the drive axles. These systems must be well matched if the truck is to function efficiently—fuel consumption may increase by as much as 25 percent if the design is poor. The truck design team will seek to match the type and power output of the engine with the type of transmission and axles.

The potential for poor fuel economy stems from the fact that the band of engine speeds at which a diesel engine operates efficiently is narrow, much narrower than in a gasoline engine. Fuel consumption can increase sharply if bad driving technique or widely spaced gear ratios cause the engine to operate outside its most efficient speed range. Hence, truck transmissions are designed to have a large number of closely spaced gears to ensure the engine can work within its optimum speed range at all times.

Transmissions that have several gear ratios are made simpler and more compact by using a secondary set of gears to provide intermediate ratios between the principal gear ratios. In this way, 12 ratios are achieved by superimposing three intermediate ratios on each of four main ratios, for example. This type of intermediate gearing is called a splitter if it connects the engine to the main transmission or a range changer if it is on

▼ The goal of this wind-tunnel test is to examine the effect of wind deflectors on air flow. Wind tunnel tests help designers minimize the drag experienced by moving trucks. The flow of air is made visible by the use of smoke and tags attached to the vehicle; smooth flow is associated with low drag.

the output side of the main transmission. The main ratios are selected by moving a lever, whereas the intermediate ratios are selected by moving a switch that controls an electric or air-operated gear-change unit. Torque from the transmission then passes through a drive shaft and a set of differential gears that allow the wheels to turn at slightly different speeds on curves.

Braking

The force require to brake heavily laden trucks is much greater than could be generated by a direct mechanical linkage to a pedal; thus, trucks use air brakes for speed control. When the driver steps on the brake pedal, compressed air rushes into a cylinder whose piston presses the friction plates of the brake together. A return spring releases the brakes when the pressure is off. Trailers must be adequately braked to reduce the risk of jack-knifing, which can happen if the momentum of the trailer pushes the tractor to one side during episodes of heavy braking.

Brakes become hot as they dissipate the energy of a moving truck. For example, a 40-ton (36-tonne) truck traveling down a one-in-ten incline at 40 mph (64 km/h) must dissipate energy at a rate of around 630 kW to maintain constant speed. Although air resistance dissipates some of this power, the rest must be dealt with by the braking system, so there is a risk of brakes overheating on long downhill stretches.

Engine braking is one way of assisting braking; the accelerator is released to cut the diesel supply and turbocharger. Leaving the truck in a low gear forces the engine to turn fast, so the intake strokes of the cylinders must then draw in air against a partial vacuum—the origin of the braking effect. The compression strokes also absorb energy in compressing air; however, most of that energy is returned during what would be the power stroke if fuel were present. Engine braking can be made much more effective by opening the exhaust valve at the end of the compression stroke; this system is called a compression-release braking system.

Drag and air resistance

Early truck designers paid little attention to aerodynamics, since maximum speeds were low and fuel economy was not a major concern. Accordingly, traditional truck designs tend to be aerodynamically inefficient, since flat facing surfaces and squared-off corners create a great deal of turbulence as a truck moves through air.

The impact of drag increases rapidly with increasing speed: if a truck uses one-third of its engine power to overcome air resistance at 45

mph (70 km/h), the same truck will use half its power for the same purpose at 55 mph (90 km/h). The effect is not just related to the speed of the truck: in a strong head wind, air resistance alone may account for an increase in fuel consumption of around 50 percent.

As cruising speeds and fuel costs have increased, truck manufacturers have pursued ways of streamlining their vehicles. The shapes of tractors and the leading edges of trailers have been redesigned, and wind deflectors have been placed on the cab roof. Much development work is based on test results from wind tunnels, but there is much less scope for design improvements in trucks than in automobiles. The curved shapes associated with low-drag designs would lead to inefficiently shaped cargo spaces if applied to trailers, and a drag-generating gap must be left between the tractor and trailer to allow for articulation of the fifth wheel when turning corners.

Fuel economy is improved when glass-reinforced plastic (GRP) replaces metal in cab and trailer construction. The benefits are twofold: first, GRP is more suited to making smoothly curved body parts that create less drag; second, the resulting components are considerably more lightweight than their metal counterparts, and a lighter body requires less fuel to accelerate.

Rather than resorting to radical design changes, truck design engineers have sought to reduce drag by concentrating on smoothing off corners and streamlining vital accessories, such as wing and door mirrors and side windows. Careful design and attention to detail can lead to a reduction in drag of about 30 percent. A further drag reduction of around 20 percent can be gained by mounting a wind deflector on the cab roof.

Health and safety

A cargo trip can require many hours or even days of driving, and a poorly designed cab environment would cause unnecessary stress and fatigue

▲ The body of this customized truck can be raised to deliver in-flight meals to the passenger doors of airliners so as to minimize the preparation time between flights.

on a single trip. Bad posture and repetitive strain can cause chronic health problems over the span of a career spent driving trucks. Also, accidents are more likely to prove fatal if the truck design fails to include adequate protective features.

The science of ergonomics has contributed a great deal to improvements in the truck driver's lot. Good posture is promoted by the use of seats that are capable of fine adjustment in relation to the steering wheel, controls, and foot pedals. Computer models and measurements of a range of human shapes are built into seat design.

The steering wheel is normally fully adjustable, and truck controls are designed and positioned to dispense with unnecessary effort and are grouped around the driving area within easy reach. Two-spoke steering wheels are chosen to facilitate a clear view of the instruments.

Comfort on long-distance journeys is seen to by the provision of sleeping accommodation where the driver can rest during stops or when a backup driver takes over the wheel. This accommodation is normally positioned behind or above the driving area; in the latter case, the sleeping compartment forms an integral part of the fairing that guides airflow over the trailer.

Road noise and vibration are major contributors to driver fatigue. The human body is prone to fatigue at certain frequencies of vibrations (between 4 and 8 Hz), and these frequencies are produced in abundance when a truck is driven. If poorly designed, the cab structure can act as a sounding board for vibrations from the engine, transmission, and the motion of tires over the road surface. Damping springs and rubber mountings can help isolate the cab from vibrations, and seating can be further isolated by its own suspension systems. Computer modeling can help identify and eliminate sources of resonance, and such studies have shown that noise in the cab can be reduced by correctly positioning the point of attachment between drivetrain and chassis.

Safety considerations address the minimization of harm to occupants of the truck itself and of other vehicles in the event of a collision. The sheer mass of truck can be a great danger to other road users, even when unladen. Hence, there has been legislation to control fender heights, and designers have striven to improve all-round visibility. The occupants of the cab are protected by the strength of the cab itself, which is boosted by reinforcing bars that help prevent the cab from being crushed in the event of a collision or if the truck rolls over for some other reason.

Safety skirts that cover the sides of trucks below the level of the load-carrying bed help prevent cars from running under the truck, and they also contribute to the smooth flow of air around the trailer. In addition, an energy-absorbing barrier, called an underrider, is suspended from the rear of the vehicle on struts. It helps prevent cars from being pushed under the truck and potentially decapitating their occupants in the event of a multiple-vehicle collision.

Instrumentation

Instrumentation in modern trucks is comprehensive. Electronics have been adopted as a route toward greater reliability, and diagnostic systems governed by microcomputers assist the driver in monitoring the vehicle's systems. Tire-pressure sensors provide information that alerts the driver if a tire becomes underinflated or flat, while other systems check for wheel imbalance, brake wear, and load shifts that could cause dangerous imbalances. These systems complement instruments that monitor fuel levels, oil pressure, battery charge, and coolant temperature.

Tachometer and speedometer outputs can produce records of engine speed and road speed, respectively, and thus can give an indication of the stress imposed on the engine and transmission. These records help in the scheduling of preventative maintenance, and some authorities require that drivers keep them as proof that they have adhered to legal restrictions, such as speed limits and the number of hours spent driving.

Satellite systems provide both a means of communicating with base and a way of tracking the movements of a truck in the event of a hijack. Global positioning systems help drivers navigate and can be interfaced with traffic-management systems that give advice on alternative routes in the event of delays or road closures.

◄ This powerful Mack rig is loaded with lumber for transporting to a paper mill. The twin axles at the rear of the tractor unit have four wheels each to spread heavy loads.

SEE ALSO: BRAKING SYSTEM • EARTHMOVING MACHINERY • INTERNAL COMBUSTION ENGINE • TRANSMISSION, AUTOMOBILE

Tsunami

Originating in the ocean depths, killer waves can travel at more than 1,000 mph (1,600 km/h). Despite the waves' impressive speed, however, any ship in their path will scarcely notice the event. Far out at sea, a killer wave may be only 3 ft. (1 m) high, but the picture changes dramatically when all the energy hits shallow coastal waters. There, the wave builds into a vast wall of water with an immensely destructive power on arrival.

Scientists call these huge waves tsunamis. The word *tsunami* is borrowed from the Japanese *tsu* meaning "harbor" and *nami* meaning "sea," colloquially, "harbor wave." The origin of the name is not surprising, because the Japanese have been by far the most frequent victims of killer waves, having been hit by devastating tsunamis at least 15 times over the past 300 years.

Tsunamis are a threat mainly to people on the shores of the Pacific Ocean. Tsunamis that travel long distances are rare in the Atlantic or other large oceans. The moving forces behind these monstrous waves are giant convulsions of Earth's crust beneath the ocean, usually earthquakes above 6.5 on the Richter scale, but sometimes submarine volcanic eruptions or even underwater

or coastal landslides. Such an upheaval of the seafloor or coastal land violently agitates the water around it. As the water vibrates, shock waves rush out in all directions. The process is like a large-scale model of what happens when a pebble hits the surface of a calm pool—the disturbance produces a series of ever-widening ripples.

The successive shock waves (wavelengths) of a tsunami in deep water are so far apart—as much as 100 miles (165 km), or a couple of hours—and so shallow that they are unique among waves in the energy they contain. The reason is that the speed of a shallow-water wave is proportional to the square root of the water depth. When a tsunami approaches shore, its forward movement is increasingly restricted as the water becomes shallower—friction with the seabed reduces the velocity of the wave. According to the formula that determines wave height against water depth the wavelengths grow shorter—they are closer together—but they also grow taller. In this way, a 3 ft. (1 m) wave traveling at 500 mph (800 km/h) in deep water becomes a towering 100 ft. (30 m) high killer pounding the shore at 30 mph (50 km/h). Occasionally, the first sign of the arrival of

▲ Tidal waves are immensely powerful and cause devastation on a large scale when they hit land. Out in the oceans, they are barely visible—it is only as they approach land that the waves begin to build in height. The biggest tsunamis have been nearly 115 ft. (35 m) tall before breaking.

a tsunami is the wave trough rather than the peak—all of the water along the coast may recede to expose the sea floor.

The strangest phenomenon of the tsunami, however, is undoubtedly the lack of height of the wave while in the deep ocean. During a 1946 tsunami that devastated Hilo, Hawaii, the crew of a freighter 1 mile (1.6 km) off the coast watched in amazement as waves broke over the top of warehouses on shore and poured into the town, while the sea around them appeared calm. Five thousand homes were smashed to matchwood during this episode.

The same Hawaiian town was struck again in 1960 by a tsunami resulting from an earthquake off Chile: this time the entire business area was destroyed. This tsunami, the worst recorded in recent history, also hit the Philippines, Okinawa in Japan, and Chile itself, killing more than 1,000 people. Even so, it pales by comparison with the massive tsunami that struck Japan in 1896, killing 27,000 people, or the shock waves from the explosion of the volcanic island of Krakatoa in 1883, which drowned 36,500 on Java and Sumatra. The Krakatoa waves, which were up to 115 ft. (35 m) high when they reached the islands, traveled two or three times around the globe and maintained their awesome power for huge distances.

Warning system

The U.S. Government's National Weather Service, in cooperation with other nations and agencies, has set up an impressive tsunami warn-ing system (TWS) in the Pacific Ocean. It provides advance warning of big waves for 14 Pacific coastal and island nations or territories, including the United States.

A diamond-shaped array of seismic detectors makes automatic calculations of the epicenter, magnitude, and possible tsunami-producing potential of any earthquakes. Meanwhile, seismographic stations around the Pacific send in their data, and a network of tide stations reports any untoward activity. Acting on this information, the Honolulu Observatory is able to estimate tsunami arrival times for each threatened community and issue advance warnings to enable them to prepare.

It is not only earth movements that produce killer waves: storms, too, can create very destructive waves; they whip the sea into a furious assault on the coast and even change its shape permanently. On tropical coasts, huge waves can be generated by violent hurricanes.

In just two days in 1960, Hurricane Donna shifted an estimated 177 million cu. ft. (5 million m³) of sand from one part of the Florida coast to another. Under normal conditions, it would take 100 years to move that amount.

As oil rigs are placed into ever-deeper waters, progress in wave research becomes increasingly important, and the equipment for investigating wave mechanisms has developed accordingly. Pressure sensors mounted on the seabed were the first tools to reveal unsuspected factors in wave behavior. Data from these sensors began to show that even ordinary waves were no random, local

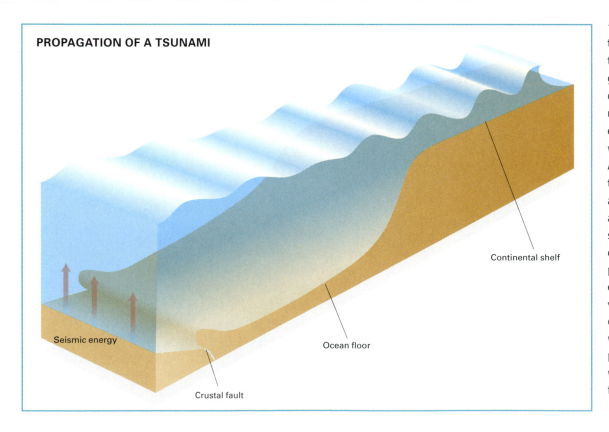

PROPAGATION OF A TSUNAMI

Seismic energy

Crustal fault

Ocean floor

Continental shelf

◄ Tsunamis undergo three distinct phases in their formation. They are generated by a seismic disturbance in the crust under the deep ocean. As energy is transmitted to the water column, it undulates. At this point, the depth of the water makes the wave appear shallow, but as it approaches the continental shelf, the wavelengths start overtaking each other; this process squeezes the energy into a smaller volume of water, and creates higher and faster waves. The inundation phase occurs as a breaking wave, a wall of water, or a flood tide.

event but originated much further afield. One study showed that waves arriving in Cornwall, Britain, had probably originated in the Antarctic.

The possibility of mapping waves and predicting their arrival worldwide is now a reality, but there are complicated factors involved. For example, a wind of a particular strength blowing uniformly over a stretch of ocean does not produce identical waves. The reason some waves are much larger than others is that sea waves have their energy locked up in a wide range of wave periods, which determine the speed of the wave. In the simple case of a sea with only two wave components, when the crest of one component overtakes the other, the result will be a higher wave. The net effect is that higher waves come in groups. As the components gradually move into phase, the wave height builds up and in so doing produces a series of waves of increasing height, which then decreases as the faster component moves away.

Measuring wave height

In a rough sea there are numerous components involved in the creation of wave height—their continual interplay makes it difficult to measure the wave height accurately. There is a guide, however, known as significant wave height, which is defined as the average of the highest one-third of all the waves. If the sea is watched for three hours, the observer will find that the height of the highest individual wave is around twice that of the significant wave height. Continuous watching and counting reveal that only one in 1,175 waves exceeds the significant height by more than three times and only one wave in 300,000 exceeds four times the average height.

Big waves are generated when many components coincide in space and time, and despite their relative rarity, their occurrence can be

◀ The effects of a tidal wave can reach far inland, devastating anything in its path.

▶ Another cause of tidal waves is the pull of the Moon on the oceans and the force of Earth's spin, which can be exacerbated when the Sun is also in alignment with Earth and the Moon.

impressive—in 1933, the USS *Ramapo* reported a wave more than 115 ft. (35 m) high.

Wave data from the world's oceans now are being processed with the aid of computers. Efforts to accurately predict tsunamis include the establishment in 1997 of the National Tsunami Hazard Mitigation Program in the United States. Its role is to assess threats, improve early detection and potential destructiveness of tsunamis, and educate communities on the action to take when a tsunami strikes. Technical improvements include the modification of coastal tide gauges to measure tsunamis and upgrading the seismic network to provide faster and more accurate reports on earthquakes at sea.

The U.S. National Oceanic and Atmospheric Administration (NOAA) is also working on the DART (Deep Ocean Assessment and Reporting of Tsunamis) project, which involves constructing a network of six deep-ocean reporting stations to track tsunamis and report them. Seismometers around the Pacific Rim will pinpoint quake locations, and computer programs will predict how long a triggered tsunami will take to reach land before detection of a wave.

The DART system relays depend on bottom pressure recorders developed at the Pacific Marine Environmental Laboratory. As the crest of a tsunami passes overhead, the bottom recorder detects the increased pressure from the extra volume of water above. The instrument is so sensitive that, even at 18,000 ft. (6,000 m) deep, it can detect a tsunami just 0.5 in. (1 cm) high. Ordinary waves created by ships or storms are not detected by the system, because they are short and the changes in pressure that they create do not transmit down to the ocean floor.

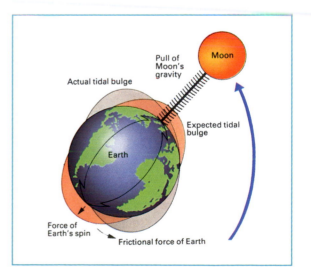

SEE ALSO: EARTHQUAKE • SEISMOLOGY • TIDE

Tunneling

Tunnels have been known for almost as long as humans have been digging holes in the ground. One of the oldest tunnels known to be for the sole purpose of transportation was constructed some 4,000 years ago to pass beneath the bed of the Euphrates River in the Middle East. The scale of the work indicates that the engineers of the time must have acquired great expertise from tunnels built even earlier, but nothing is known of these earlier constructions. Records show that various other tunnels were constructed at an early date in the Middle East. By 600 B.C.E, tunnels had been driven from both ends for distances exceeding 1,800 ft. (550 m), showing a skill in surveying that would be acceptable today.

Tunnels can be either bored or built by the cut-and-cover method—that is, by digging a trench and filling in part of the excavation to form a roof over the top of it. Before the development of techniques for supporting weak ground (such as gravels below the water table level), tunnels were only driven through self-supporting ground.

The canal era in the 18th and early 19th centuries involved the construction of many major tunnels with temporary timber supports and permanent brickwork linings. With the coming of the railways, larger sections of tunnel had to be constructed, and the temporary supports in soft ground became more and more complex, in some cases even hampering the erection of the permanent lining. This situation called for new methods of support, which have become standard features of soft-ground tunneling worldwide.

The most important development was the invention by the British engineer Marc Isambard Brunel of the tunnel shield for the construction of his tunnel under the Thames River in England between 1827 and 1842. This shield was rectangular in section and was advanced by screw jacks thrusting off the front of completed lining, which was made of brick. Modern tunnel shields owe their inception to James H. Greathead, who developed a circular shield for another tunnel beneath the Thames in 1869, this time driven

▲ A comprehensive all-purpose (CAP) tunneling machine, which is suitable for both hard and soft rock. Hydraulic power does much of the work (note the bank of hydraulic valves left of center).

through nonwaterbearing clay and lined with cast iron, another important innovation.

The shield is a movable frame that supports the face of the tunnel and the ground immediately behind the face, affording protection to the tunnel miners who carry out both the excavation of the face and the erection of the lining. It consists of an outer envelope, or skin, made of steel. This envelope is slightly larger than the external diameter of the tunnel lining, which is stiffened internally by diaphragms or, in the case of larger shields, with a heavy framework of structural steel. Mounted integrally at the leading edge of the skin is a thick cutting edge of steel, which trims the excavation to the shape of the tunnel. Powerful hydraulic jacks are mounted on the rear of the shield inside the skin, and they push the shield forward as the tunnel progresses. Towed behind the shield is a series of sledges that carry all the paraphernalia of modern tunneling, principally dirt-handling and grouting equipment.

Methods of tunneling

There are two distinct forms of tunneling—hard-ground and soft-ground tunneling. In both cases, a pilot tunnel may be driven before the main tunnel—to check the geological conditions, to allow free movement of personnel and equipment, and to provide ventilation for the main work face. Such pilot tunnels may be either opened out into the main tunnel or left as separate service tunnels.

When tunneling through hard ground without a tunneling machine, the rock face is drilled by pneumatically or hydraulically operated drills so that explosives can be inserted into the drill holes and detonated with time delays to give the desired fragmentation to the rock debris and profile to the tunnel. Where space allows, the drills are mounted on a drill carriage, or jumbo, which allows the drill operator to control a number of drills at the same time. The drill bits have tungsten carbide tips to allow rapid drilling with minimum tip wear. The drill rods are hollow, and water is supplied to the cutting edge through the drill to flush the rock cuttings out of the bore.

The pattern of drilling is carefully controlled to provide the maximum length of pull (depth of excavation) for each detonation. Generally, two methods of drilling are adopted—the wedge cut and the burn cut. In the wedge cut, holes are drilled in a converging pattern toward the center of the face. When the charges are set off, the rock is blown back toward the center of the tunnel. The burn cut, where a large central hole is drilled in the tunnel face and the other holes are drilled parallel to the longitudinal axis of the tunnel, requires less skill than a wedge cut, and greater

lengths of pull are usually obtainable, but it consumes a greater amount of explosives.

In both cases, the pattern of rock fragmentation is similar. The explosions are timed so that the blast commences in the center of the tunnel face, creating a space into which rock is blown by succeeding charges. As the blast progresses, concentric rings of rock are blown inward. The central area, although never larger than the volume of broken rock being forced into it, provides sufficient space for the debris to accumulate.

A number of different working methods are used in rock tunneling. In sound rock, full-face working may be used—the tunnel is opened out to full size with each blasting operation. In the top-heading method, the top section of the tunnel, the heading, is driven first, with the bottom portion of the tunnel, the bench, removed subsequently. The heading-and-bench method is similar, except that the bench is removed immediately behind the heading. With poor rock conditions, where falls are likely, the face is worked in a set of drifts to allow the insertion of supports before all the rock is removed.

The techniques of tunneling on soft ground evolved from mining methods and consisted of placing a series of boards, or runners, closely around the perimeter of the tunnel face. They were driven forward into the ground as a form of horizontal sheet piling, suitably strutted and braced. The face of the excavation itself had to be

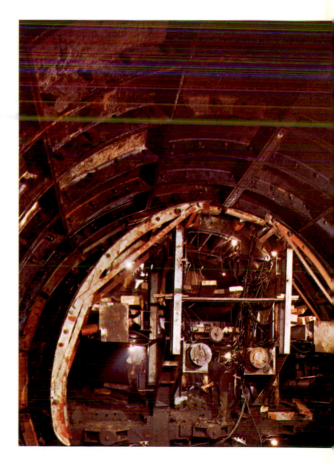

▶ The shield and ringing machine—which puts up the rings supporting the roof—used to build the Jubilee subway line in London, England.

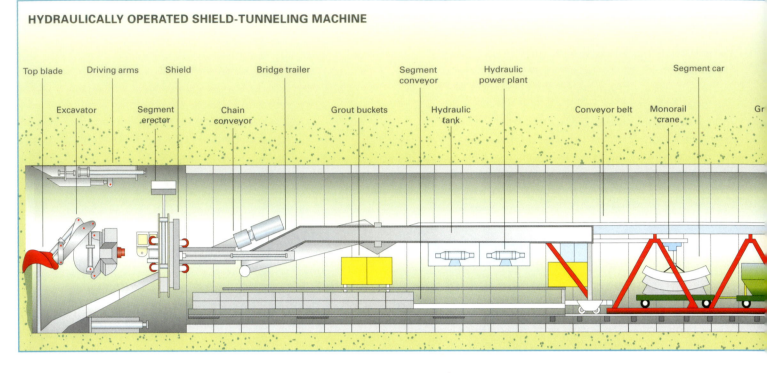

HYDRAULICALLY OPERATED SHIELD-TUNNELING MACHINE

kept closely boarded with horizontal boards that were removed one at a time, and a small area of ground was then excavated so that the board could be replaced a short distance ahead of the face and secured. This process was repeated until sufficient space had been created to insert a fresh length of runners and strutting. Progress was very slow because great care had to be exercised at every step to prevent movement of the ground in any direction. In spite of this caution, accidents did occur, and roof falls were frequent.

Tunnel-excavating machines are of two kinds: full face and partial face. The full-face machine must necessarily be circular, since the entire front face of the shield rotates. Depending on the hardness of the ground, the arrangements for excavation vary. In soft ground, plates pressing against the tunnel face may be used; they are adjusted to allow only a certain amount of ground to be excavated at any one time. For harder ground and rock, individual teeth, cutting disks, or rollers may be used. The hardness of the ground is not the only criterion that dictates the choice of teeth; abrasiveness also has to be taken into account.

More recently, full-face mechanization has been applied to the process of tunneling through water-bearing sands and gravels with the introduction of the bentonite tunneling machine. This technique makes use of the clay mineral bentonite in a sealed pressure chamber in front of the shield to provide a stabilizing effect on the unstable ground at the tunnel face, at the same time allowing mechanical excavation at a much faster rate than was previously possible by hand. The excavated material, mixed with the bentonite slurry, is

▲ A tunneling machine and its ancillary equipment; hydraulic rams can thrust the head of a machine with a diameter of 33 ft. (10 m) against the rock with a force of up to 2.5 million lbs. (11 MN).

extracted from the pressure chamber and taken to the surface by hydraulic pumping. On the surface, bentonite is separated from the sand and gravel, so it can be recirculated, and the sand and gravel are taken away in trucks.

Partial-face mechanization takes the form of a rail-mounted machine with a cutting head attached to a hydraulically controlled boom, which can range over the entire area of the tunnel face. In some cases, the cutting boom is mounted within a tunnel shield, the cutting profile being controlled by a guide ring in the shield.

Tunnel linings
Of the various considerations governing the choice of lining for a tunnel, one of the most important is the need to withstand any load imposed on it during and after erection. If a shield is to be used, the lining must be capable of withstanding the thrust of the shield and also any other stresses induced by handling. It should have a high strength-to-weight ratio so that its thickness can be minimized to save unnecessary excavation. Tunnels blasted through solid rock may not need lining. Where appropriate, rock bolts are used to retain loose sections of rock, and arch supports are used for the roof—and sometimes the walls—in broken rock.

Factors that must be taken into account when designing tunnel linings include water and ground loadings, rock-loosening loads, the construction of subsequent tunnels, and any special characteristics of the ground. The response of the ground to the actions of tunneling must also be considered. The initial process of excavating a

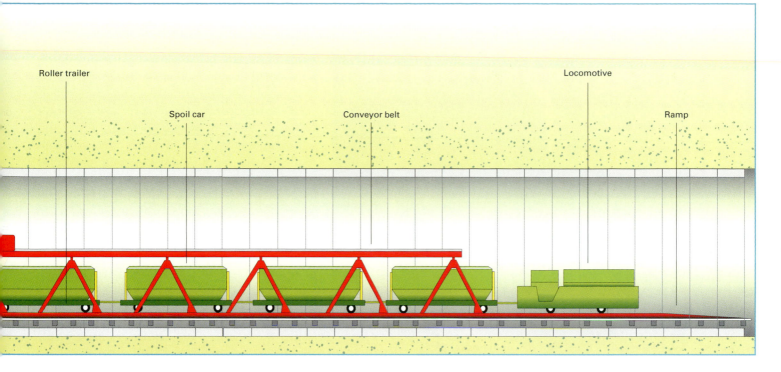

Roller trailer

Locomotive

Spoil car

Conveyor belt

Ramp

hole in the ground is followed by the erection of a structural lining. The time interval between these two operations greatly affects the loads that the lining can carry, and it is important to know how long a tunnel can safely remain unlined.

In the case of soft-ground tunneling, the lining is usually installed immediately behind, and under the protection of, the shield as tunneling proceeds. Linings may be of cast iron or reinforced concrete and are usually expanded into place against the tunnel walls. Alternatively, grouting (liquid cement) may be injected to fill any space between the lining and the tunnel.

Specialized techniques

The presence of water in the ground has a tremendous effect on the construction of tunnels, and techniques employing compressed air, ground injection, and freezing are available, particularly when tunneling through soft ground.

Although the principle of compressed air as a means of excluding water from diving bells had been known for centuries, it was not until the 19th century that James Greathead first used compressed air in tunneling operations. Previously the development of compressed-air methods had been hampered by lack of sufficient technology. The air lock, permitting the passage from one pressure to another, was not invented until 1830.

The main reason for using compressed air is to prevent water from entering the tunnel, but it also provides an important function in increasing the load on the tunnel face, in some cases allowing a reduction in the quantity of timbering. There are risks in using compressed air—nitro-

gen in the air is forced into the blood under pressure, and if decompression is uncontrolled, the nitrogen forms bubbles in its attempt to leave the bloodstream, causing the condition known as the bends. Each country has its own standards, but the use of compressed air is now governed by strict regulations to ensure that both compression and decompression are performed safely.

In addition to compressed air, ground treatment can also be used to reduce the flow of water into a tunnel. It is now possible to inject all but the most finely grained ground materials with cement or chemical grouts that form a matrix that fills the voids between the soil particles and binds them together. The injected materials range from

▶ The cutting head of this Denmag full-face tunnel-boring machine is rotated by electric motors with clutches linked to speed reducers.

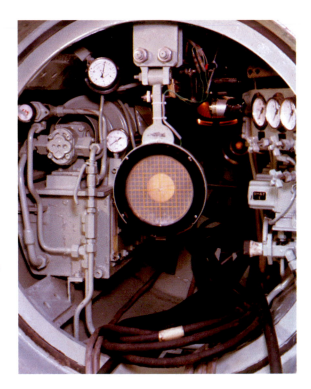

cement and clay, used for filling the larger voids, to polymers and low-viscosity grouts for fine sands, the cost depending to a large extent on the material being injected.

Refrigeration techniques have also been employed since the first freezing plant was set up for shaft sinking in 1883. The temperature of the soil is lowered significantly by drilling or driving tubes into potentially unstable soil and then circulating a low-temperature liquid such as cooled brine or liquid nitrogen. The water in the soil gradually freezes around the probes, and ice cylinders build up to form a continuous wall of frozen ground, which provides an effective barrier against unwanted soil and water entering the tunnel.

Although the costs of tunneling are often greater than for other forms of construction, increasing awareness of environmental issues is prompting many people to consider tunneling preferable to large-scale surface disruption caused in urban areas by working from the surface.

The latest techniques

A more recent alternative to expensive bentonite, used as a slurry to enable tunneling through water-bearing ground, is ordinary water, with the soil filter in the tunnel itself. This process was speeded by replacing the water pumps and filter apparatus with an Archimedes' screw, the result being the earth pressure balance (EPB) machine,

▲ The prefabricated sections of a tunnel that was built under the harbor in Hong Kong. After being towed to the correct position and sunk, the sections were welded together, and water was pumped out.

▶ This microtunneling machine uses a laser guidance system to direct its forward movement. A beam is directed at the center of the target. If the beam shifts, the machine is off line. An operator on the surface can correct the beam by using joystick controls linked to a cathode-ray tube.

in which the soil is forced into the chamber behind the cutterhead, where the screw drives it through the machine to a conveyor belt, a process obviating the need for slurry, hydraulic pumps, and filters. This method led in turn to the development of computer-controlled tunneling equipment—mechanical earth pressure counter balance (MEPCB) machines. These machines, which, in their smaller forms, can be remote controlled, work on the older bentonite principle. Slurry can be used as a hydraulic fluid to increase and decrease the pressure of the cutterhead on the tunnel face; doing so equalizes the cutterhead pressure and the ground pressure.

Another major improvement was the use of a laser guidance system to ensure that the tunnel was dug straight. It consists of a laser transmitter mounted in the mouth of the tunnel, shining down toward the digger. A target board shows where the laser is pointing. If the beam is off-center, the computer controlling the operation raises the alarm, and a single operator at the surface can return the machine to its original track.

Microtunnelling machines use principles similar to those of larger slurry- or rock-cutting machines but are always remote controlled and used for nonman entry tunnels of under 6 ft. (2 m) in diameter. Even smaller machines, known as moles, whose forward thrust is provided by air pressure, can be used to drive nondisruptive holes for small-diameter pipe connections to houses.

SEE ALSO: CIVIL ENGINEERING • EXPLOSIVE • MINING TECHNIQUES

Turbine

A turbine is a rotary machine that converts some of the energy in a flowing stream of fluid (either liquid or gas) into rotational energy. This energy can then be used to do useful work, such as generating electricity in a power plant. The word *turbine* comes from the Latin word *turbo*, a "whirl," and was first used by a French engineering professor, Claude Burdin, whose pupil Benôit Fourneyron designed the first practical turbines.

The power developed by a turbine for a unit flow of fluid is equal to the difference in a fluid property called specific stagnation enthalpy. This property is made up of two parts: enthalpy, relating to the pressure and temperature, and kinetic energy, from the motion. For steam, the enthalpy depends on the pressure and temperature; for water, the difference of stagnation enthalpy is equal to the difference in water pressure across the machine divided by the density of water.

The use of stagnation enthalpy assumes the working fluid is flowing steadily through the turbine, the transfer of heat through the casing is negligible, and the fluid entry and exit connections are not too great a vertical distance apart.

Because of imperfections in the flow owing to viscous effects, the power developed is somewhat less than this theoretical ideal.

Water turbines

At the beginning of the Industrial Revolution, an alternative to the water mill, or waterwheel, was being sought because of the limitations of rotational speed. About 1740, Barker's mill was invented. This device, later called the Scotch mill, comprised a vertical tube with two hollow arms at the base. The machine was mounted in bearings, and a tangential hole was cut in each arm, so when water flowed down the tube, it spurted out of the holes, and the machine turned in reaction to the jets. This type of reaction turbine proved to have little potential.

The first reaction turbine to combine all the features of a modern turbine was that of Fourneyron in 1827. In this turbine, water traveled radially outward through a set of stationary guide blades. The blades were shaped with a converging passage, the result being an outward, swirling flow. The rotor, or runner, was arranged around

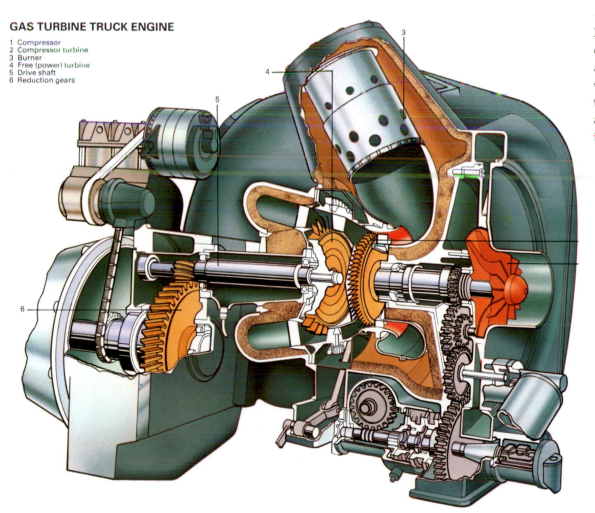

GAS TURBINE TRUCK ENGINE

1 Compressor
2 Compressor turbine
3 Burner
4 Free (power) turbine
5 Drive shaft
6 Reduction gears

◄ A gas turbine engine. It is started by a 24-volt electric motor that accelerates the compressor while fuel is sprayed into the combustion chamber and ignited by an electric ignitor plug.

◀ A steam turbogenerator, driven by heat converted from nuclear energy in a nuclear power plant.

the guide blades and was supported in bearings via a vertical shaft and a series of spokes. It too contained converging passages, so the swirl in the flow was reduced as it passed through the rotating runner. This action exerted a torque on the runner, which then delivered power to the shaft.

This turbine was a great advance but suffered from two disadvantages: the awkward shape of the runner support, which had to be displaced axially to contain the guide blade assembly, and the fact that centrifugal force assisted the flow of water. The latter posed a problem in controlling the turbine—the rotor tended to increase in speed, the increase allowing more flow through the machine, which increased the speed even more.

About 1850, inward-flow reaction turbines were independently developed by a Scottish engineer, James Thomson, and a U.S. engineer, James B. Francis. These turbines were similar to Fourneyron's machine but were arranged with the rotor within the guide blades. They proved to be stable and robust machines—and the Francis turbine is still the most common type because of the wide range of heads of water with which it can be used. (The head is the energy per unit weight of a fluid, a function of its elevation, velocity, and pressure.)

More recent developments include the introduction of an axial-flow reaction turbine with variable-pitch rotor blades by an Austrian inventor, Victor Kaplan, in 1920, and a mixed-flow (semi-axial, semi-inward) machine by a Swiss engineer, Paul Deriaz, in 1956, which also has variable-pitch blades. The Kaplan machine is suitable for very low heads, while the Deriaz machine is more robust because there is more room for the pitch-varying mechanism. In all of these turbines, the pressure in the water is reduced in flowing through both the guide blades and the rotor blades—they are sometimes described as 50 percent reaction.

Another completely separate type of turbine is the impulse turbine. It is suitable for very high heads of water, where the high pressure forces the incoming water through one axisymmetric nozzle, which produces a coherent, high-velocity jet that impinges on buckets attached to the periphery of a wheel. First used in the gold workings in

◀ A steam turbine being assembled. The work is done slowly, and the sequence of operations is carefully planned to avoid damage to delicate vanes and precision-machined surfaces.

California, this type was developed as a tangential-flow machine (called the Pelton wheel) by Lester Allen Pelton, a U.S. millwright in the 1880s, and as an axial-flow machine (called the turbo impulse) in the 1920s. In both cases, control is given by an axially adjustable spear in the nozzle that varies the flow-rate of the water. Both types are still in use.

Steam turbines

In the 1880s, power engineers were dissatisfied with the steam engines of the day. The Swedish engineer Carl G. P. De Laval developed a single-stage impulse machine, while the British engineer Sir Charles Algernon Parsons worked on a multi-stage 50 percent reaction turbine. Both were of the axial-flow type.

These machines were very different in appearance from water turbines, because steam, unlike water, is a compressible substance of low density. By condensing the exhaust steam from the turbine in a water-cooled heat exchanger, it is possible to use a steam outlet pressure as low as $\frac{1}{20}$ of an atmosphere. Even with the modest boiler pressures then used, about 4 atmospheres, complete expansion in a nozzle would have given steam velocities several times that of the Pelton wheel, which had the highest water head available.

For a simple impulse machine, the blades of the rotor should move at about half the speed of the jet, so a single-stage machine of this type had to have a fairly high rotor speed, which put great stress on the rotor. This problem is overcome in a pressure-compounding machine (several De Laval-type stages built in a series, reducing the pressure difference over each) and in a velocity-compounding machine (where two or more rotors are interspersed by stators, which reverse the direction of the swirl in the flow of the steam).

Turbine development

Most of the accessible water-power potential is now exploited, using Kaplan, Deriaz, Francis, and Pelton machines, in order of ascending available

▼ Francis turbines (right) can be used with a wide range of heads of water. The Kaplan turbine (left) is suitable for very low heads of water.

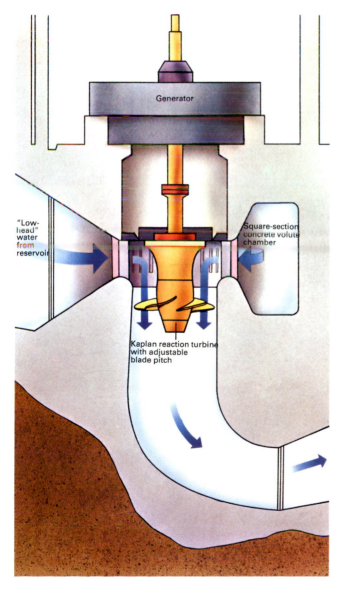

"Low-head" water from reservoir

Square-section concrete volute chamber

Kaplan reaction turbine with adjustable blade pitch

Generator

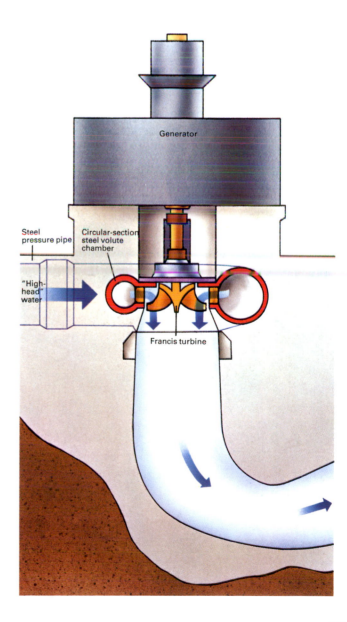

Generator

Steel pressure pipe

Circular-section steel volute chamber

"High-head" water

Francis turbine

water head. These machines, especially large versions of the first two types, are about 90 percent efficient and highly reliable. Modern hydroelectric power plants have several Francis turbines and are capable of producing over 700 MW. The 1,000 MW Neuquen plant in Argentina produces enough electricity for a million homes. Building such power plants is often politically sensitive, as large areas of land can be submerged under water.

An interesting development is the pumped-storage scheme. Water is pumped from a low-level to a high-level reservoir at times of abundant power from thermal sources—for example, late at night from a nuclear reactor plant. Then at times of peak demand for electricity, the water flow is reversed, and hydroelectric power is fed into the grid. This system requires either separate pumps and turbines with disengagement clutches or a universal machine that can perform both functions through reversal of its blade settings. A large, pumped-storage facility at the Hoover Dam in the United States, for example, has 17 Francis turbines, each of which can store and deliver between 40 and 130 MW. The United States has more than 30 pumped-storage plants.

In today's large coal- or oil-fired power plants, steam turbines of 600 to 750 MW are often used. In PWR (pressurized-water reactor) or BWR (boiling-water reactor) nuclear plants, unit ratings of 1,200 MW and higher are common. Steam emerges from fossil-fuel-fired boilers at about 160 atmospheres, superheated and reheated to 1022°F (550°C). The density of the steam as it enters the turbine can be 2,000 times higher than at the outlet.

Significantly more powerful steam turbines are not expected to be built in the near future because of the practical limitations of the turbine components and surrounding plant. Industrial turbines are typically very large and difficult to transport. They require special load vehicles that are 165 ft. (50 m) long and travel at only 3 mph (5 km/h). They can take days to reach their destination and can cause significant traffic problems.

Blade erosion

Both water and steam turbines have problems with erosion of the blade. In some water turbines, a low local pressure develops in the water flow, and pockets of water vapor are formed. When these pockets move into a region of higher pressure, they suddenly collapse. This process is called cavitation, and if it occurs on the surface of a blade, the metal is eroded and may fail. This problem is avoided by careful design and especially by the use of variable-pitch blading.

◄ The fully bladed low-pressure rotors of a 600 MW steam turbine used to generate electricity.

In steam turbines, water droplets form, which can strike the rotor blades at a very high velocity; erosion of the edge of the blade can result. Reheating the steam after it has passed through the high-pressure cylinder not only improves the overall cycle efficiency but also makes the steam drier, so it carries smaller water droplets by the time it reaches the low-pressure stages.

Wind and wave turbines

As the evidence grows of global warming and climate change, there is pressure today to exploit renewable forms of energy and reduce carbon dioxide emissions. Many people believe that wind and wave power could play a large part in future electricity production. In a wind turbine, the blades are mounted around a hub, as in an aircraft propeller, at the top of a tall mast; this hub drives an electricity generator. Modern wind turbines can be more than 200 ft. (60 m) tall and generate power in excess of 1 MW. By placing several such turbines together in a wind farm, significant amounts of power can be generated. The Horns Rev farm, off the coast of Denmark, is set to supply 150 MW when it comes on line in 2002.

There is also growing interest in wave power, in which tidal movements drive a turbine. However, wave turbines are still at an early stage of commercial development.

SEE ALSO: Gas turbine • Hydroelectric power • Power plant • Tidal power • Water mill • Wave power • Wind power

Typewriter

The first known patent for a typewriter was issued in England by Queen Anne to Henry Mill in 1714, but it is not known how the machine worked or if it was ever built. Many designs were produced during the first half of the 19th century, but the first practical typewriter was built in the United States by two inventors, Christopher Sholes and Carlos Glidden.

Development of the Sholes and Glidden machines was taken up by the U.S. company Remington and Sons, and the first typewriters it made went on sale in early 1874. By the end of the 19th century, many companies were engaged in the design and production of typewriters, and following the introduction of electric and electronic machines in the mid-20th century, typewriter manufacture became a major industry.

Manual typewriters

To produce a good printed image on manual typewriters, there needs to be a thin, even film of ink covering the typeface, a firm, even impression of the typeface against the paper, and a resilient backing for the paper. The quality of inking of the typeface has improved as new and better inks have been developed along with improved ribbon materials to hold the ink. One of the most important advances in this area was the introduction of polyethylene ribbons coated on one side, somewhat like carbon paper, with a layer of ink. This ink contains a much higher density of carbon than could be used on an ordinary fabric ribbon.

The platen, or rubber roller, on a typewriter provides a base for the paper that is resilient and yet sufficiently flexible to give a little under pressure, and these characteristics aid a complete transfer of ink from the ribbon to the paper. The design of the platen and of the moving carriage that carries it must ensure that the paper is kept in perfect alignment as it moves.

The character images on traditional machines are cast on small pieces of metal called typeslugs, which are fixed to the ends of the typebars. The typebars are mounted on a slotted semicircular casting called a segment, and the complete set of typebars is called the typebasket.

The downward motion of the key lever on the keyboard is converted, by a series of linkages, into a downward and forward motion of the lower end of the typebar. The typebar is pivoted a little way above its lower end, so this motion moves the other end of the typebar (carrying the typeslug) upward and rearward to strike the ribbon against the paper and print the character.

The type slugs usually have two characters cast on them, one above the other. In the case of alphabetical characters, the upper character on the slug is the capital (uppercase) letter and the lower one is the small (lowercase) letter. The design of the type slug and the curvature of the paper around the platen ensure that only one of these characters can print at a time. The type basket is mounted on vertical guides, and when it is at the top of the guides, the lowercase characters are printed. Operating the shift key moves the basket to the bottom of the guides so that the uppercase characters are printed. A shift lock enables the operator to lock the machine into its uppercase position.

As the typebar moves up under the action of the key lever, other linkages bring the escapement and ribbon mechanisms into operation. The ribbon feed advances the ribbon slightly to bring a fresh area of ribbon into use, and the ribbon-lift mechanism lifts the ribbon up into place in front of the paper. When the machine is used for typing stencils, setting the ribbon-control lever in the stencil position prevents the operation of the ribbon lift so that the typeslug hits the stencil directly.

◄ Electronics have made modern typewriters much easier to use. Most have a liquid crystal display screen that allows the user to see what is being written and correct any mistakes before the line is printed out. The memory can store frequently used phrases or whole pages of text for repeat printing.

Escapement mechanism

The escapement mechanism controls the horizontal motion of the carriage, which is pulled to the left by a coiled spring that is rewound each time the carriage is moved back to the right to begin a new line. The escapement mechanism is a form of ratchet that allows the carriage to move one letter space to the left each time a character is printed or when the space bar is depressed to provide the space between words. The backspace mechanism pulls the carriage one space to the right when the backspace button is depressed. The left- and right-hand margins are controlled by movable stops mounted on a rack on the carriage, which engage with a fixed stop on the frame.

Carriage return is operated by means of a lever extending forward from the left-hand end of the carriage. The initial movement of this lever drives a link with a tooth-shaped end that engages with a ratchet mounted on the left-hand end of the platen, and this ratchet rotates the platen to give the desired vertical spacing of the paper. When the platen has been rotated (indexed) the correct amount, the drive link contacts a stop that prevents it from moving any farther. The pull on the carriage-return lever is transferred to the carriage itself, and the carriage moves to the right. Operating the carriage-return lever when the carriage is at the left margin results in indexing, or line spacing, of the platen.

The tabulation (tab) mechanism allows the carriage to be moved rapidly leftward to preset positions along the writing line. A rack carrying a set of movable stops, one for each letter position along the line, is mounted on the carriage. To set a tab stop, the carriage is moved to the position required, and the tab set button is pressed; the tab stop for that position is then fixed.

When a tab operation is performed, the escapement ratchet is released, and the carriage moves to the left under the action of the escapement spring. When the carriage reaches the point at which the tab stop was set, the stop contacts the tab mechanism fixed to the frame of the machine. This action stops the carriage and brings the escapement ratchet into operation.

Electric typewriters

The first commercially successful electric typewriter was developed by International Business Machines (IBM) in the United States in 1935, but it took many years and much technological development before the electric machine began to compete effectively with the manual machines. Few of the other typewriter manufacturers produced electric machines before 1950.

Since the 1950s, the design of electric typewriters has undergone radical changes. The first involved the perfection of the driving mechanism. In the early machines, the typebar vibrated exces-

▲ Early variants of the typewriter show different methods of selecting letters for printing. Of these three 19th-century attempts to produce a single-element typewriter, only Blick's (right) is a true example, having a keyboard and a cylindrical typehead.

sively as the character was printed, the vibration causing some blurring of the image. Much of the development work was aimed at reducing the number of linkages in the mechanisms.

Single-element machines

The next stage of development involved the introduction of single-element, or golf-ball, typewriters. The first successful single-element machine was the IBM Selectric, introduced at the beginning of the 1960s. The main difference between single-element typewriters and conventional typebar machines is that the carriage assembly remains stationary in the single-element machine, while the typing element moves along the typing line with each keystroke.

Instead of the type characters being carried on a set of typebars, they are all carried on the single typing element, referred to as a golf ball because of its rounded shape and its size. The single-element machine has the advantage that its typestyle can be changed quickly and simply by removing the element and replacing it with one of a different typestyle.

Another advantage of single-element machines is that, unlike the typebar machines, they are not prone to damage or misalignment of the characters owing to typebar clash. With all the characters located on a single element, only one character can be selected at a time. The typing element carries the 44 lowercase characters on one half and the 44 uppercase characters on the other half. Shifting from lowercase to uppercase means turning the element through 180 degrees. The characters on the nickel-plated plastic element are arranged in four horizontal bands (tilt positions); thus, there are a total of 22 vertical columns with four characters in each.

When a character is to be printed, the element must be turned to the rotate position of the character, tilted to the appropriate tilt position, and then driven against the ribbon with sufficient force to print the image on the paper. The rotate motion is transmitted from the selection mechanism to the typehead by a thin steel tape, and the tilt motion is transmitted by a tape or by a shaft running across the machine in line with the platen. Once the typehead has been moved to the correct position, it is detented (locked) in place to ensure accurate alignment during printing.

The selection mechanism is driven by a set of cams, and the amount of motion transmitted to the typehead is controlled by a set of levers and latches. When a key is depressed, it operates a mechanism that sets up the correct combination of latches or levers to give the required amount of rotate-and-tilt motion for that particular character.

Carrier assembly operation

The typehead is carried along the typing line by the carrier assembly, which travels along a shaft (the print shaft) in front of the platen. This shaft has a groove machined along its length, and it passes through a hollow sleeve inside the carrier. The sleeve has a set of cams mounted on it and a metal peg or key that fits into the groove on the shaft so that when the shaft rotates during a print operation, the sleeve and its cams turn with it.

The ribbon, together with the ribbon lift and ribbon-feed mechanisms, is mounted on the carrier so that it moves along with the typehead.

The cams on the sleeve provide the motion to drive the typehead to the platen and print the character, to operate the detents that hold the head in its selected position, and to drive the ribbon lift and feed. The print shaft is driven by the motor via a clutch assembly that is actuated when a key lever is depressed, and it makes one revolution for each print operation.

After the character has been printed, the carrier moves along to the next printing position. This movement is powered by a spring that is rewound when the carrier is moved to the left to start a new line. On most machines, the spring turns a drum that winds on a nylon cord attached to the carrier. The amount the carrier moves is controlled by a pawl assembly mounted on it, which engages with a toothed rack running along the machine below the platen.

Electronic typewriters

Instead of a golf-ball element, electronic typewriters use a type wheel, or daisy wheel. Because only one movement on its axis is required for an impression to be made, the daisy wheel is more accurate, quieter, and faster than the golf ball and still allows for an easy change of typeface.

Accuracy and speed are further aided by the automation of most functions on many models—for example, automatic new line selection and paragraph indentation. Most important, however, electronic typewriters use the latest microprocessor technology. The TA Adler-Royal PowerWriter MD, for example, has a LCD display; a permanent memory facility of 40,000 characters for storing text, frequently used pages, or page formats; a second memory for automatic correction of the last 500 characters typed; and an 80,000-word spell-check facility. Most electronic typewriters can be connected to a personal computer to act as a high-quality printer.

 SEE ALSO: COMPUTER • COMPUTER PRINTER • INK • WORD PROCESSOR

Ultralight Aircraft

Ultralights are small, light airplanes, usually with motors of less than 100 horsepower and often with only a single seat. They first appeared in the 1920s, realizing the dream of pilots who wanted simple flying for fun and for those who wanted to build their own airplane. Famous early ultralights were the Aeronca C-2 of 1930 in the United States and the DH53 of 1923 and Dart Kitten of 1936 designed in Britain. However, the lack of reliable lightweight engines prevented greater use of ultralight aircraft in those early days.

The United States is the cradle of homebuilt aircraft, including ultralights. Many scale replicas (usually in ⅞ scale) of famous airplanes, such as the Thomas Morse Scout of World War I and the P-51 Mustang of World War II, have also been built. Ultralight flyers have grouped together to form the Experimental Aircraft Association (EAA), whose annual fly-in at Oshkosh, Wisconsin, attracts 10,000 airplanes, including all varieties of ultralights, and even World War II bombers rebuilt with loving care. Many of the craft are microlights, which in the United States fall within the general category of ultralight aircraft. A precise international definition of a microlight does in fact exist, although the term ultralight—with its more general, all-inclusive meaning—is still widely used to refer to them. Generally, the fact that microlights are direct descendants of hang glider technology, differentiates them from other types of ultralight aircraft.

History

In the 1960s, some individuals in California, who disliked the increasing complexity, regulation, and cost of conventional aviation, began flying stick-and-string gliders by running into the air from hilltops, as had the German aviation pioneer Otto Lilienthal in Germany in the 1890s. Some used as their model the experimental delta-shaped soft wing designed by the NASA aeronautics engineer Francis Rogallo as a possible retrieval system for spacecraft. No aircraft could have been simpler; it was merely a large triangle of sailcloth fastened over a triangle of bamboo or, in later models, aluminum tubes. Despite the skepticism of conventional aircraft designers, it worked and quickly became popular worldwide; subsequently, much research was undertaken to make it per-

▼ An Eagle microlight aircraft flying above the Severn suspension bridge in Britain. The Eagle is basically a hang glider and consists of a delta-shaped nylon wing and an alloy tube framework that supports the pilot and provides rigging points. With two-stroke engine included, the aircraft can remain airborne under its own power.

form better. Many new ideas were tried in the process, and one of them was to attach a small snowmobile two-stroke engine to the frame.

This new method of powered flying quickly caught the public imagination, because it offered flying to thousands who could not afford expensive airplanes or who did not wish to fly from concrete airports. Microlights differed from conventional airplanes in that they were controlled by weight shift—the pilot swinging his or her body weight in the required direction so that control surfaces were not needed.

Control systems
By the early 1970s, as well as the Rogallos, there were also hang gliders with rigid wings, like the weight-shift Quicksilver or tailless Fledge, and some of these were soon fitted with small engines. Within a few years, the powered hang gliders, as they were known at the time, were being built with the pilot's seat in a tubular framework together with the engine, fuel tank, and wheels. Control was still by weight shift, using the control frame attached to the hang glider wing. These soft-wing, powered hang gliders soon became known as trikes, because of their three landing wheels; the rigid-wing types, such as the later Quicksilver and the Goldwing canard, were called three-axis machines. This name was intended to indicate that control was by stick and rudder, as in conventional airplanes, although several of the early three-axis aircraft were only aerodynamically controlled in one or two axes. Some made turns using only a tail rudder, or wing-tip rudders if tailless, while weight-shift control in pitch lingered on for some time. It was cheap and effective, but so many varieties of three-axis systems caused confusion among pilots, and now all rigid-wing microlights have normal airplane controls.

Definition of a microlight
Initially, microlights were technically classified as airplanes by many civil aviation authorities—thus, in theory they remained subject to their stringent airplane regulations. To avoid excessive control over the new air sport, the microlight committee of the Fédération Aéronautique Internationale (FAI) determined an international definition of a microlight so that the difference between it and a larger, heavier airplane would be clear. The definition finally decided upon described a microlight as a one- or two-seat airplane having an empty (dry) weight not exceeding 330 lbs. (150 kg) and a wing area not less than the weight divided by ten and in no case less than 108 sq. ft. (10 m²). The objective was to ensure that the microlight

remained a light and relatively slow aircraft of low kinetic energy, characteristics that would allow full development of the craft for sporting purposes, while ensuring that it remained safe in the hands of inexperienced pilots.

Most national authorities have now accepted the simple microlight as air-sports equipment and leave regulation of its activities to national aero clubs or specialist microlight associations. This is the case in the United States and France, but not in Britain, where they are regulated by the state. Although microlight pilots in the United States do not require a pilot's licence, there are operational restrictions, and they include the following: no flying over towns or cities; no flying around airports without prior permission; no commercial operations other than instruction; no passengers allowed except for instruction; no flying at night or above or in clouds; and microlights must give right-of-way to all other aircraft.

Microlights generally have wing spans of around 33 ft. (10 m) and wing areas of about 161 sq. ft. (15 m²). One of the smallest, the U.S.-designed Hiperlight biplane, has a span of only 22 ft. (6.7 m), but it still falls within the definition of a microlight, as its wing area is 140 sq. ft. (13 m²) for an empty weight of 246 lbs. (112 kg). Most microlights weigh 260 to 330 lbs. (120–150 kg). From their hang glider origins, they have inherited the very low stall speed necessary if the pilot is to take off by running. With engine and fuselage weight, the stall speed is slightly higher, but most are in the range 25 to 28 mph (40–45 km/h).

▲ A Canadian Lazair ultralight aircraft on floats. It is powered by two 9.8 horsepower engines and can land on calm water. The Lazair is designed to be easily rigged and dismantled, and the materials used are light and strong—alloy tube frames, and a waterproof Mylar film over the wing and tail. Lazairs can be used in competitive flying, including landing-accuracy tests.

Microlight performance

Cruise speed for cross-country flying depends on aircraft drag and engine power. Trikes, with their soft wing and wire bracing, have a fairly high drag configuration, which is reduced by installing a more powerful engine. A single-seater trike usually has a power unit of 30 horsepower, while a two-seater needs over 40 horsepower. It is easier to reduce the profile drag on an airplane-configuration microlight, and single-seaters, such as the Sirocco or Falcon, can achieve satisfactory speeds on 28 horsepower. In general, cruise speeds are on the order of 60 mph (95 km/h).

All aircraft have a known redline, or maximum speed, that should never be exceeded. For microlights in current production, the average is 75 mph (120 km/h). Microlights are not normally certificated for aerobatics.

Microlights are not usually flown above 5,000 ft. (1,500 m), but altitudes of over 23,000 ft. (6,900 m) have been reached in ultralights and high-performance models have exceeded 30,000 ft. (10,000 m). Above, 5,000 ft., however, low temperatures make flying open aircraft less enjoyable, while above 12,000 ft. (3,600 m), the FAA requires pilots to have a supplementary supply of oxygen.

Microlight takeoff and landing runs are short. Takeoff in nil wind requires around 115 ft. (35 m), and landing 230 ft. (70 m). Rate of climb is around 8 to 10 ft. per sec. (2.5–3 m/s), although carrying a passenger reduces this rate noticeably, as a typical aircraft weighs less than double that of its pilot; with two people on board, however, the aircraft weight may be significantly less than the load it is carrying. The performance differs accordingly.

The amount of fuel carried is limited by law in some countries, but a normal tank has a capacity of 5 to 7 gallons (19–26 l). It gives a still-air range of about 112 miles (180 km), although range is usually less, about 75 miles (120 km), on two-seater trikes. Microlights are now much quieter than the earlier experimental aircraft and comply with national noise requirements—70 to 80 dB at 500 ft. (150 m) would be typical.

The low performance of a microlight compared with that of an airplane, such as a Cessna 152, demands that its pilot have a good understanding of meteorology and in particular the local effects of wind and thermal turbulence. Almost all microlights are able to cope with quite rough weather, but it will be more of a problem for a beginner than it would be for an experienced pilot.

Nearly all microlight power units are two-strokes. They were developed from small industrial engines and no longer suffer from the old problems, oiled-up plugs and refusal to start when hot. As they are basically simple engines, maintenance is mostly done by the owner, and thus the cost of flying is kept down. Two-strokes are, how-

▲ Like many home built aircraft, Rutan's canard wing VariEze is difficult to classify, falling as it does between the light aircraft and ultralight categories.

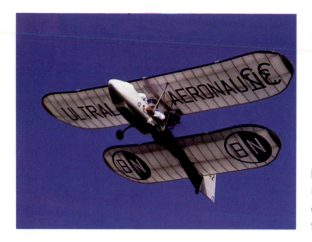

◀ A Belgian Butterfly aircraft, which has a tandem wing and weighs 154 lbs. (70 kg).

▶ A recoil-started microlight trike. The pilot can pull the starter cord from his or her seat.

ever, fairly thirsty on fuel, which is why a four-stroke engine would be more economical for a frequently flown two-seater used for teaching.

A single-cylinder two-stroke, as might be fitted to a very light microlight weighing about 154 lbs. (70 kg), weighs 41 lbs. (18 kg), while a single giving 26 horsepower at 6,500 rpm weighs 53 lbs. (24 kg). The big Rotax 462, which might be fitted for special purposes, such as airtowing hang gliders, gives 52 horsepower at 6,500 rpm and weighs 71 lbs. (32 kg). Reduction drives of about 2:1 via tooth or V belts are normal. Most engines are fitted with a recoil starter, though an electric start is an option on bigger engines.

Flying ultralights

Although there is no reason why a microlight could not be flown coast to coast—given plenty of time—most pilots get their enjoyment from flying in company with friends in other microlights to a club meet or simply from flying around the sky on a summer evening looking at the countryside. Open-cockpit designs are usually preferred for this kind of flying. Most ultralights can also be fitted with floats or with skis for flying off snow or ice in winter. Ultralights, of any configuration, are designed to be easily rigged or dismantled, and many can be transported on the roof of an automobile.

In any air sport, there is some form of competition flying. With microlights, it ranges from club spot-landing contests to the long navigational tasks of world championships. In world championships, pilots are limited to 6.9 gallons (25 l) of fuel. One test is to fly as far as possible around selected turn points and to return home without running out of gas. Failure results in lost points, but there is no difficulty in landing the ultralight safely even in small fields. The skills needed to win such tests include accurate navigation, precise fuel management, and the ability to soar well in thermals or in ridge lift, as with a glider. The ultralight's low stall speed allows it to

circle in quite small upcurrents, and during a championship, pilots have achieved distances of over 310 miles (500 km) and six hours' duration on an allowance of 6.9 gallons (26 l) of fuel. Landing-accuracy tests are also popular and are always carried out with the engine being stopped at 1,000 ft. (305 m) or above. The FAI world championships are held in a different country every two years, with continental championships taking place in the intervening years. The FAI, based in Switzerland, is also the governing body responsible for establishing world records for ultralights.

Improved technology

In recent years ultralights have developed fast, with manufacturers and home builders producing or working on 450 different types of aircraft and over 50 engines. They have brought into practical use not only many new materials but also digital instrumentation panels and ballistic parachutes, which lower both aircraft and pilot together in complete safety. Ballistic parachutes are fired out of a container using either an explosive charge or a chemical rocket, which aids rapid deployment of the chute—around 2 seconds—and enables it to be deployed from altitudes as low as 100 ft. (30 m).

These technological and safety improvements show that ultralights are excellent vehicles for experimenting with new ideas both quickly and inexpensively. Development has naturally been different across the world. In the United States, with its long and successful airplane traditions, development has concentrated on more conventional airplane configurations with a leaning toward nostalgia. In Europe, unlike the United States, there are large numbers of trikes, possibly because they are cheap to buy and operate and are more stable in windy climates.

SEE ALSO: Aerodynamics • Aircraft design • Hang glider

Ultrasonics

Ultrasonics is the study and use of longitudinal pressure waves that propagate through matter in the same manner as that of sound waves but whose frequencies lie above the audible range. Such waves arise when an object vibrates at an appropriately high frequency in a medium whose constituent particles are close enough to interact with one another. This condition is satisfied in solids, liquids, and most samples of gases. A vacuum fails to support the propagation of pressure waves, as do highly rarefied samples of gases.

When a compressional wave passes through a medium, there is a net back-and-forth motion of the particles in that medium superimposed on their random thermal motion. The motion along the direction of propagation classifies this type of wave as longitudinal (as opposed to transverse waves, which are characterized by motion perpendicular to the axis of propagation). Principal wave characteristics include frequency (the number of vibrations per second), amplitude (the maximum displacement of a vibrating particle), and wavelength (the distance between two points at the same stage of the oscillation).

A human ear is sensitive to pressure waves with frequencies between 20 Hz and 20,000 Hz, which are classed as acoustic sound waves. Vibrations with frequencies above 20,000 Hz are too fast to be detected by a typical human ear and are classified as ultrasonic, although animals such as bats and dogs hear frequencies above this value. The upper-frequency limit of ultrasonic vibrations is set by the capabilities of the generators available and is currently around 10 GHz.

A feature that distinguishes ultrasound from acoustic sound is that it can be focused into beams by oscillators of a convenient size, because the focusing process requires the source to be of dimensions significantly greater than the wavelength of the sound. The wavelength at 20,000 Hz is around 0.67 in. (1.7 cm), so a transducer around an inch (2.54 cm) in diameter can produce a focused beam at this frequency. Higher frequencies are easily focused by even smaller transducers, since wavelength is inversely proportionate to frequency. For comparison, an audible frequency of 600 Hz has a wavelength of 22.6 in. (57.3 cm) and so would require a much larger transducer surface for focusing.

The ease of focusing makes ultrasound a useful means of carrying energy along a specific route or to a specific position, an essential property in many of its applications. The other advantage of ultrasound is its inaudibility; thus, it is

▲ A selection of heads for ultrasonic cutting tools. The heads move back and forth at high frequency, and the shapes of the resulting holes match the shapes of the tools.

easier to work with than audible sound. No ear protection is necessary, and there is no problem of noise in the working environment.

Sources and detectors

Ultrasonic waves are generated by means similar to those used to produce sound waves. Most techniques use a vibrating surface to instigate the waves, as occurs with loudspeakers in the audible range; some use oscillations set up in resonant cavities, as is the case with organ pipes and whistles for audible sound. Ultrasonic "whistles" have low maximum frequencies, however, so their scope as ultrasound sources is limited.

Most ultrasonic generators produce the desired vibrations by the conversion of electric or magnetic energy into mechanical energy. Such converters are examples of transducers, and they rely on piezoelectric, electrostriction, and magnetostriction phenomena to produce ultrasound.

Piezoelectric transducers. Certain crystals, such as those of quartz and Rochelle salt, exhibit a phenomenon called piezoelectricity. When pressure is exerted on a quartz crystal, deformations in the crystal structure result in an electrical potential difference and an electric current can be produced. Since acoustic waves consist of an alternating series of pressure changes, such vibrations

◄ This apparatus is an acoustic microscope. It uses pulses of ultrasound from a zinc oxide transducer to probe test objects. A processor calculates the positions of discontinuities, such as flaws, from the time taken for the reflected pulses to reach a second transducer.

around a Ti^{4+} ion. The cavity within the unit cell is large enough for the Ti^{4+} ion to move around, creating an electrical dipole when it is off center.

A strong electrical field can cause unit cells in such a material to distort, the distortion creating an electrical dipole that persists until the material is subjected to another strong field. This behavior is called ferroelectricity by analogy to the magnetization of ferromagnetic materials, such as iron. Ferroelectric materials exhibit the piezoelectric effect when charged and so can be used as generators or detectors of ultrasonic waves.

A major advantage of ferromagnetic ceramics over crystalline piezoelectrics is that the former can be molded into a variety of shapes and then exposed to an electrical field to create an ultrasonic transducer. This property extends the usefulness of ultrasound by making it possible to create various forms of wave fronts: disk-shaped transducers produce narrow beams that can travel over long distances, whereas concave transducers produce waves that converge on a point. Also, ferroelectric transducers are more efficient than crystalline piezoelectric transducers, and they are not constrained to working at a resonant frequency in order to be efficient.

Electrostrictive transducers. Ferroelectrics such as barium titanate, calcium titanate ($CaTiO_3$), and calcium zirconate ($CaZrO_3$) can be used in an alternative manner to that described above. The application of an electrical field causes them to contract—an effect called electrostriction—and the degree of contraction increases with the strength of field. An oscillating electrical field causes such a material to vibrate at twice its frequency, since the contraction reaches its maximum when the field reaches both its positive and negative peaks. This behavior can be used as the basis for making ultrasonic transducers.

Magnetostrictive transducers. Ferromagnetic materials, such as iron, can be made to vibrate by applying an oscillating magnetic field, because they contract when subjected to a magnetic field. As with electrostriction, magnetostriction occurs at twice the frequency of the field oscillation. Magnetostrictive transducers have the advantage that the field can be applied through an electromagnetic coil that does not have to be in direct contact with the transducer. Materials that exhibit magnetostriction include nickel, a number of nickel alloys, and mixed metal oxides called ferrites, which are based on Fe_2O_3.

Scanning applications

The potential of ultrasound pulses for surveying and scanning purposes is demonstrated by the way that bats sound out their environments using

striking the crystal give rise to an electrical field that varies in time with the incident vibrations. Appropriately placed electrodes produce a current that varies with the field, so a piezoelectric crystal can be used as an ultrasound detector.

The converse piezoelectric effect—changes in crystal size caused by an applied electrical field—can be used to produce ultrasonic vibrations. The process is most efficient when the frequency of the applied alternating field coincides with the resonant frequency for the mechanical vibration of the crystal: the rate at which electrical energy converts into mechanical energy reaches its maximum in this condition. Since the resonant frequency of the piezoelectric crystal depends on its dimensions, an effective ultrasound generator can be made by cutting a crystal of the appropriate size and applying a matching oscillating field.

Ferroelectrics. The principal disadvantage of crystalline piezoelectrics stems from the need to cut single crystals precisely along specific crystal axes for maximum effect. This problem is obviated by the use of certain ceramic mixed-metal oxides, such as barium titanate ($BaTiO_3$). The unit cell of this material consists of a cubic cage of Ba^{2+} (corners) and O^{2-} ions (faces) centered

▲ This ultrasonic scanner provides a nondestructive means of testing for flaws in railroad tracks.

ultrasonic pulses. The delay in the returning echo indicates the distance between the bat and reflecting objects, and the slight differences in the delays for reaching each ear provide information on the direction of the incoming echo pulse.

Underwater surveying. One of the earliest uses of sound at ultrasonic frequencies was to improve depth-sounding methods at sea. The narrow, directed beams available by the use of ultrasonics are not absorbed by water as easily as lower-frequency sounds in the audible region. Ultrasonic scanning enables accurate mapping of the seabed by measuring the time delay between the transmission and detection of the subsequently reflected waves. Information about the rock strata under the seabed is also obtainable and has been used in prospecting for underwater mineral deposits such as oil and natural gas.

Sonar. Sonar (*so*und *na*vigation and *r*anging) equipment uses pulses of ultrasound to survey underwater terrain and detect submerged objects in a way that mimics a bat's sighting technique. The use of ultrasound rather than audible sound improves this technique by improving its resolution, because resolution—the minimum separation between two points for them to be discerned as separate—is determined by the wavelength of the scanning vibration.

Ultrasonic sonar can also be used in the Doppler mode, which uses slight shifts in the frequency of the reflected pulse to identify the relative speed of the reflecting object along the path of reflection. Doppler sonar, like Doppler radar, can filter out a background of reflections from stationary objects to highlight moving reflectors. This ability, combined with a resolving power that can discern individual fish, helps trawlers locate shoals of fish below the surface.

▲ This device is an ultrasonic disintegrator. It is used to break up animal tissue cells for analysis.

▼ This virtual reality image of a fetus has been derived from ultrasound scans. Researchers hope to use the system in real-time situations to allow a doctor to see the fetus in its actual position during an examination.

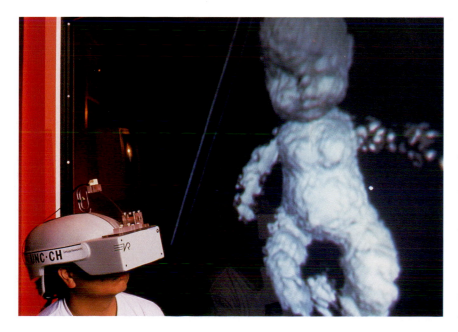

Nondestructive testing. Ultrasonic vibrations are used to probe for defects deep within castings and other manufactured objects and to measure the thicknesses of such objects. In many cases, ultrasonic methods have replaced more hazardous and expensive radiographic techniques.

The test method relies on the fact that ultrasound reflects off discontinuities within materials. Examples of discontinuities include the opposite face of the object, an internal flaw or cavity, or an inclusion (an impurity or lump of foreign matter). When pulses are transmitted into an object under examination, the time they take in returning to the transducer gives an indication of the depth of the reflecting surface, so a scan of its surface can produce a map that shows the depth of flaws and the thickness of the material. As with other ultrasonic techniques, the resolving power increases with higher frequencies of ultrasound.

Body scanning. One of the growth areas of ultrasonic scanning in recent years has been in medicine, where it offers an alternative to techniques such as magnetic resonance imaging (MRI) and X-ray scanning. The technique works because different types of tissues in the human body—bone, muscle, and fat, for example—reflect and absorb ultrasound in different ways. By scanning a portion of the body with a suitable ultrasonic beam and detecting the reflected signals, it is possible to produce a picture of the area of interest. The resolution is almost equivalent to that of viewing an object with the naked eye.

Ultrasound scanning is noninvasive, and the low-intensity sound waves present no hazard to humans, so the technique is safe for repeated applications. In many ways, ultrasonic imaging is comparable to X-ray radiography, but without the harmful effects of radiation. Also, ultrasonic imaging can reveal details in the soft body structures, such as fat and muscle, that do not show up on X rays. The picture is formed in real time, so surgeons can use ultrasound images to ensure the correct positioning of endoscopes and sampling needles without having to make large incisions.

Ultrasonic scans are now used routinely to monitor fetal development, helping identify sex and the number of fetuses in the uterus and providing a means of detecting abnormalities at an early stage. In children and adults, ultrasound is used to detect inclusions, tumors, and other abnormalities in organs such as the brain and kidneys and to monitor the effects of hemorrhages. Doppler ultrasound can even monitor the flow of fluids, such as blood, around the body because of the slight frequency shifts that occur when ultrasound bounces off objects suspended in the moving fluid, such as blood cells.

Therapy

Focused high-energy ultrasound beams are used as a therapeutic alternative to surgery for a number of medical conditions. One application is in the treatment of kidney stones: an ultrasound beam focuses on the stones, breaking them down to a size that can easily pass out of the body through the urinary system. The beam is of such an intensity that it causes damage only within a small radius of its focal point, so other body structures are unharmed. Alternatively, kidney stones can be broken up by a probe that delivers ultrasonic vibrations through a keyhole incision.

High-energy beams have an associated heating effect that can be put to therapeutic use. Gentle heating can be used to soothe joint pain, for example, whereas intensive heating can be used to attack tumors as an alternative to more generally destructive chemotherapy and radiotherapy.

Cutting and machining

Ultrasound offers a versatile alternative to drilling and other techniques for machining hard objects. A suitable cutting tool is attached to an ultrasonic transducer, which causes it to vibrate back and forth at high frequency. An abrasive paste or slurry provides the means for cutting as the tool rubs its particles against the surface of the workpiece. Since the motion of the cutter is oscillatory—as opposed to the rotary motion of a conventional drill—the hole that forms matches the cross section of the tool. This machining technique is particularly effective on brittle materials such as germanium, silicon, and ferrites.

At the other end of the hardness scale, ultrasonic blades can be used to cut sticky, semisolid materials, such as soft cheeses. The rapid sawing motion of the blade prevents the material from sticking, so a cleaner cut can be achieved than would be possible using a conventional knife.

Cavitation

When ultrasonic waves are generated in liquids, tiny voids repeatedly form and collapse in a process called cavitation. Within these spaces, a partial vacuum is set up that exerts a pull on particles on the surfaces of immersed objects, greatly assisting solvent action in the cleaning of objects as diverse as computer components and jewelry.

Cavitation helps emulsify immiscible liquids, such as oil and water, and helps remove air bubbles from liquid metals prior to casting. Cavitation also increases the rates of many chemical reactions where the ultrasound energy is thought to be delivered through the fluctuations of electrical dipoles, as voids form and collapse.

◄ This long-eared bat uses ultrasonic pulses—a natural version of sonar—to find its way around.

FACT FILE

- Information currently discarded during scans could be processed by computer to reveal a huge variety of tissue conditions. Different diseases, such as cirrhosis and hepatitis, each have specific ultrasound signatures. Exploratory surgery and biopsies could be virtually replaced by highly efficient computerized scanning techniques.

- High-intensity ultrasound pulses may soon be used for brain exploration without the use of electrodes. Ultrasound is capable of triggering brain nerve cells to react, and tests have shown that localized neuron groups can be "switched on" in animal subjects. It is technically feasible that the visual cortex of some blind patients could be stimulated by ultrasound.

- Digital imaging systems have been created that can process large quantities of data from ultrasonic materials testing. A map of the object under test is displayed on a screen that reveals in false colors the sizes, types, and locations of flaws. This technique is widely used on large metal structures, such as gas pipelines and oil well caps.

SEE ALSO: CERAMICS • DOPPLER EFFECT • PIEZOELECTRIC MATERIAL • SONAR • TRANSDUCER AND SENSOR

Ultraviolet Lamp

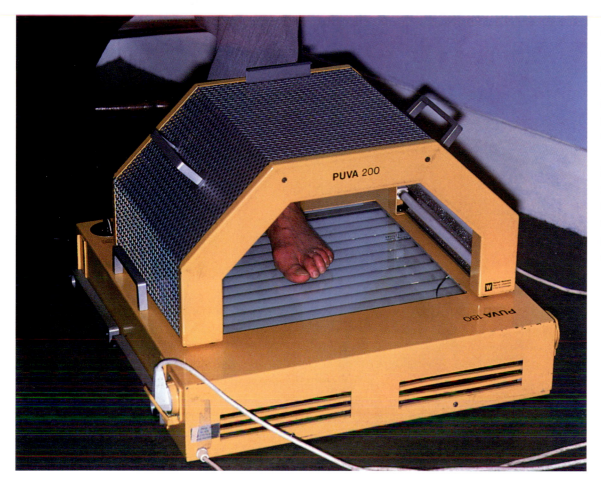

Ultraviolet light is similar to visible light—both are forms of electromagnetic radiation—but ultraviolet waves are shorter, ranging from the wavelength of violet light, which is 390 nm (a nanometer is a billionth of a meter), down to the beginning of the X-ray region (1 nm).

Earth's atmosphere absorbs radiation from the Sun that has wavelengths shorter than 280 nm (the far ultraviolet); known as UVC, these wavelengths are energetic enough to be harmful to living cells. Slightly longer waves, the middle ultraviolet (280 to 320 nm), or UVB, cause the skin reactions that show as suntan and sunburn. Glass absorbs these wavelengths, which is why people do not tan through glass. The longer wavelengths between 320 nm and visible violet light, known as UVA, are the near ultraviolet.

Lamps and their uses

Lamps for producing ultraviolet light are discharge tubes employing an electric discharge through mercury vapor. The electrons in the mercury atoms gain energy from the discharge and lose it again as radiation at a few particular wavelengths that occur in both the ultraviolet and visible parts of the electromagnetic spectrum.

The pressure of the mercury vapor can be varied to produce ultraviolet lamps that operate most efficiently in the far, middle, or near region of the spectrum, while the unwanted wavelengths can be screened out by using an envelope (of quartz or certain types of glass) that is transparent only to the required ultraviolet region.

Far-ultraviolet lamps are used for sterilizing perishable foodstuffs. The radiation that destroys the bacteria will also damage human skin cells, so precautions must be taken. High-intensity ultraviolet arc lamps are very efficient at destroying waterborne microorganisms, bacteria, viruses, and molds. The applications for ultraviolet water disinfection systems include drinking-water treatment (where ultraviolet has replaced the traditional chlorination plant) and process-water treatment in the brewing and soft-drinks industries.

Sunlamps

Mercury lamps, which produce most of their radiation in the middle ultraviolet and screen out the dangerous shorter wavelengths, are sold commercially as sunlamps. These lamps are used mainly for cosmetic purposes, to give a suntan, but they also have a medical application in the treatment of

◄ An apparatus used for sterilizing water on ships by means of ultraviolet light. Ultraviolet light disrupts processes in the cells of organisms; thus, it is effective for killing bacteria and algae that may be present in a water supply.

some skin diseases, such as eczema. Sunlamps usually incorporate an additional electrically heated filament that emits infrared radiation to warm the skin while it is tanned. In the medical field, high-intensity ultraviolet lamps are routinely used for the localized healing of sores, ulcers, and postoperative infections. In some lamps, the intensity can be varied from half to full power through an intensity regulator that varies the heat according to the patient's needs.

It is UVB rays that cause most of the problems related to sun exposure—such as eye damage, immune system changes, wrinkles, premature aging of the skin, and skin cancers. Ninety-nine percent of the Sun's radiation at sea level is UVA. However, the UVA rays emitted from sunlamps are two to three times more powerful than natural UVA rays. UVA rays have a suspected link to malignant melanoma, the most serious type of skin cancer, and like UVB rays, they also may be linked to damage to the immune system.

Fluorescence

The principal use of near ultraviolet (UVA), sometimes known as black light, is in causing substances to fluoresce. This effect is due to the fact that the electrons in any material can only have particular energies, and when they change from one energy state to another, they emit or absorb electromagnetic energy. If an electron is excited into a higher energy state by ultraviolet, it can either return to its original state by reemitting ultraviolet of the same wavelength or pass through intermediate energy states, each time emitting radiation at a longer wavelength than the original ultraviolet. The radiation from the latter process (fluorescence) is often visible

light—a fluorescent substance glows in the dark when ultraviolet radiation is shone on it.

This phenomenon is used to good effect in the theater and in night clubs. It also has practical uses in the analysis of mineral specimens (different chemical compounds fluoresce at different wavelengths) and in the detection of small cracks in the surface of metals and other materials. In this case, a fluorescent dye is applied to the surface and wiped off; dye that has penetrated into cracks shows up brilliantly under an ultraviolet lamp.

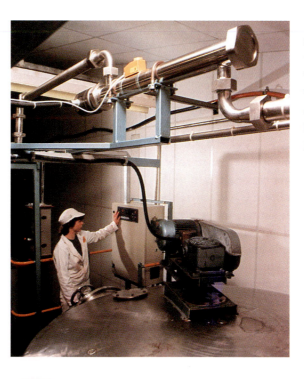

◄ Disinfecting sugar syrup for use in soft drink manufacture. The syrup is pumped from the tank into the pipework containing ultraviolet light, which destroys bacteria and viruses.

SEE ALSO: DISCHARGE TUBE • ELECTROMAGNETIC RADIATION • FOOD PRESERVATION AND PACKAGING • LIGHT AND OPTICS • MERCURY • PHOTOTHERAPY • WATER SUPPLY • X-RAY IMAGING

Undercarriage, Retractable

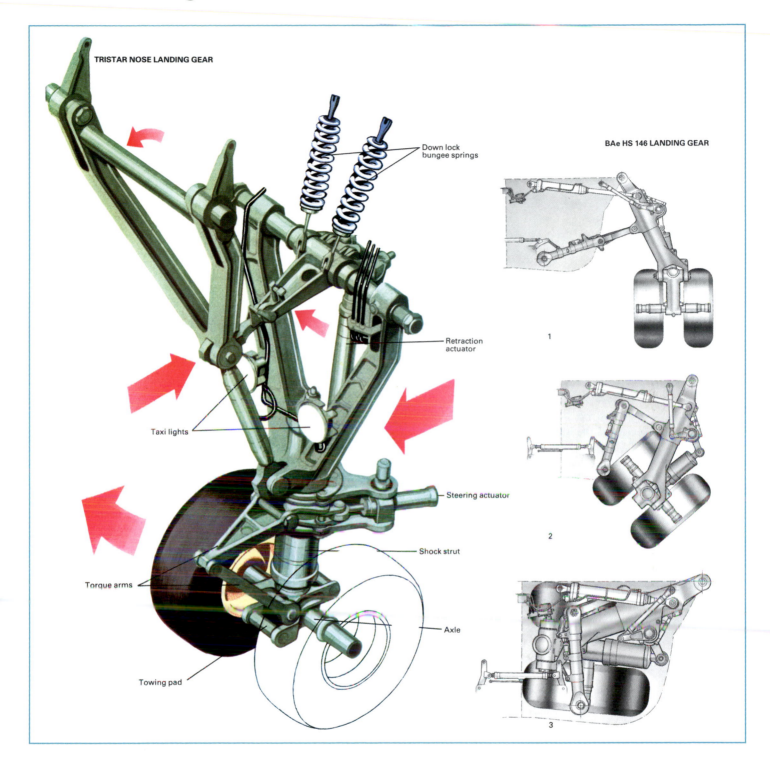

TRISTAR NOSE LANDING GEAR

Down lock bungee springs

Retraction actuator

Taxi lights

Steering actuator

Shock strut

Torque arms

Axle

Towing pad

BAe HS 146 LANDING GEAR

1

2

3

The benefits of streamlining have been recognized from the earliest days of flying. By smoothing the profiles of airplanes and as far as possible removing awkward protrusions, their speed could be increased and their range extended. An obvious candidate for this treatment is the undercarriage, or landing gear, which is not only large but serves no purpose once the aircraft has left the ground. The undercarriage comprises the wheels, axles, brakes, and supporting structure and is inevitably bulky—it has to be strong enough to absorb the stresses of takeoff, landing, taxiing, and towing. The drag of these units (their resistance to motion through the air) is great even at low speeds and increases sharply as the plane accelerates.

Mechanical gear

The first mechanically operated retractable undercarriage was tried out in 1908 by an American, Matthew Sellers, who fitted it to an aircraft he built. It was patented in the United States three years later.

▲ Left: the retractable nose landing gear of the Lockheed L-1011 Tristar, with the red arrows showing the direction in which the links move as the gear retracts. Right: the landing gear of the BAe HS 146 airliner retracts into a very small space in the fuselage.

In the surge of enthusiasm for aviation that appeared following the successes of airplanes in World War I, it was the racing-plane builders who made the first demands on technology. The Dayton-Wright monoplane, which competed in France in the 1920 Gordon Bennett air race, had the first improved retractable landing gear. It was followed in 1922 by a British airplane, the Bristol Monoplane racer. U.S. airplanes had wheels that retracted into circular recesses in the fuselage in a way that was to characterize U.S. single-engined fighters for many years afterward. Those of the British racer folded into circular wells in the underside of the wing.

By the late 1930s, most of the new commercial and military airplanes were able to employ retractable landing gear because of developments in the technology of high-pressure hydraulic mechanisms. The undercarriages of even the smallest planes are heavy, and great force is needed during retraction to overcome the weight and wind-resistance forces. These difficulties increase with speed. Some of the early planes, such as the Avro Anson, had a mechanical screw-jack device for winding the wheels up by hand. Others, for example, the early marks of Spitfires, used rudimentary hydraulic circuits energized by hand pumps. These methods were not suitable for bigger, commercial airplanes, for which high-pressure circuits, energized by pumps driven by the engines, were eventually developed. All modern retractable landing gear systems are hydraulic.

In the days of piston-engine airplanes, the wheels of multi-engine planes were usually pulled up into the engine nacelles (housings). In many cases, the nacelles were not deep enough to enclose the wheels completely, and the tire was left protruding, but the loss of performance was small because the wheels were of smooth contour and produced little drag. On single-engine planes, the wheels commonly folded away into the wings. The wings of modern fighters are so thin that they cannot accommodate the landing gear, and complicated arrangements are necessary to fold the wheels in such a way that they take up the least possible space in the fuselage.

Emergencies

Occasionally the landing gear fails to work properly. It is not dangerous if it does not retract after takeoff—the plane will simply have to overcome some extra drag—but it could be a disaster if the hydraulics failed to push the gear down for landing. The wheels are now designed to drop down under the pull of gravity as soon as the locks holding the gear inside the fuselage are released.

▲ Like many modern military airplanes, the BAe-Sepecat Jaguar's wings are too thin to accommodate the wheels, so they must be folded away into the fuselage during flight.

 SEE ALSO: AERODYNAMICS • AIRCRAFT DESIGN • HYDRAULICS • TIRE

Undersea Habitat

There have been many different attempts to remain underwater for prolonged periods since the 1970s, but no technique has so far been found to overcome the main obstacle to subsurface living—that of decompression, that is, when nitrogen bubbles form in the bloodstream of a diver returning to the surface. In the 1960s, that obstacle thwarted the ambitious hopes of divers who wanted to remain submerged for long periods to enable them to work on either commercial or scientific projects. Instead, the most that has been achieved is the ability to reduce the number of times divers have to undergo decompression, by keeping them in pressure vessels onboard ship between dives. Only a few marine biologists stay underwater on long surveys.

The bends

As soon as a diver submerges, his or her body undergoes subtle changes as a result of the increased pressure. The greater the depth, the greater is the weight of water above the diver and the greater the pressure. At greater pressures, increased amounts of nitrogen gas dissolve in the bloodstream. As the diver begins to ascend, the amount of dissolved nitrogen is greater than the blood can hold. If the return to the surface is slow, the diver can expel the excess nitrogen naturally with no ill effects. If he or she rises too fast, however, the excess nitrogen will not be expelled rapidly enough, resulting in the formation of nitrogen bubbles in the bloodstream. This leads to the condition familiarly known as the bends with symptoms ranging from pain in the joints and nausea to paralysis and possibly death.

The only known reliable way of avoiding these problems is a slow, controlled decompression. However, owing to the great depth of modern dives, decompression times are long. A dive of about 590 ft. (180 m) for 1 hour requires a decompression time of 57 hours, and a dive for 4 hours requires a decompression time of 170 hours.

Saturation diving

The key to solving this problem lies in a phenomenon known as saturation diving. After a certain length of time at any given depth, a diver's body becomes saturated with the inert gas he or she has been breathing, and no more is absorbed. After saturation, decompression time does not increase, however long a diver stays at pressure. It therefore follows that any device that can enable a diver to stay at pressure will extend the time available for useful work. After spending 4 hours or more at depth, a diver is considered to be in saturation, and it does not matter how much longer he or she spends at depth—whether an extra 2 hours or 2 weeks, the decompression time remains identical. From a depth in the region of 590 ft. (180 m) it would take just over a week.

One solution to the problem that has appealed to many marine scientists is the underwater habitat. In a "home underwater" a diver could actually live at working depth. He or she could leave the habitat to work, return "home" at the end of a work period to be comfortable, warm, and dry while resting and eating before the next work period. Only at the end of a shift lasting several days would the diver come to the surface, go through decompression once in a pressure vessel on a ship, and return to normal life.

Scientists working on early habitats calculated that a diver using a habitat would be able to do three times as much work for the amount of time spent on the project as a whole, compared with the inefficient dive-and-decompress system.

In 1962, the French diver Jacques Cousteau launched the era of habitat experiments when he submerged the barrel-shaped vessel *Diogenes* in 34 ft. (10.5 m) of water in the bay of Marseilles. Two divers lived in it for a week. In their simple steel capsule, anchored to the seabed to counter its buoyancy, they had two bunks, a supply of breathing gas, and food ferried down to them by divers. On the first day, they showed symptoms of anxiety. By the fifth day, however, they had become completely acclimated to their way of life.

In 1963, Cousteau set up another project, *Conshelf II*, in which five aquanauts stayed for a month at a depth of 36 ft. (11 m). In 1964, two separate programs tackled one of the most serious of the problems of habitat living—atmosphere.

Breathing underwater

The problem with air, which is principally a mixture of 78 percent nitrogen with 21 percent oxygen, is that, at depths of 100 ft. (30 m) and more, it causes divers to suffer nitrogen narcosis. The nitrogen dissolved in the blood reaches the nervous system and results in lethargy, hallucinations, and loss of control. These symptoms, known as "rapture of the deep," can be fatal.

Nitrogen is not involed in the human metabolism and can therefore be replaced by another gas in the mixture that divers breathe. Helium appears to be the best substitute. It does not cause diver narcosis, but it does have other disadvantages. Helium removes heat from the body several times faster than air, both in respiration and through the skin. At 590 ft. (180 m), the heat lost through breathing is estimated to be the same as the total metabolic rate of the human body. So marine engineers have had to give serious attention to the problems of insulating and heating a helium-rich atmosphere.

Helium also gives rise to helium tremors, especially as a result of over-rapid compression, which can lead to painful joints, loss of balance, and dizziness. For the diver in the habitat, helium affects the vocal cords, so speech takes on a "Donald Duck" effect, and support crews can barely distinguish between the simple responses "positive" and "negative" sent up from the habitat without the use of a helium unscrambler.

The U.S. Navy later embarked on the Sealab program, and in *Sealab I*, four men spent 9 days breathing a mixture of 4 percent oxygen, 17 percent nitrogen, and 79 percent helium. In *Sealab II*, at a depth of 205 ft. (62.5 m), relays of divers—a total of 29 men—spent 15-day shifts, one of them enduring a 30-day stretch, breathing and working with no ill effects.

At the same time, Cousteau was engaged in an extended-stay program in *Conshelf III*, a sphere 18 ft. (6 m) in diameter in which his team of six aquanauts spent 27 days at 328 ft. (100 m) followed by a three-day decompression during their tow back to Monaco. The emphasis in these experiments

▼ A technician relays life-support data back to the shore base. Conditions in the *Aquarius* are closely monitored, as is the health of the researchers during their stay onboard.

was on the use of a liquefied gas generator, which supplied oxygen and also removed humidity and carbon monoxide from the atmosphere.

In 1965 the U.S. Navy mounted its third Sealab experiment by submerging the laboratory to a record 590 ft. (180 m) off the Californian coast. Unfortunately, a diver on an inspection mission suffered from exhaustion, cold, and carbon dioxide poisoning and died. His death focused attention on the risks inherent in this research, and for some time, enthusiasm for undersea habitat experiments diminished.

Surface support

The U.S. Navy called off its program, but the cessation of underwater research was brief. In 1969, the German underwater laboratory (UWL) *Helgoland* went into operation in the North Sea. It was a pressure-proof cylinder comprising two rooms, a wet room and a workroom. In a departure from conventional practice, it took its power and breathing gas supplies from a buoy on the surface, which was moored adjacent to the UWL and was therefore largely independent of support ships.

It also adopted an unconventional solution to the problem of surface contact. The basic idea behind an underwater habitat is that it should liberate the users from the limitations imposed by surface life. Yet, paradoxically, the more advanced the habitat became and the deeper it went, the greater its dependence on the support ship on the surface. The greater its dependence on the support ship, the greater the danger, since there was always the possibility that the support ship would be unable to maintain station for days at a time because of surface weather. *Helgoland*'s independent, onboard life-support systems, as well as the contact with the unattended surface buoy, offered one solution to this problem.

The best known of the civilian projects in the United States was the GEC *Tektite* mission of 1968, in which four men spent 50 days at 49 ft. (15 m) studying behavior, physiology, and the usefulness of undersea habitats. They also put special emphasis on saturation diving. In the follow-up experiment a year later, saturation research was again a major feature, and 53 aquanauts were subjected to nitrogen–oxygen saturation.

It was another U.S. enterprise, the Perry Foundation, which held the distinction of building the longest-serving undersea laboratory. The *Hydrolab* was 15 ft. 9 in. (4.8 m) long and 9 ft. (2.8 m) in diameter and was submerged in 49 ft. (15 m) of water 1.18 miles (1.9 km) off Grand Bahama island. *Hydrolab*, like the UWL, took its life-support supplies remotely, through an umbilical cord from a crewless support boat.

▲ The *Aquarius* is periodically brought back up to the surface for an overhaul. The main body of the vessel is divided into a living and work area and a bunk room. Air and power are supplied to the *Aquarius* by an umbilical connection, but emergency batteries and breathing equipment are kept onboard in case of a main power failure.

Habitats still promise to serve certain purposes, not least among them being the leisure industry. Millions of amateur scuba divers might, once the cost becomes realistic, welcome the chance to extend their diving to greater depths and overcome the inconvenience of frequent periods in decompression.

The other most promising area of development continues to be marine biology. The optimum time and depth for a stay in a habitat appears to be approximately one week at about 80 to 120 ft. (24–36 m). A diver using scuba equipment can range from there over half a mile.

These conditions suit the marine biologist well. The habitat offers the marine biologist, geologist, and archaeologist the chance to live for several days at a time among the subjects they are studying without the need to resurface.

Aquarius

One of the latest undersea habitats is *Aquarius*, an ocean laboratory sited near Key Largo, 60 ft. (20 m) deep in the Florida Keys National Marine Sanctuary. The laboratory, constructed in 1987, lies 3.5 miles (5.6 km) offshore on the sands beside the Key's deep coral reefs. Scientists take part in ten-day missions in *Aquarius*, which is owned by the National Oceanic and Atmospheric Administration (NOAA) and operated by the National Undersea Research Center at the University of North Carolina at Wilmington. The laboratory has also been used by NASA to train astronauts in a situation that is said to be "surprisingly similar" to that of the International Space Station.

The laboratory is attached to a base plate that holds the underwater habitat about 13 ft. (4.1 m) off the protected seabed, so the working depth of the laboratory is about 50 ft. (16.6 m). Inside the 81-ton (73-tonne), 43 x 20 x 16.5 ft. (14.3 x 6.6 x 5.5 m) module are six bunks, washing and kitchen facilities, air conditioning, and computers linked to shore by wireless telemetry.

Key Largo is also home to the world's only underwater hotel. Jules' Undersea Lodge, named in honor of author Jules Verne, can hold up to a dozen guests for an underwater wedding or be used for diving holidays. Guests have to use scuba gear and dive 21 ft. (7 m) to enter it through the "moon pool" in the floor of the habitat. The lodge started life as the La Chalupa research laboratory, which was used to explore the continental shelf off the coast of Puerto Rico.

A similarly long-running project has been mounted in the Sublimnos Igloo, near Tobermory, Ontario, Canada, which is situated 30 ft. (9 m) under Lake Huron.

When the idea of undersea habitats first appeared, scientists entertained ambitious notions of their solving an extraordinary range of problems—providing a working base for engineers to repair and service submerged pipelines and work on undersea wellheads and offshore rigs, as well as giving marine biologists, geologists, and archaeologists freedom to work for long periods at a time without the constraints of decompression.

The technology improved rapidly. Autonomy of operating seemed possible. In particular, the system of lowering the habitat by crane gave way to the use of ballast and variable-buoyancy tanks, as used by submarines, which allowed the crew to control their own descent. Nevertheless, however much the engineers improved the habitat, it has still proved impossible to free it from the need to maintain expensive surface support.

▲ Divers secure the *Aquarius* to its base plate. Because divers do not return to the surface during their stay onboard, they avoid the problems of decompression sickness and can make longer dives than when using conventional surface-based diving techniques.

SEE ALSO: DIVING SUIT • OCEANOGRAPHY • SUBMERSIBLE

Underwater Photography

Underwater photography is both an interesting hobby and an important aspect of scientific research into conditions and life in the lakes, rivers, seas, and oceans of our planet.

For the photographer and the diver, the sea can be thought of as consisting of three distinct layers. The first layer extends about 16 ft. (5 m) down from the surface, and in this region, only a face mask and snorkel are required. In this layer, photography is comparatively simple, because daylight penetrates the water and provides sufficient natural illumination for taking pictures, and pressure is low enough to allow the use of the simplest of cameras.

The second layer extends from about 16 ft. (5 m) down to about 160 ft. (50 m). Scuba gear (self-contained underwater breathing apparatus) is essential at these depths. Furthermore, because much less daylight penetrates this far, artificial light is needed for photography. The increased water pressure also means that cameras must be equipped with specially-built housings.

Beyond the 160 ft. (50 m) range, humans cannot dive without special deep-sea equipment, but underwater cameras can still be used as long as enough artificial illumination can be provided to light the subject.

As far as photography is concerned, the most interesting and attractive region of the sea lies within about 30 ft. (10 m) of the surface, where the ample daylight nourishes a great variety of fish and plant life. In warm water especially, there are often interesting photographic subjects, such as coral reefs, only 10 ft. (3 m) or so below the surface of the water.

Apart from the problem of keeping water out of the camera, one of the most important considerations for the underwater photographer is that of refraction. When light passes from water, through glass, and into air, it is refracted, phenomenon that makes the subject look closer than it really is. Refraction increases the effective focal length of the camera lens by 25 percent. As a result, the angle of view of the lens is reduced when it is used underwater, and the depth of field is reduced also. However, this situation does not present focusing problems with a single-lens reflex (SLR) camera. Provided that the photographer can get an eye close enough to the focusing screen of the camera's viewfinder, he or she will see the view that the camera will record; the photographer can thus focus the camera in the ordinary way, even though everything seems nearer than it really is.

▲ A range of underwater cameras, including (left to right) the 110 Weathermatic, Ikelite housing, Nikonos IVa, Ricohamarine AD-1 housing with camera, and the Hanimex Amphibian. The housings allow photographs to be taken underwater using conventional cameras.

With nonreflex cameras, however, focusing is often a matter of guesswork. The focusing scale on the camera can still be used, but it must be set to the apparent distance rather than the actual distance. Cameras specially designed for underwater use can be equipped with an adapted distance scale so that the actual distance can be measured and set on the scale to produce a sharp photograph.

The narrower angle of view and reduced depth of field present more difficult problems. Seawater is often very murky, and vision is limited to 30 to 60 ft. (10–20 m). Most underwater photographs are taken at distances of less than 10 ft. (3 m), so the angle of view is very important.

A lens for a 35 mm camera, which has a focal length of 35 mm in air, becomes the equivalent of 47 mm when used underwater. If this lens were used to take a full-length picture of another diver, the camera would need to be about 13 ft. (4 m) from the subject. At this distance, the dirt and plankton suspended in the water between camera and subject is often sufficient to reduce contrast and definition considerably, and there is no alternative but to move in closer to the subject to get a sharper result.

Naturally, doing so means that less of the subject appears in the picture, unless a wide-angle lens is used. With a simple fixed-lens amphibious camera, changing lenses is impossible, and such cameras are of limited use for this reason. With a more advanced underwater camera, such as the Nikonos or an SLR in an underwater housing, a lens with a shorter focal length can be fitted to take in more of the subject. The clear glass front of the camera housing also acts as a lens, and this feature needs to be considered when lenses of different focal lengths are being fitted. When a wide-angle lens is used with a housed camera, a dome port should be fitted over the front of the housing. The dome port is a large, deeply curved front glass that corrects for refraction. For the Nikonos camera, there is a corrected auxiliary lens that clips over the standard lens. This lens can be fitted underwater to convert the camera to wide-angle use.

Color and exposure

Water not only refracts light but also reflects and absorbs it. Thus, some of the daylight that falls on the surface of the sea never penetrates the water and the light that does penetrate becomes dimmer with increasing depth. Even in quite clear, shallow water 15 to 30 ft. (5–10 m) down, one or two stops more exposure are required than for a photograph on the surface. The photographer must also remember that all the light underwater comes from above, so if the camera is pointed upward, an incorrect light reading may result.

If the underwater camera has a built-in light meter, exposure measurement is unlikely to be a problem, but for other cameras, a separate hand-held meter in an underwater housing is required. Relying on a light meter is usually accurate enough for negative films, but slide film has a very limited exposure latitude, and it is advisable to take a bracket of exposures of the same subject to be sure of getting correctly exposed slides.

◀ This underwater photograph, taken with flash, demonstrates the low-contrast effect of backscatter.

Light absorption by water is not even across the spectrum but is differential—red light, for example, is absorbed more than blue. Seawater has a pale blue tinge that is increasingly noticeable as light travels through greater and greater depths of water. Its effect is gradually and progressively to filter out all colors of light except blue as the diver swims down from the surface of the sea. Photographs taken at increasing depths have a stronger and stronger blue cast. Even in clear water, red light is missing from the spectrum at a depth of 16 ft. (5 m), and red objects appear dark gray or black at these depths and below. At 65 ft. (20 m), only blue light remains, and photographs taken at this depth by available light appear monochromatic—just blue and black. Underwater photographers are often disappointed by the colors in their photographs, because although the human eye can compensate for the missing colors in the spectrum, film cannot do the same. The blue-black tones of a color picture taken underwater cannot be improved by filters: a filter can only remove colors, not replace them. The only way to photograph submarine objects in all their natural vividness is to use flash or a strobe light.

The most important consideration when using underwater flash or strobe is to keep the axis of the flash gun as far from the camera as possible, to avoid backscatter, which is the reflection of light back to the camera from suspended particles in the water. Backscatter shows up as tiny white dots across the whole frame.

A close-up photograph of a sea horse. Most colors are easily absorbed by water, so close-up photography using flash or strobe lights provides the most colorful results.

Types of underwater cameras

There are a number of types of underwater cameras. The simplest types are disposable and have built-in flash. The degree of water protection and the power of the flash limit these cameras to shallow-water use.

More sophisticated is the custom-built underwater camera, designed for use in deeper waters. An example of this type is the Nikonos, for which a range of accessories is available. The Nikonos is fully waterproofed and does not need a separate housing. For close-up work, there is a frame finder, which is placed in contact with the subject to be photographed and ensures that the focus is correct. In 1992, Nikonos produced the world's first underwater SLR camera, the Nikonos-RS. Prior to the introduction of this model, the only way of achieving SLR capabilities was to use an SLR camera inside a housing. The Nikonos-RS is designed to be used to depths of 330 ft. (100 m) and has useful features, such as automatic focusing and focus tracking. On land, it weighs 4.5 lbs. (2 kg), and although it reduces to 2 lbs. (0.9 kg)

underwater, the mass of this camera combined with its expense made it less popular than anticipated, and its manufacture has been discontinued.

One of the problems in using underwater cameras is the risk of flood damage, which may cost hundreds of dollars to repair. Water-tight seals called O-rings prevent water from entering the camera, but even the slightest defect or piece of dirt on a seal can result in flooding. One solution to this problem is the use of a safety device called the Subalert, which is used to assess the water-tightness of underwater cameras and housings. This device compresses the O-rings using a high vacuum that creates the same degree of pressure found at a depth of 23 ft. (7 m). An electronic system is then used to detect any leaks.

Underwater housings are available for ordinary 35 mm cameras and for digital cameras. These housings have external controls that link up with the camera's own controls. The housing remains waterproof at great depths—in fact, increasing water pressure tends to close up the seals of the housing, and water is more likely to get into the camera in shallower water, where the pressure is less. For serious professional use, there are waterproof housings for medium-format cameras, such as the Hasselblad.

SEE ALSO: CAMERA • CAMERA, DIGITAL • LENS • OCEANOGRAPHY • SUBMERSIBLE • UNDERSEA HABITAT

Universal Joint

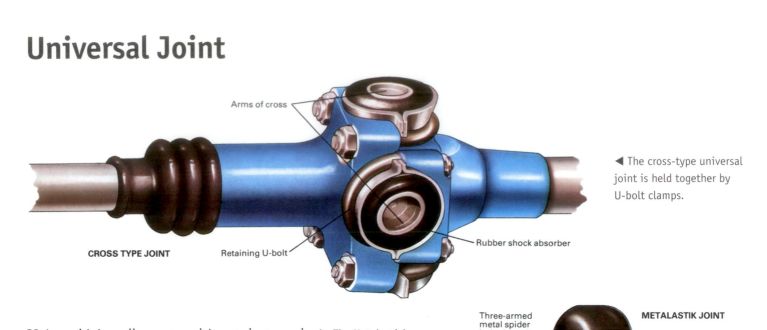

Arms of cross

CROSS TYPE JOINT

Retaining U-bolt

Rubber shock absorber

◀ The cross-type universal joint is held together by U-bolt clamps.

Universal joints allow rotary drives to be turned through varying angles. They have been in use for hundreds of years. The design of the first is usually attributed to Girolamo Cardano, a 16th-century Italian mathematician (hence the term *Cardan shaft*), but the first practical unit was invented about a hundred years later by an English scientist, Robert Hooke. This design was used to manipulate mirrors in a solar astronomical device called a helioscope and consisted simply of two stirrups, one on each end of the two shafts, connected by an X-shaped crosspiece. The modern Hooke joint works on exactly the same principle, the only major difference being that needle roller bearings are used instead of plain bearings.

Variations of the basic Hooke joint include the ring type, which replaces the crosspiece with a ring; the ball type, in which the forked ends of the shafts slide in machined grooves in a ball; and the de Dion type, which has a T-piece on one shaft and a hollow-grooved cylindrical pot on the

▶ The Metalastick universal joint allows relative movement of the shafts.

METALASTIK JOINT

Three-armed metal spider bolted to doughnut

Rubber doughnut

Identical spider on the other side

▼ The Birfield–Rzeppa is a constant-velocity joint, its ball race always bisecting the shafts' angles.

BIRFIELD-RZEPPA CONSTANT VELOCITY JOINT

Socket

Caged ball race

Outer element

Inner element

Shaft splined into inner element

other. Mounted on bearings on the end of the T-piece are blocks that have a curved outer surface and fit into the grooves or slots in the pot. The bearings allow rotation perpendicular to the plane of the T-piece and also in the plane of the T-piece by the curved edges sliding in the groove.

Where the relative angles between shafts are small or where unwanted torque reversals and vibrations occur, the joining member between the two shafts can be made of or covered with rubber to give a degree of damping. The most commonly used are the ring type, or doughnut (used in the rear driveshafts of some BMWs), which also give a degree of relative movement of the shafts toward or away from each other, and the cross type, a Hooke joint with a rubber-covered crosspiece, used on the inner end of the driveshafts of some front-wheel drive (FWD) cars.

Constant-velocity joints

Unfortunately, especially for front-wheel drive cars, these flexible couplings and the ordinary universal joints suffer from an unwanted charac-

teristic—if one shaft is rotated at a constant speed and the other shaft is not exactly in line, the second will rotate at a speed that varies cyclically during each revolution. Although both sides of the joint complete any given revolution in the same time, the speed of one varies sinusoidally with respect to the other.

There is not much of a problem in linking the transmission and differential of a front-engine, rear-wheel drive car, where the angles are fairly small. However, in a front-wheel drive (FWD) car, where the outer universal joint has to cope with steering angles of 40 degrees or more, the drive would be unacceptably jerky, so it is necessary to use a constant-velocity joint.

All modern front-wheel drive cars use constant-velocity joints on the outer ends of driveshafts. Some early FWD models, such as the Traction Avant Citroëns from France, used a Hooke joint at each end of the shaft, but constant-velocity joints are more suitable for applications where large variations in angles are found. Some car manufacturers fit constant-velocity joints in the propeller shafts of rear-wheel-drive models; these joints make the drive smoother than it would be if Hooke joints were used.

The condition for constant velocity is that the points through which the torque is transmitted from one side to the other lie on a plane that bisects the angle between the two shafts. There is a simpler way of avoiding the unwanted speed differentials—by arranging two Hooke joints in such a way that the oscillations cancel each other out. A double Hooke joint is rather long, so in most instances, a constant-velocity joint is used. The best known of these is the Birfield–Rzeppa unit, in which the drive is transmitted through a set of ball bearings held in a caged ball race and rolling in grooves between a ball and socket: the plane containing the balls always bisects the angle between the input and output shafts.

Another type of constant-velocity universal joint is the Bendix–Weiss. This type differs from the Birfield–Rzeppa in that the balls are not held in a cage. The rotary force is provided by four large balls, while a fifth ball, which rotates on a pin connected to the outer race, acts as a spacer.

◄ This type of universal joint, used with sets of sockets, helps turn nuts and bolts.

▶ The rubber doughnut universal joint is used in the transmission propshafts of certain car models. These three pictures show a doughnut being removed, compressed, and replaced.

A third type of constant-velocity joint is the tripod, or ball-and-housing, joint, which usually has three ball bearings fitted around a spider that in turn fits within a slotted yoke. This arrangement allows the balls to swivel and slide.

Constant-velocity joints need to be kept lubricated, so they are covered by flexible gaiters, which are clipped to the driveshaft. The gaiter keeps the lubricant in the joint and prevents road dirt from finding its way into the joint. Despite receiving continuous lubrication, constant-velocity joints eventually wear out and need to be renewed. A failed joint will leave the car immobile, but the driver is warned of a worn joint by its rattling sound.

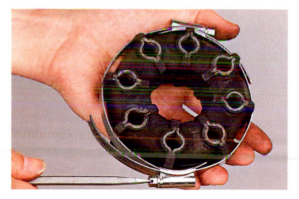

SEE ALSO: Automobile • Gear • Steering system • Transmission, automobile

Uranium

Uranium was discovered by the German chemist Martin H. Klaproth in 1789 in pitchblende ore from the Joachimstal Mountains of Bohemia in Czechoslovakia. The deep and varied colors of some of its compounds led to their use in ceramic glazes, and much later some of its ores were mined for their valuable radium content. For nearly 150 years, uranium was of practically no industrial significance, and interest lay mainly in its having the highest atomic weight (238) and occupying the top place in the periodic table with an atomic number of 92. In 1896, the French scientist Henry Becquerel noticed that uranium compounds blackened photographic plates even when wrapped in paper: this was the first observation of the phenomenon of radioactivity. In sharp contrast to its early history, uranium is now one of the world's most important industrial resources, and its main scientific interest is in its nuclear properties. The change in its importance dates from the discovery, in 1939, of nuclear fission.

The chemistry of uranium accords with its position in the periodic table, where it falls immediately below neodymium, the third of the rare earth elements, with which it shares many characteristics. It exists in several different valency states corresponding to the filling up of the inner 5f electron shell: for example, it forms several oxides, of which the most important are U_3O_8 and UO_3, which are yellow, and UO_2, which is black and much more stable when heated than the others. Also of technical importance are the green tetrafluoride, UF_4, and the very reactive hexafluo-ride, UF_6 (hex), which vaporizes readily below 212°F (100°C). Uranium also forms a positively charged uranyl ion, $[UO_2]^{2+}$, which is soluble in water and many organic solvents, and a negatively charged diuranate ion, $[U_2O_7]^{2-}$. Freshly exposed uranium metal is silvery, but it very quickly forms a dark oxide film that protects the bulk metal; when in powder form, however, it ignites very readily to form the oxide UO_2.

Occurrence and extraction

Some of the richest uranium ores, and among those that were the first to be exploited, are found in the Democratic Republic of the Congo, and in 1939, these ores were already being mined for radium. Other important vein deposits are worked in Canada, Australia, South America, and several European countries, both east and west. The other major type of uranium occurrence, probably containing the greater part of the world's reserves, is in sedimentary deposits containing only about 0.02 percent to 4 percent uranium. There are very large amounts in the United States and Canada and also in South Africa, where uranium is found with gold and is recovered from existing waste as well as being mined directly.

Uranium is always accompanied in nature by its radioactive daughter products, so gamma-ray detectors such as Geiger counters are of great help to the prospector, both in aerial surveys of large or inaccessible areas and in the detailed study of individual outcrops.

◀ Nuclear waste containing plutonium is stored in drums that are handled remotely from a control room.

Once a deposit has been located and its extent determined, ordinary open-pit or deep-mining techniques are used to win the uranium ore. Precautions have to be taken, especially in deep mining of rich ores, against the health hazard of inhaling radioactive dust or gases; the radioactivity of uranium itself, however, presents little danger to health. The extracted ore is sorted and crushed, the uranium is dissolved out by strong acid or alkali, filtered, and recovered either by precipitation or by an ion-exchange process (similar to water softening). The resulting yellow cake, containing up to 50 percent uranium oxide, is shipped to the refinery to be made into fuel for nuclear power plants.

Refining has to be extremely thorough, because a few parts per million of some common impurities in the fuel may absorb so many neutrons that they can effectively prevent the nuclear reactor from working. The yellow cake is dissolved in nitric acid, and the solution is agitated repeatedly with an organic solvent mixture, such as tributyl phosphate and kerosene, which dissolves out the uranyl nitrate while leaving the impurities in the acid solution. The pure uranyl nitrate is then redissolved in water and converted to the trioxide UO_3, either by precipitation as ammonium diuranate and heating or by heat alone. The trioxide is reduced by heating in hydrogen to give pure uranium dioxide, UO_2, which may then be compacted into pellets and sealed into zirconium alloy or stainless steel protective cans to form the fuel elements used in most designs of nuclear power reactors. For some other reactors, the dioxide is first converted to the green tetrafluoride, by reacting it with dry hydrogen fluoride gas, and then to the metal, by reduction with magnesium turnings; the metal is cast into rods,

▶ Pellets of uranium-plutonium oxide are used as fuel in fast breeder nuclear reactors. Fast neutrons given off in the reaction convert uranium into plutonium, which in turn breeds more plutonium.

which are machined to close tolerances and sealed in magnesium alloy cans. The object of the canning is to protect the fuel material from reacting with the gas or liquid that carries the heat from the fuel to the turbines and to prevent radioactive fission products from escaping into the environment. Sometimes the cans have an extended or finned surface to improve heat transfer.

Nuclear properties

Uranium consists almost entirely of two isotopes, uranium-238 (99.27 percent) and uranium-235 (0.73 percent). Both are long-lived alpha-particle emitters that give rise to long chains of radioactive daughter products, the chains ending eventually with lead. Uranium-235 is alone among natural materials in undergoing nuclear fission on being struck by a slow-moving neutron, the process liberating further neutrons and thus making a self-sustaining chain reaction possible, with the production of an extremely large amount of nuclear energy in the form of heat. Uranium-238 does not fission in these circumstances, but it can absorb a neutron and undergo a rapid sequence of radioactive changes leading to the formation of the synthetic element plutonium, which can be fissioned by neutrons. Thus, it is possible not only to use the fission of naturally occurring uranium-235 for nuclear power production but also to use some of the neutrons arising in the fission process to convert the much more abundant uranium-238 atoms into plutonium and to use this as well.

Isotope enrichment

Most of the world's nuclear power reactors, with the exception of the British Magnox and the Canadian CANDU designs, require their fuel to be enriched with a concentration of the fissionable isotope (uranium-235) higher than the 0.73 percent normally found. The first large-scale technique used for this purpose was gaseous diffusion, with the uranium being converted to the gas uranium hexafluoride (UF_6) for processing. The rate at which the gas diffuses through a porous membrane depends on its density, with molecules containing the lighter U-235 passing through the membrane more readily than molecules of the heavier isotopes. The proportion of the lighter isotope is thus slightly increased during the diffusion process, and repeated processing through a series of many stages gives the required concentration—usually about 1.5 to 2.5 percent uranium-235. However, the diffusion process requires large and expensive plants with high running costs, and consequently more efficient processes have been developed.

In the centrifugal process, the gas is passed through a rapidly rotating cylinder; the centrifugal forces have a greater effect on the heavier isotopes, which move to the outside of the cylinder, where they are removed. This process gives an increased concentration of the required lighter isotope in the gas passing through the centrifugal stage. Repeating the process produces the required concentration. After enrichment, the uranium hexafluoride is reconverted into the dioxide (UO_2) by reacting it with steam and hydrogen.

Laser enrichment of uranium depends on the fact that vaporized atoms of the different isotopes

Billets of uranium metal being chemically cleaned, after which residual slag is chipped off by hand. The metal will be made into fuel elements or converted into uranium hexafluoride.

can be selectively excited by laser light of the appropriate frequency. Further excitation of the atoms ionizes them, so they can be separated by the use of magnetic and electric fields. With all enrichment processes, the depleted material containing the excess uranium-238 can be converted into plutonium (for use as a reactor fuel or for atomic weapons) in a fast breeder reactor.

Applications

Although the main use of uranium is as a reactor fuel, depleted uranium metal (industrial uranium) is sometimes used in applications where its great density (it is 18 times as dense as water and nearly 1.7 times the density of lead) makes it valuable. It is used, for example, for gyroscope weights and for radiation shielding of high-energy X rays or gamma-ray sources. The metal has also been used in specialized ammunition and even for the keel of a racing yacht, where the high density resulted in a smaller keel with less drag in the water. It is also useful in a few special alloys, and some of its compounds are still used for coloring ceramic glasses.

 SEE ALSO: ATOMIC STRUCTURE • ELEMENT, CHEMICAL • NUCLEAR FUEL CYCLE • NUCLEAR REACTOR • NUCLEAR WASTE DISPOSAL • PERIODIC TABLE • RADIOACTIVITY

FACT FILE

- In World War I and later, uranium was used in steels produced for toolmaking, by acting as a hardener. From 1914 to 1916, large quantities of this "ferro-uranium" material were manufactured and used, containing up to 30 percent uranium.

- When released by fission, the energy in a pound of uranium is equivalent to the energy released by perfect combustion from some 1,650 tons (1,485 tonnes) of coal. One gram of uranium can release 20 million calories. In contrast, boron, which is the highest-energy chemical fuel, releases only 14,000 calories per gram.

Urology

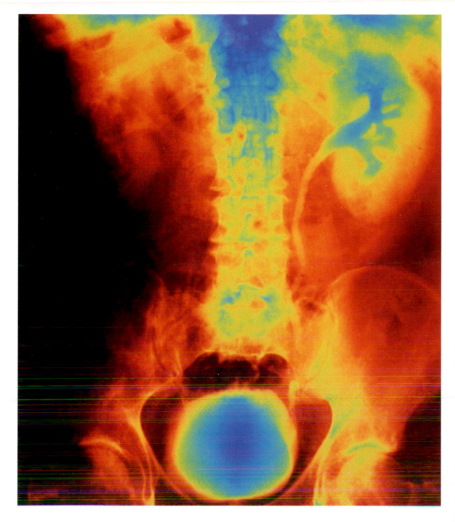

The science of urology deals with the urinary organs and their diseases. The human urinary system comprises two kidneys, two ureters, bladder and urethra. The kidneys act as natural filters, removing dissolved waste products from the blood in the form of urine. They have other important functions, including maintaining a stable balance of salts and other substances in the blood. The kidneys also produce the hormones renin and erythropoietin, which, respectively, regulate blood pressure and the formation of red blood cells. Urine passes from the kidneys via two narrow tubes called the ureters, which lead to the bladder, a triangular organ in the lower abdomen. Urine is then eliminated through the urethra.

One of the most significant recent advances in urology is the development of laparoscopic, or "keyhole," surgery, an advanced technique that has had repercussions throughout the whole of surgery. Laparoscopic surgery avoids the need for a major incision through skin and muscle. Instead, two or three small puncture wounds (keyholes) are made in the skin, through which the surgeon passes fine tubes bearing surgical instruments.

▲ Urograms are used to look for blockages in the urinary system. This patient has a staghorn kidney stone, shown as a branched blue structure at upper right, blocking the ureter between the kidney and the bladder (blue area at bottom). Stones can be removed by surgery or by lithotripsy, which shatters the stones from outside the body using high-frequency shock waves.

The manipulation that goes on inside the body can be seen with the help of small telescopes called endoscopes. Fiber optics allow light to pass along these, illuminating the field of view. The image can be displayed on television monitors in the operating theater. Sometimes such surgery is carried out while the surgeon watches the maneuver on an ultrasound or CAT scan.

New treatment for kidney problems

Formation of stones (renal calculi) in the kidney or bladder is one of the most common urological complaints. The stone or stones may cause few symptoms, although when a kidney stone enters the ureter, it causes severe pain.

Several other new techniques, in addition to laparoscopic surgery, have improved the treatment of kidney stones. One of these, called extra-corporeal shock-wave lithotripsy, involves directing high-frequency shock waves at the stone through the patient's skin. The waves cause the stone to disintegrate into small pieces, which can then be passed out in the urine.

Larger fragments remaining after lithotripsy (and small stones in general) can be removed by passing fine tubes into the kidney through a small puncture wound, the tubes carrying instruments that crush the stone and suck the pieces out. Sometimes a laser is passed down the tube into the kidney to shatter the stone to fine dust or sand.

Knowledge about why stones form and what they are made of has helped doctors to advise patients how to reduce their risks of developing further stones. It may be possible with the help of drugs and dietary restrictions: avoiding high intakes of the minerals that are to blame.

People who develop kidney failure today have a very different prospect in front of them from those who suffered this condition even in the early 1980s. Many of them now can have their dialysis using a new technique called continuous ambulatory peritoneal dialysis (CAPD), which eliminates the need for them to make several trips to a hospital each week.

In a conventional kidney machine, the patient's blood circulates along many feet of tubing, which are bathed by fluid. Impurities in the blood, such as urea, diffuse across the tubing, which is made of a semipermeable membrane, into the surrounding fluid. The cleaned blood is then reinfused into the patient's veins.

Someone who is going to have CAPD first has a tube inserted into his or her abdomen, connecting the peritoneal cavity to the outside. The

Endoscopic view of a kidney stone clamped in the jaws of a second endoscope, prior to being withdrawn from the body. The incision needed for this operation is comparatively tiny.

patient runs about 4 pints (2 l) of dialysis fluid into the cavity. Impurities, such as urea, diffuse out of the numerous blood vessels in the membranes present in the abdomen and into the fluid. A few hours later, the patient drains the fluid off and throws it away. The process is repeated three to four times in every 24 hours. During the treatment, the patient can carry on with normal activities at home and work.

Prostate operations

A common urological problem that affects men is enlargement of the prostate gland, a condition called benign prostatic hypertrophy. The prostate gland encircles the urethra, so when the prostate enlarges, the bladder cannot empty properly. Urine may back up in the ureters to the kidneys, the result being eventual kidney damage.

This condition can be tackled with an operation called transurethral resection of the prostate. The surgeon passes a fine tube through the urethra, allowing removal of the part of the gland that is causing the blockage. The operation is best done by experienced urologists, otherwise the patient risks suffering side effects such as incontinence, hemorrhage, and impotence.

Because of the risk of adverse effects from surgery, doctors have tried to find other ways of reducing the enlargement of the prostate. As yet, there has been little success in developing drugs that have this effect.

Innovations and breakthroughs

New surgical techniques hold out greater promise. One approach has been to insert a probe into the rectum (one wall of which lies next to the prostate) and direct microwaves at the enlarged gland. Alternatively, a laser that can cut away at the gland, a few cells at a time, from within the urethra, may make it possible to improve the accuracy of transurethral resection.

Advances are also being made in the early detection of prostate cancer. Ultrasound screening of the prostate, by inserting a probe into the rectum, may soon be able to give an early warning of the presence of this dangerous disease.

Innovative surgical techniques have also helped people born with abnormalities of the urinary tract. Some of them used to be fatal, while others resulted in lifelong urinary incontinence. It is now possible, for example, to reconstruct the bladder with a piece of the patient's colon. If the bladder sphincter does not work, it may be possible to insert a mechanical sphincter. Another option is to transfer the patient's appendix so that it forms a conduit between the inside of the bladder and the outside of the abdominal wall. The patient can be taught to insert a catheter into the bladder, via the tube formed, to drain the bladder.

Lasers have been helpful in treating bladder cancer, but for those patients who need to have the bladder removed, it is possible to bring the ureters to the surface of the abdomen with the help of part of the patient's ileum (part of the small intestine) so that the urine drains into a collecting bag on the outside of the abdomen.

Other ailments

The remaining most common urological problems are urinary incontinence, interstitial cystitis, urinary tract infections, and polycystic kidney disease. Figures show that kidney and urologic diseases affect over 13 million people in the United States and claim 260,000 lives annually. Women are particularly prone to urinary tract infections, although the reasons are poorly understood.

Normal urine is sterile and contains fluids, salts, and waste products, but it does not contain bacteria, viruses, or fungi. An infection initially occurs when microorganisms, usually bacteria from the digestive tract, adhere to the opening of the urethra and begin to multiply there.

▶ Lithotripsy uses ultrasound to break up kidney stones. The patient is immersed in a water bath, while the two sound sources focus blasts of ultrasound onto the stones. A surgeon monitors progress using a scanner.

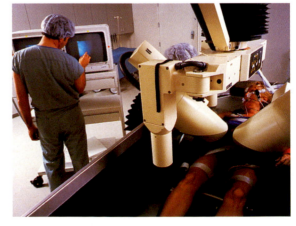

SEE ALSO: Cancer treatment • Dialysis machine • Endoscope • Surgery • Transplant • Ultrasonics

V/STOL Aircraft

V/STOL, standing for vertical or short takeoff and landing, is a term used to describe the ability of a special class of aircraft to ascend or descend vertically, so permitting them to operate from very confined spaces on the ground. The description now specifically applies to aircraft having a more or less fixed-wing layout but possessing special features that permit them to hover or land or takeoff without significant forward motion. The term VTOL, for vertical takeoff and landing, is synonymous with V/STOL and was current some years ago. However, designers now recognize that significant increases in payload or range may be secured where circumstances permit a short ground run, and the newer term more accurately reflects this benefit. The term STOL in isolation denotes a type of aircraft that, though capable of operating from very short runways, cannot land or takeoff vertically.

V/STOL airplanes share some of the benefits and drawbacks of both fixed-wing types and helicopters. They may be regarded as extending the low-speed capability of the former and improving the high-speed performance of the latter.

Although of outstanding versatility, helicopters have the fundamental disadvantage of being slow. While a few can attain 250 mph (400 km/h), most can cruise at only half that speed. They are essentially short-range vehicles, and their value as a means of transport has been largely overshadowed by their usefulness for tasks demanding an ability to hover or fly slowly for long periods or to land and takeoff from restricted spaces or unprepared surfaces. In general, their special abilities are obtained at the expense of generally low structural, aerodynamic, and propulsive efficiency.

Since the 1950s, many attempts have been made to improve the speed of helicopters by

▲ A U.S. Marine Corps AV-8A at take-off, using its four nozzles swiveled downward.

adding engines and propellers to give forward thrust and small wings to relieve the load on the rotor so that at high speed it provides no lift but simply freewheels. By these means, some of the more undesirable effects of compelling the rotor to generate lift and thrust simultaneously at speed are postponed. Although a number of compound helicopters, as they are called, have been built and flown experimentally, their performance has not justified the extra complexity and cost.

The convertiplane

The next step was the convertiplane, the simplest form of which has a conventional fuselage and tailplane and a small wing having two rotors at its tips, similar to those of a helicopter but of smaller diameter. For takeoff and landing, they rotate horizontally, as on a helicopter, but are turned to spin in a vertical plane for forward flight, when they act as outsize propellers. Convertiplanes have been investigated in more detail than probably any other form of V/STOL configuration, because in the opinion of many designers, they offer a more acceptable set of compromises. Wide variations of the basic idea are possible; the LTV-Hiller-Ryan XC-142, designed in the United States, was a four-engine transport in which the entire wing, carrying the engines and large propellers, rotated about a horizontal axis so that the propellers could be moved in unison. Germany's VFW-designed VC-400, though it never flew, had two rotors on the tips of each of its tandem wings—four in all. An alternative approach uses ducted fans instead of the propellers, with the fan assemblies being tilted to the vertical position for takeoff and horizontally for cruising. This design was used in the Bell X-22A research aircraft, which had tail-mounted General Electric T58 turbine engines, driving four ducted fans through a transmission system that maintained drive to all the fans, even when one of the engines failed. The ducted propellers were mounted on the wings and tailplane and directed downward for takeoff and hovering. During hovering, control of the aircraft pitch and roll movements was achieved by appropriate adjustment of the propeller pitch. For horizontal flight, the ducted fans were moved to the horizontal position. Exhaust from the engine turbines was directed at 65 degrees to the horizontal to give additional lift.

The V-22 Osprey, developed by Bell Helicopters and Boeing Vertol, uses a pair of tilting engines mounted at the ends of the wings. This aircraft can travel at twice the speed of a helicopter and is used by the U.S. Department of Defense for purposes such as transport of troops and cargo and search and rescue operations.

Jet power

In all the configurations described, lift and thrust have been obtained by the use of rotors or propellers. However, an equally large number of experimental types have been built and flown on the power of conventional jet engines. Perhaps the most ambitious of these was the German company Dornier's D031, a medium-sized transport that used a combination of special vectored-thrust and lift engines supplied by Rolls Royce of Britain and was thought in the late 1960s to have commercial possibilities. (In a vectored-thrust engine, the thrust can be directed downward for lift or rearward for propulsion.)

In the early 1970s, the West German air force and the German airline Lufthansa together held a competition to select a 100-seat transport suitable for both civil and military applications. No fewer than four projects were put forward by industry, and one of them was chosen as the winner. However, when the design was analyzed in great detail, the drawbacks and technical difficulties were seen to be too great, and the idea was shelved.

At about the same time in Britain investigations were being made into V/STOL airliners with virtually the same operational requirements, and Hawker Siddeley (now British Aerospace) made a proposal for a 100-seat transport with a range of 500 miles (800 km) and a speed of Mach 0.85. The propulsion system was based on the discrete lift-thrust technique, which for any V/STOL airplane is the alternative to vectored thrust. Instead of varying the direction of the thrust for one or more engines to give the required proportion of lift to propulsive force, the two forces are generated by separate sets of engines. The HS.141 was designed around two large engines for cruising power and a battery of 16 small engines to be switched on at the beginning and end of the flight to generate the lift required to keep the aircraft in the air when the small, swept wing could no longer generate sufficient lift. Evaluation showed, again, that despite the application of very advanced technology, the design would be technically risky and commercially unattractive.

Vectored thrust

Jet engines can be tilted as propellers can to give another version of the convertiplane concept. Various experimental aircraft of this type—such as the Bell X-15—have been produced.

The most successful—and simplest—technique used in V/STOL aircraft is the vectored-thrust approach, in which rotating nozzles are used to deflect the engine thrust from the horizontal to the vertical direction. This design is

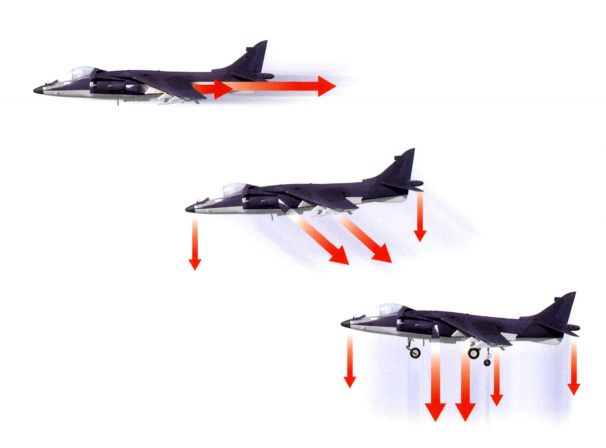

◄ Airplanes that takeoff vertically use nozzles to direct the thrust from the engine. As the plane lifts off, all the thrust is directed toward the ground (bottom). As it begins to move forward (middle), the main nozzles begin to rotate to provide forward thrust, while the nose, wing, and tail puffers maintain stability. In flight (top), only the main engine nozzles operate to push the airplane forward. The process is reversed for landing.

used in the British Aerospace Harrier fighter, a version of which is also built by McDonnell Douglas as the AV-8B for the U.S. Marine Corps.

This fighter plane is powered by a single Rolls Royce Pegasus jet engine in which the propulsive exhaust is ejected through four vectored-thrust nozzles. The fighter is not dependent on runways vulnerable to bombs but can fly from any small clearing a few miles or so from the battle or from an assault ship and is ideally suited for the close support of troops in the field.

In the Harrier, the nozzles project through the sides of the aircraft fuselage, with the front nozzles being ahead of the aircraft's center of gravity (cg), while the rear nozzles are behind the cg to give a balanced lift. The foreward nozzles are supplied with cold air from the turbofan section of the engine, and the hot jet gases from the turbine are used for the rear nozzles. For takeoff and hovering, the nozzles are pointed downward, and when the aircraft is airborne, the nozzles are rotated backward so as to give forward thrust. Control of the rotation is by a single lever in the cockpit, with the drive system interlocked to ensure that the nozzles remain aligned at all times. For normal flight, the nozzles are turned to point fully backward, but it is also possible to point them slightly forward for braking purposes.

During V/STOL operation, the normal aircraft attitude controls (for pitch and roll) are ineffective, because they rely on the aerodynamic effects caused by the airflow over them. Accordingly, a separate control system is built into the aircraft, a system using reaction jets fitted at the nose and tail of the fuselage and at the wingtips. These jets are supplied with high-pressure air bled from the engine and are coupled to the conventional control surfaces, so they are operated by the normal flying controls.

Harrier performance

The AV-8B/Harrier engine has sufficient power to lift the aircraft vertically at takeoff and is about twice as powerful as the power plant fitted to a conventional fighter of equivalent size and performance; accordingly, for a given fuel weight, the Harrier can fly only half as far. However, in view of its flexibility this limitation is no penalty. If a ground roll of 1,000 ft. (305 m) or so is available—and conventional fighters need 10,000 ft. to 12,000 ft. (3,050–3,660 m)—a much heavier bomb load can be carried, because the aerodynamic lift produced by the forward movement acts together with the vectored thrust.

New development

As of 2002, the Lockheed Martin X-35 joint strike fighter has been under joint development by the United States and the United Kingdom. This short takeoff and vertical landing (STOVL) airplane will use engines based on the Pratt & Whitney F119 and is expected to be operational by 2008.

SEE ALSO: Aircraft design • Aircraft engine • Gas turbine • Helicopter • Propeller

Vaccine

The purpose of a vaccine is to create a state of immunity in an individual—either to prevent the development of a specific infectious disease or to treat an existing infection by introducing into the body dead or attenuated (weakened) microorganisms, which stimulate the body cells to form new globulins, called antibodies, specifically against the invading disease. The antibodies fight subsequent invasions of the disease or help control the spread of an existing infection.

History

By the 18th century, the Turks and the Chinese had developed methods of immunizing against smallpox by scratching the crusts from mild smallpox lesions into the arms of persons to be immunized. This procedure, known as inoculation, or variolation, was introduced to Britain but was not without risks—some persons so treated developed full smallpox and died.

The credit for discovering that infectious materials from cowpox (vaccinia) could be inoculated artificially into a person's skin and so give immunity against smallpox belongs to the British physician Edward Jenner. In 1796, he inoculated an eight-year-old boy with matter from the cowpox vesicles on the hands of a milkmaid. He was inspired by an old country belief that cowpox sufferers become immune to smallpox. In 1798, he published his findings and soon began a program of mass inoculations—or vaccinations as they became known—which reduced the death rate from smallpox in London, England, by two-thirds within 18 months. (At first the terms *vaccine* and *vaccination* were used only for immunization against smallpox with the vaccinia virus, but later they became the general terms for all inoculations against specific diseases.)

The French scientist Louis Pasteur developed the next group of vaccines in 1879, when an epidemic of chicken cholera had destroyed 10 percent of the chickens in France. He discovered, almost by accident, a method of reducing the virulence of the microbes in a culture by leaving it alone for several months. At the same time, he found that chickens inoculated with the mild form of the

▼ A medical team vaccinates villagers in the Democratic Republic of the Congo, Africa, in an attempt to control disease endemic in that part of the world. Such diseases include polio, tetanus, and diphtheria. Keeping vaccines cool is an important part of the vaccination program in hot countries where refrigeration may be limited or nonexistent, because heat can inactivate many vaccines.

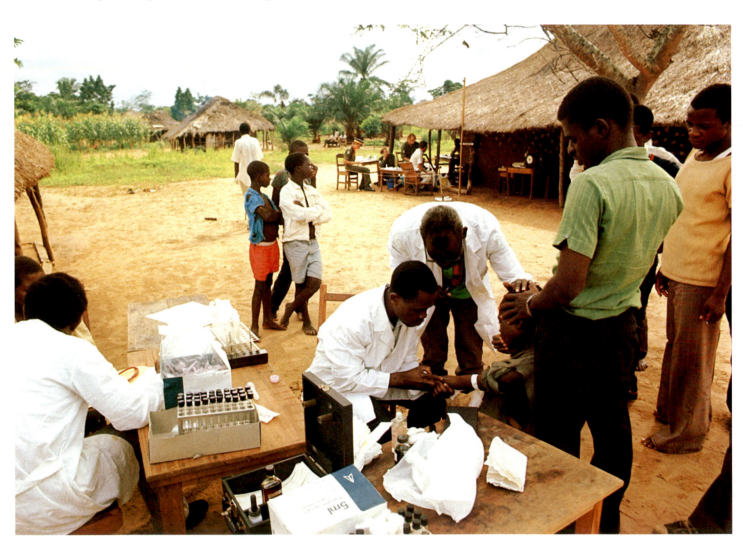

culture became immune to the effects of the virulent form. This was the first time that immunization had been observed in a microbial disease, smallpox being a virus.

Soon after, Pasteur developed a vaccine for anthrax in animals. Then, in 1885, came his greatest immunological triumph—the inoculation, with dried tissues, of a nine-year-old boy who had been bitten by a rabid dog. These tissues had been taken from infected animals but were weakened by heating and the passage of time. Within a year, Pasteur inoculated 350 patients, of whom only one died. Thousands of people came to him in subsequent years for rabies treatment—with a mortality rate of less than 1 percent. (In the 20th century, dead vaccines were found to be safer than Pasteur's live vaccine.)

The successes with smallpox and rabies encouraged attempts to develop vaccines for many other diseases. Effective vaccines were developed against typhoid, paratyphoid, cholera, yellow fever, tetanus, bubonic plague, tuberculosis, encephalitis, and typhus, among others.

In 1953 the U.S. research scientist Jonas Edward Salk announced the development of a trial polio vaccine. Within two years, the Salk vaccine, which used killed virus, had been widely accepted, and the rate of polio cases began to decline steeply. A longer-lasting vaccine using live viruses was developed in 1961 by another U.S. researcher, Albert Bruce Sabin. This vaccine could be taken by mouth. Since then, the number of people infected with polio has declined dramatically, although the disease has not yet been eradicated. In 1988, the World Health Organization (WHO) resolved to eradicate polio worldwide by 2005. Since polio affects only humans, the strategy is based on the premise that the polio virus will die out if it loses its human host through immunization. This strategy is similar to the one used to eradicate smallpox in 1977, which is the only disease so far to have been eradicated.

In the 1970s, a similar urgency accompanied the ultimately successful search for a vaccine against hepatitis B, a viral disease that causes a form of liver cancer. A safe and effective vaccine has been available since 1982 that is 95 percent effective in preventing people from developing chronic infection if they have not yet been infected. It is, effectively, the first anticancer drug.

Since the 1980s, attention has been focused on the attempts to find a vaccine against HIV (human immunodeficiency virus), the precursor of AIDS (acquired immune deficiency syndrome). Since the appearance of the epidemic, HIV has infected almost 58 million people, and nearly 25 million have died from AIDS. The United

▶ Large-scale production of anaerobic vaccines requires stringent safety measures to prevent the bacteria or virus being cultivated from escaping into the environment.

Nations Program on HIV/AIDS (UNAIDS) and WHO joined forces to establish the HIV Vaccine Initiative (HVI) to boost HIV/AIDS vaccine research. So far, scientists have failed to find an effective vaccine, although clinical trials over the past ten years show some promise that a vaccine will soon be found.

There was a renewal of interest in leprosy vaccines in the 1970s, but the situation regarding leprosy control has since changed. In the early 1980s, a strategy of treating leprosy (*Mycobacterium leprae*) with a combination of drugs—called multidrug therapy (MDT)—was implemented and has proved to be highly effective in curing the disease. Although Indian scientists have developed a vaccine that has been successful in clinical trials, the need for a vaccine has reduced as the incidence of the disease itself has declined.

Work continues on the search for a vaccine against malaria, which is still killing millions in the developing world. Malaria is caused by a parasite that infects the blood and is transmitted by the bite of an infected mosquito. There are signs that the disease is becoming resistant to certain drugs that are currently used to prevent and treat it.

Types of vaccines
There are three main types of vaccines—weakend, or attenuated vaccines, inactivated vaccines, and subunit vaccines. Attenuated vaccines are

made up of microorganisms that can no longer cause serious disease but that are able to stimulate immunity. Attenuated vaccines include those for measles, mumps, polio (the Sabin vaccine), rubella, and tuberculosis.

Inactivated vaccines contain organisms that have been killed or inactivated by heat or chemicals. They are less effective than attenuated vaccines, and therefore greater amounts of them need to be given. Vaccines against rabies, polio (the Salk vaccine), some types of influenza, and cholera are made from inactivated organisms.

Subunit vaccines, such as those for hepatitis B and influenza, are made from proteins found on the surface of infectious agents (pathogens). For the prevention of tetanus and diphtheria, diseases in which the chief symptoms stem mainly from the effects of the bacterial toxins in the body, the vaccine consists of modified toxins (toxoids) and is therefore antitoxic rather than antibacterial.

Viral and bacterial vaccines are prepared in a similar way—except that viral microorganisms need to be cultivated in the presence of living animal cells. If the vaccine is composed of intact bacterial cells, the microorganisms are killed either by heating to 140°F (60°C) for one hour or by the addition of some material. If the vaccines

▼ Polio vaccine is given to small babies in a syrup, which is put into a dropper and squeezed into the baby's throat. The first polio vaccine could be given only in a series of injections, named Salk shots for their discoverer, Jonas Salk. Modern vaccines, usually taken orally, date from Albert Sabin's development in 1961 of a vaccine using live polio viruses.

are to be composed of fragments of bacterial protoplasm rather than intact bacteria, the bacteria are destroyed by breaking up the cells: by repeated freezing and thawing, by grinding in a ball mill, by ultraviolet irradiation, or by ultrasonic irradiation. The resulting mixture is tested for sterility to make certain it is not infectious, and a preservative, such as phenol, is added.

Advances in vaccine development

In the late 20th century, scientists were able to refine their approach to vaccine development. Today they can identify the genes of a pathogen (disease-causing microorganism) that encode the protein (or proteins) that stimulate an immune response (called antigens), and the antigens can then be mass-produced and used in vaccines. Scientists are also able to genetically modify pathogens and produce weakened strains of viruses. Thus, if harmful proteins from pathogens can be altered or deleted, a way to make safer and more effective vaccines can come to pass.

Recombinant DNA technology is also proving useful in manufacturing both viral and bacterial vaccines. Genetic material that codes for a particular antigen is placed inside the attenuated form of a large virus, such as vaccinia, or a modified bacterium. The altered virus or bacterium then carries the foreign genes, "piggyback" style, and can stimulate the production of antibodies and confer immunity against several diseases at once.

Naked DNA therapy is a method in which DNA that encodes a foreign protein is injected into muscle cells. These muscle cells produce the foreign antigen, stimulating an immune response.

Multiple, or combination, vaccines combine the antigens from several different diseases in one vaccine. They have been administered for nearly 30 years. The MMR vaccine, for example, combines the antigens for measles, mumps, and rubella in one vaccine; the DTaP vaccine combines those for diptheria, tetanus, and pertussis (whooping cough). Such combination vaccines are usually given to babies and young children, but questions have been raised about potential adverse effects. The MMR vaccine, for example, has been linked to autism by at least one research team and continues to be controversial.

Antigenic drift and shift

Once a person reaches adulthood, the only vaccines generally required are those to protect against tropical diseases. One exception to this rule is the influenza vaccine, which is encouraged for anyone with a history of respiratory illness and for the elderly. Unlike manufacturers of most vaccines, those that supply flu vaccines have to

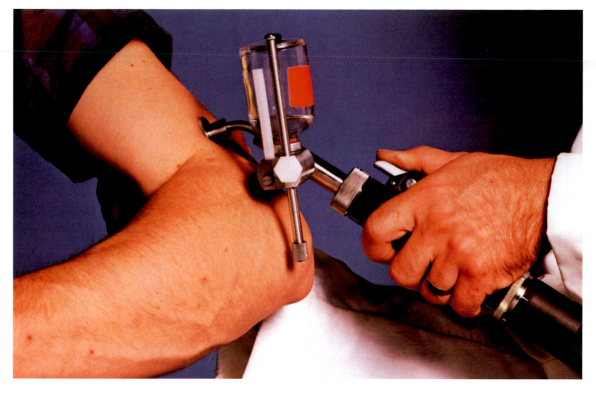

◀ This vaccine-administering device uses air pressure to propel multiple vaccines in a spray form. It does not puncture the skin in the way that a normal syringe needle does. The device is particularly useful for mass vaccinations against diseases such as influenza and others in which virus strains are constantly changing. It is also used for diabetics' insulin injections.

change the components almost every year, according to the amount of antigenic change that occurs in the viral cells each year.

The influenza vaccine contains killed strains of two types of virus—the A strain and the B strain. Within the A strain, there is an infinite variety of antigenic drift; that is to say, slight differences in antigenic characteristics occur every year. However, every few years, there is a major change called an antigenic shift, and as a result, scientists have to devise large modifications to previous vaccines. WHO keeps a watchful eye on new strains of influenza as they appear all over the world. For example, the flu vaccine prepared for the winter of 1980 contained killed strains of virus originally identified as far apart as Bangkok in Thailand, Brazil, and the former Soviet Union.

Slightly less difficult has been the development of a vaccine against the numerous types of bacteria that can cause pneumonia. In 1979, one drug company began to market vaccine that, it claimed, could prevent 80 percent of cases of pneumonia. To get this result, material from 14 of the 80-odd varieties of pneumococcus bacteria had to be incorporated into the vaccine.

Effectiveness of vaccines

It is difficult to evaluate accurately the efficacy of vaccine prophylaxis in many diseases. Although the triumphs of, for example, the polio or diphtheria vaccines are clear-cut and incontestable, it is often impossible to arrange experiments with large enough numbers of individuals in inoculated groups and uninoculated control groups to ensure statistically significant results. Evaluation is especially difficult in diseases with short incubation periods or where exposure to the disease is unpredictable or irregular.

Typhoid and cholera, for example, are similar waterborne diseases against which vaccines have been developed. The typhoid vaccine, however, is estimated to confer a 70 to 90 percent immunity, while that for cholera gives only 50 percent. Also, the typhoid vaccine gives protection for three years, while that for cholera lasts only six months. Influenza vaccines are normally of only limited value because the influenza virus is constantly changing its antigenic structure and the vaccine can produce a reaction nearly as unpleasant as influenza itself. (The typhoid vaccine also produces disagreeable reactions in most people, but because typhoid can be a fatal disease, these side effects are considered acceptable.)

Vaccines are much less effective if they are exposed to heat and must be kept at the correct temperature from the time they are manufactured until the time they are used. Keeping vaccines cold in developing countries, which often lack refrigeration, is especially important. The equipment and people that keep vaccines cold during their journey are together called the cold chain. Equipment for storage and transport has to meet performance standards defined by WHO and the UN Children's Fund (UNICEF).

 SEE ALSO: Cancer treatment • Epidemiology • Immunology • Medicine • Pharmaceuticals

Vacuum

▲ This vacuum-sealing machine is being used to pack cherries for shipment. The absence of oxygen in the pack inhibits the growth of microorganisms that could otherwise spoil the produce before it reaches its customers.

In its strictest sense, the term *vacuum* describes a complete absence of matter or a space where absolutely nothing exists. Since such a state is impossible to achieve—except possibly in deepest space—more realistic usage of the word refers to a space where pressure has been reduced from its normal value, since pressure indicates the amount of gaseous matter per unit volume. Such a state is described as a partial vacuum.

Although humans are seldom directly aware of the amount of matter present in air at sea level, standard conditions of 1 atmosphere (14.7 psi; 101,325 Pa) and 77°F (25°C) correspond to approximately 7×10^{23} gas molecules per cu. ft. (2.5×10^{25} molecules/m³). Atmospheric pressure decreases with increasing altitude, falling to around 0.3 atmospheres (4.3 psi; 30,400 Pa) at 30,000 ft. (9,100 m), the normal cruising altitude of conventional airliners, and continuing to trail off toward the outer limits of Earth's atmosphere. By 1,200 miles (1,930 km) above Earth's surface, the conditions are so close to a perfect vacuum that satellites can orbit Earth for years without

suffering appreciable decreases in their orbital energies due to collisions with particles.

An alternative unit for reporting pressures—including those of partial vacuums—is the torr, or mmHg (millimeter of mercury; Hg is the symbol for mercury), which originated from the use of mercury barometers to measure pressure. When an evacuated tube is inverted in a bowl of mercury, a column of mercury rises up the tube owing to the action of pressure on the surface of the mercury in the bowl. The standard atmospheric pressure of 14.7 psi (101,325 Pa) supports a column 760 mm high, so it can be expressed as 760 mmHg, or 760 torr; 1 torr is around 133 Pa.

Vacuum pumps

A vacuum pump is a device that can remove fluid—usually a gas—from a sealed container so as to create a partial vacuum. The various types of vacuum pumps each have characteristic capacities that make them suitable for different tasks.

Rotary pump. The most common vacuum pump for general applications is the rotary pump. Such a device consists of a static chamber, or stator, in which a rotor turns when powered by an external motor. In one form of rotary pump, the rotor is set off center in the stator, and flexible vanes create spaces of varying size between the rotor and stator. Each space is at its largest when aligned with the inlet port and decreases to a minimum volume when aligned with the outlet port. In another type of rotary pump, an off-center wheel mounted on the rotor produces a cavity between itself and the stator that diminishes in size as the rotor turns, compressing the gas within it. These types of pumps are immersed in an oil that lubricates the pump and helps prevent leaks.

The pumping efficiency of a rotary pump is at its greatest when the inlet pressure is close to the external pressure. Efficiency decreases at lower pressures, and the pump ceases to function when the inlet pressure is so low that the pressure of the air in the pump just matches external pressure even after compression, which happens at inlet pressures around 7×10^{-4} psi (5 Pa) for a single pump. The use of two pumps in series can reduce this value to around 7×10^{-5} psi (0.5 Pa).

One concern with crude rotary pumps is that the compression stroke can cause the water content of the gas to condense out and contaminate the lubricating oil. To overcome this problem, most pumps are now fitted with a gas ballast facility that restricts the intake volume so that the pressure during the compression stroke remains below the pressure at which water vapor condenses. The oil must be replaced on a regular basis, since the presence of condensed water and low-boiling substances formed by decomposition of the oil creates a significant vapor pressure that sets a lower limit on the achievable pressure.

Vapor-diffusion pump. Operating at pressures below 1.5×10^{-3} psi (10 Pa), vapor diffusion enables a rotary pump to produce vacuums better than 1.5×10^{-13} psi (10^{-9} Pa). In most cases, however, it is used for vacuums of around 1.5×10^{-8} psi (10^{-4} Pa). A vapor-diffusion pump has a boiler that heats a high-boiling oil until it evaporates. The vapor then passes through jets into the space to be evacuated. The high-speed streams of vapor drag gas molecules with them toward an air-cooled or refrigerated wall, where the oil condenses before returning to the boiler. The momentum of the gas molecules increases their pressure when they strike the wall, and they pass from there to the inlet port of the rotary pump.

Other types. A variety of pumps use chemical and physical means to remove most of the molecules that remain after rotary pumping; the result is extremely good vacuums. Sorption pumps use molecular sieves, such as zeolites, that adsorb gas molecules on the internal surfaces they possess by virtue of their porous structures. Cryopumps use liquid-helium refrigeration to condense all but the lightest gases from the evacuated space. Sublimation pumps use heat to vaporize a reactive metal, such as titanium, that combines with reactive molecules to form salts and complexes that condense or solidify when they cool. These three types of pumps are free of moving parts, so they cause none of the vibrations that can interfere with some sensitive measuring devices.

Measurement

While the mercury barometer already described is in principal simple to use, its size makes it inconvenient for many applications. Also, the presence of mercury vapor above the mercury column distorts the reading, and small variations in pressure are practically impossible to read. For these reasons, a number of other pressure gauges have been developed, each using a physical property to measure low pressures.

Relative pressure. One of the most common ways of measuring vacuum is by means of the capsule gauge,

▼ These radioactively labeled samples are held under vacuum in sealed ampoules. The seal is made by playing a flame on the neck so as to soften it while connected to a vacuum line. The glass then collapses and forms a perfect seal at the neck.

similar to an aneroid barometer, in which pressure is measured by the deflection of a thin diaphragm. This small deflection is normally magnified by a mechanical linkage that connects to an indicator needle on a dial. In another form of capsule gauge, a metal rod is fitted to the diaphragm. As the rod moves with the diaphragm, it changes the inductive load in an electrical circuit. In most cases, the change is shown on a dial, but a digital indication is also possible. Capsule gauges measure pressures from atmospheric down to around 0.015 psi (100 Pa).

Thermal conductivity. Vacuums from 0.15 psi (1,000 Pa) down to around 1.5×10^{-5} psi (0.1 Pa) are calculated from measurements of thermal conductivity. These are based on the equilibrium temperature of a filament heated by an electrical current, and that temperature depends on the rate of heat loss. At moderate pressures, the filament loses heat by a combination of radiation and conduction. The temperature then settles at a value for which the rate of heat loss balances the rate of heat development. As pressure falls, the rate of conductive heat loss decreases as the frequency of collisions with gas molecules falls. The temperature of the filament then rises until the rate of heat loss by infrared radiation—which increases with increasing temperature—matches the shortfall in heat loss by conduction.

Ionization. Still harder vacuums are measured by their ability to yield ions when probed by a beam of electrons. Free electrons are produced by either a cold cathode at high negative potential or a thermionic emitter of the type used in vacuum tubes. These electrons are then accelerated by an electrical field formed between the cathode and a suitable anode. As their kinetic energy increases, the fast-moving free electrons become capable of knocking further electrons out of atoms and molecules they encounter; this process forms positive ions and releases more electrons.

The cations and electrons formed by such collisions can then conduct electricity between the electrodes, so the ionization process is detected by an increase in the current in the gauge. The rate of ionization depends on the ionization probability of the residual gases and the frequency of collisions between electron and gas molecules—a function of the pressure of the gas. Hence the ion current in the gauge is a direct indication of pressure that can be amplified and measured. This method works only at low pressures, since the frequent collisions in a gas at moderate pressure usually prevent electrons from acquiring sufficient kinetic energy to induce ionization.

Applications

A number of industrial and scientific applications benefit from or require the use of a vacuum. Depending on the process, the vacuum can be hard (close to a perfect vacuum) or soft (closer to atmospheric pressure).

Distillation. Distillation is an important process for the separation of mixtures in processes such as oil refining and chemical manufacture and in the preparation of pure compounds for chemical and pharmaceutical research programs. In some cases, the temperature needed to boil a substance at atmospheric pressure is sufficient to cause its decomposition and the procedure is useless. The boiling points of substances fall as pressure decreases, however, so distillation at reduced pressure is useful for distilling high-boiling or heat-sensitive substances.

Inert atmospheres. Air and its components can be extremely damaging to sensitive materials. Aerial oxidation causes some substances to corrode, burn, or even explode, and microbial processes can cause the degradation of food. A vacuum protects against these effects by excluding the components of air that cause them. Thus, a vacuum is used to pack certain types of foods and for the handling of chemical substances that can ignite in contact with air.

Vacuums are also used in the processing of certain metals and alloys. This is the case in the heat treatment of titanium blades for gas turbines, where gases that dissolve in the hot metal could weaken the blades and cause failures in use.

Mechanical handling. Automated production lines make use of suction cups to hold workpieces in machinery and to transfer articles between sections of lines. The soft suction cups mold themselves to a variety of surface profiles without causing damage to the surface. Pressures around 0.15 to 1.5 psi (1,000–10,000 Pa) are usually sufficiently low, since they equate to the atmosphere exerting around 14.5 psi (100,000 Pa) on the opposite side of the workpiece. Vacuum handling is particularly useful for items made of card, paper, plastics, and nonferrous metals—materials that cannot be picked up by electromagnets.

Insulation. One of the principal methods by which heat transfers between bodies is conduction, a process whereby particles acquire heat from hot bodies in the form of kinetic energy and then transfer that heat to cooler bodies through

▲ A vacuum deposition chamber for the silvering of headlights. The filaments from which the silvering metal evaporates are visible at center.

collisions. The absence of matter in the space occupied by a vacuum prevents this mechanism; in this way, the vacuum jacket of a Thermos flask helps prevent heat transfer.

Vacuums also inhibit the transmission of sound, which requires an elastic medium, such as a gas, that can propagate sound waves. Thus, the evacuated gaps between the panes of double-glazed windows help in soundproofing.

Vapor deposition. A number of processes require the transfer of material in its vapor state from a hot vaporizing source to a cool surface, where it forms a surface film. Such processes are assisted if the space between the source and the deposition surface is evacuated, both in terms of easing the vaporization process and protecting the vaporized material from oxidation and other forms of chemical attack. Examples of vapor deposition include the formation of antireflective lens coatings and the deposition of mirroring in headlights.

Particle beams. Some experimental and analytical apparatuses require particles to travel at great speeds without colliding with other particles for great distances. Extremely hard vacuums make this situation possible: at 1.5×10^{-12} psi (10^{-8} Pa), a typical gas molecule travels an average distance of 300 miles (480 km) between collisions. Such conditions are necessary in particle accelerators and storage rings, where charged subatomic particles are accelerated and stored before being subjected to planned collisions with target species.

SEE ALSO: COMPRESSOR AND PUMP • PRESSURE • PRESSURE GAUGE • THERMOS BOTTLE • VACUUM TUBE

Vacuum Cleaner

Matter is constantly being degraded into small particles; even the human body sheds thousands of dead cells every minute. All this wear and tear produces great quantities of dust, which must be removed for esthetic and hygienic reasons.

The first practical vacuum cleaner, patented by Hubert Cecil Booth in 1901, used a five-horsepower piston engine. Later types included cleaners that were hand operated with bellows, vacuum pumps with gas engines, air blowers working from the inlet side, and venturi systems run on compressed air.

Today the term *vacuum cleaner* usually refers to an electrically powered fan unit, often multistage, designed to create an airstream moving at high speed through a pickup nozzle, which is usually connected to a flexible hose. As the fan rotates, air is discharged from the periphery by centrifugal force, which causes a partial vacuum at the center of the fan into which air rushes through the nozzle and hose. The amount of vacuum is determined by the design, number, and size of the fan blades, and the volume of air flow depends on the size of the fan.

Vacuum potential is measured in inches water gauge (an instrument for measuring vacuum; one inch wg = 0.036 psi) or millimeters water gauge and in cubic feet or cubic meters of air displaced per minute. The greatest amount of suction is created when the nozzle is pressed hard against a surface, and the highest air flow, when it is fully open. During cleaning, with the nozzle working over surfaces of varying texture and flexibility, the contact made by the orifice of the cleaning tool will vary from moment to moment. Therefore the amount of air flowing through will also vary.

Upright cleaners may have a filter to remove objects that could damage the fan blades. The filter system is usually a paper or cloth bag or a screen of woven fabric. The material must retain the dust yet not restrict the flow of air. On most vacuum cleaners, the filter will retain particles down to five microns. Most vacuum cleaners made today use disposable dust bags. In industry, there may be dangerous dusts that would be harmful for people to breathe. These dusts can be controlled by special filters. Special filters are also needed in hospitals to prevent cross-infection by the spreading of germ-laden dust.

Household cleaners fall into two main groups: uprights and canister (or suction) cleaners. Optional tool kits are usually available for upright cleaners. The flexible hose, suction tubes, floor-cleaning head, dusting brush, crevice tool, and multipurpose nozzle enable the upright cleaner to be used for a wide variety of cleaning jobs.

Suction cleaners tend to have more powerful motors because they rely entirely on the vacuum to remove the dirt. They are supplied with a range of cleaning tools for all cleaning tasks. Another type of cleaner is the wet-and-dry canister machine. It contains a tank that will hold either dry dirt or water from a blocked sink. Mounted on top of the tank is a bypass motor, which does not allow air from the nozzle and hose to pass over the electric parts. Wet-and-dry cleaners can be fitted with large-diameter hoses that will cope with wood shavings and rubble.

Cyclone vacuum cleaners

One problem with conventional vacuum cleaners is that when the collecting bag begins to fill with dust, the flow of air becomes restricted, and thus the effectiveness of the cleaner is reduced. In 1978, a British inventor, James Dyson, began working on proto-

▶ This upright Dyson vacuum cleaner uses a dual cyclone to provide greater cleaning power. The first cyclone removes larger particles of dust before the air travels into the second, faster cyclone, which removes microscopic particles.

UPRIGHT VACUUM CLEANER

As well as producing a vacuum using a fan, upright cleaners have a rotating beater bar, which has a series of spiralling brushes that beat against the carpet as the bar rotates. This beating action loosens dirt and helps sweep surface litter into the cleaner. The suction created by the vacuum also lifts the carpet so that more dust and dirt are released. The air containing the dust then passes into the collecting bag in the upright section of the cleaner and then through very fine holes in the bag and out of an exhaust port in the handle. The dust particles, however, are too large to pass through the fine holes and so are retained in the bag.

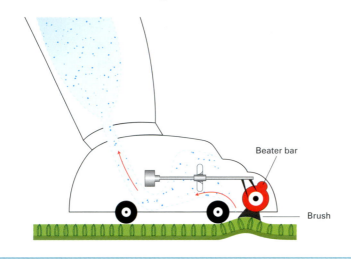

Beater bar

Brush

▶ This Electrolux vacuum cleaner uses a high-speed spiral of air, or cyclone, to produce the vacuum. Cyclone systems do not require a collecting bag or filter and so do not lose suction as they fill with dust.

types of a new kind of vacuum cleaner that dispenses with bags and filters and instead uses a fast-moving spiral of air to create a vacuum. This cyclone action causes dust to be drawn into the cleaner in a spiral path, which creates a centrifugal force that flings the dust to the inner surface of the collecting cylinder. The dust then falls downward and collects at the bottom of the cylinder. Because there is no collecting bag, the level of suction does not decrease as the cylinder fills with dust. In a dual cyclone system, larger particles of dust are first removed using an outer cyclone before the air passes into an inner, faster cyclone that removes even finer particles. One of the most recent models of cyclone cleaner uses eight smaller cyclones to produce still more suction. A further development in vacuum cleaner technology is the use of robot cleaners, such as the Dyson DC06, which contains three computers and 50 sensors to enable the cleaner to guide itself efficiently around obstacles in a room.

SEE ALSO: ELECTRIC MOTOR • VACUUM • VENTURI EFFECT

Vacuum Tube

The term *vacuum tube* is used to describe a variety of electronic devices, also called thermionic valves, that use the emission of electrons from certain heated metals to control the flow of electrical current. All have two characteristics in common: their working parts are enclosed in an evacuated glass envelope (electrical contacts are made through contacts in the base of the container) and all have a thermionic electron emitter heated by an electric element.

Thermionic emission

The emission of electrons from hot metals was first observed in 1877 by the British physicist Joseph John Thomson. This phenomenon forms the basis for the operation of all vacuum tubes.

The electrons in a metal fall into two categories: those that are firmly bound to specific nuclei and those that occupy molecular orbitals that extend throughout the sample of metal—"free" electrons. Free electrons are responsible for metallic bonding and conduction; they can be thought of as roaming throughout the metal. The average speed of motion of free electrons increases with temperature. At low temperatures, an electron that reaches the surface of a metal will overrun the surface only by an extremely short distance before electrostatic attraction to the positive nuclei pull it back into the body of the sample. This situation changes at high temperatures, when significant numbers of electrons possess enough thermal kinetic energy to break free of the pull of the nuclei, just as a space rocket breaks free of Earth's gravity.

In the presence of air or another gas, the escaping electrons are soon trapped as they form anions by combining with gas molecules. The masses of such ions are many thousands of times greater than the mass of a free electron, so ions accelerate slowly in all but the very strongest of electrical fields. In a vacuum, however, the escaping electrons remain free and are easily accelerated by any electrical fields that are present.

Diode

The invention of the first practical vacuum tube device is generally attributed to the British engineer John Alexander Fleming, who produced a vacuum tube diode in 1904. In this device, the thermionic emitter was a graphite or tungsten filament heated to around 4500°F (2500°C) by the flow of an electrical current. (Although not a metal, graphite has a delocalized bonding system similar to those of metals—a property that permits graphite to conduct electricity.) The emitter is alternatively called a cathode by analogy with electrolytic cells, in which the cathode is the source of negative charge.

◀ Vacuum tubes, as seen here in this exhibit in the Boston Science Museum, were once common in radio and telephone systems. They were, however, extremely bulky, unlike modern devices, which are becoming ever smaller thanks to the silicon chip.

Also within the tube was a metal plate, called the plate electrode, or collector. It was placed around one inch (2.5 cm) from the filament, and the whole assembly was mounted in an evacuated glass bulb. If the plate was then set at a positive voltage with respect to the filament by means of an external battery, negatively charged electrons from the filament would be attracted to the plate, and an electrical current would flow. If the plate was made negative, electrons at the emitter would be repelled. Since the plate electrode did not emit thermionic electrons, no current would flow.

This type of vacuum tube is called a diode, since it has two electrodes. It behaves as a nonreturn valve for electrical current, that is, it permits current to flow in one direction only—hence the term valve. At low voltages, the amount of current that flows through a vacuum tube diode increases in direct proportion to the potential difference between the emitter and the plate electrode, provided the emitter is negative relative to the plate electrode, a condition called forward bias. Above a certain voltage, the flow of current remains constant, as it is limited by the rate at which electrons escape from the emitter. This condition is called saturation, and the voltage at which it occurs depends on the composition of the emitter and the rate of heating. Saturation causes distortion

when a diode is forced to operate beyond its capacity, since the output signal is clipped by saturation. The condition where voltages are reversed and no current flows is called reverse bias.

The Fleming diode found use as a detector in early amplitude-modulated (AM) radio sets, and continues to be used as a means of rectifying alternating current—that is, filtering out one direction of current flow to produce a direct current for one half of the alternating cycle. While a diode can filter out one direction of current flow from an alternating signal, it cannot amplify the part of the signal it allows to pass—a distinct drawback in early radio receivers.

Triode

In 1907, Lee de Forest, a U.S. scientist, solved the problem of amplification by introducing a third electrode, called the control electrode, or grid, between the emitter and collector. This electrode was a perforated plate or wire grid, and its purpose was to regulate the flow of electrons from the emitter to the collector, which were set at a permanent forward bias by connection to an external direct-current power supply.

When the grid was at a negative voltage relative to the emitter, its repulsive electrical field would negate the attractive field of the collector

▼ This diagram illustrates, from left to right, a diode, a triode, and a tetrode. In each case, the emitter, or cathode, is the heated element at the center of the tube, and the collector, or anode, is the cylindrical outer sleeve. The triode and tetrode devices have, respectively, one and two grid electrodes between the main electrodes.

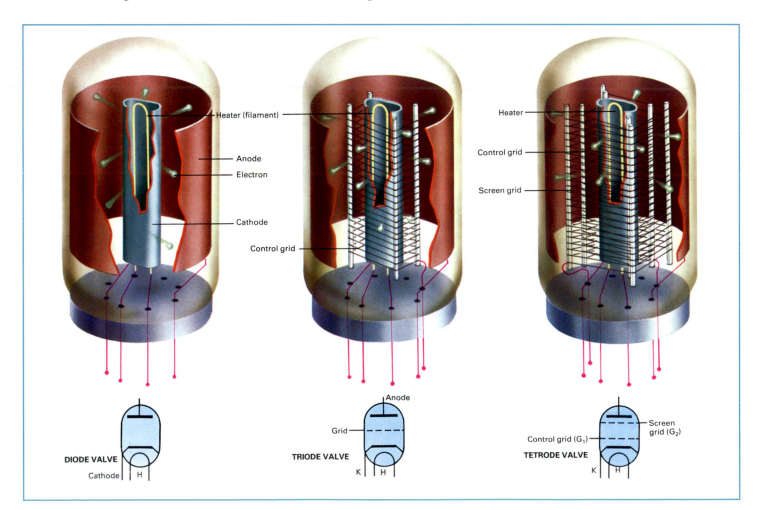

Heater (filament)
Anode
Electron
Cathode
Control grid

DIODE VALVE
Cathode | H

Heater
Control grid
Screen grid

Anode
Grid
TRIODE VALVE
K | H

Heater
Control grid
Screen grid

Screen grid (G₂)
Control grid (G₁)
TETRODE VALVE
K | H

and impede the flow of electrons. When the grid was neutral with respect to the emitter, the triode would act as a normal diode in forward bias. When the grid was positive with respect to the emitter, its attractive electrical field would add to the attractive field of the collector and boost the flow of electrons to the collector.

Since the grid was placed nearer to the emitter than to the collector, small variations in grid voltage would cause a much larger variation in the anode-to-cathode current. The triode could therefore be used as a kind of amplifier.

Improvements

Improvements in the vacuum of tubes made possible the introduction of more efficient electron emitters that would have burned up in soft vacuums. An important example was the thoriated tungsten filament, introduced in 1915, which was made by adding 1 to 2 percent thorium oxide (ThO_2) to tungsten powder before melting and drawing it as a wire. The addition improved the emission efficiency of the filament—the number of electrons produce at a given rate of heating—and extended its life. Its operating temperature was also lower, at around 3600°F (2000°C).

Another improvement introduced around this time was the indirectly heated cathode. Whereas early electron emitters took the form of fine wire filament heated directly by the passage of electrical current, the indirectly heated emitter took the form of an oxide-coated nickel sleeve surrounding an insulated tungsten heating filament. This structure improved the emission qualities of the cathode by keeping the heater electrically separate from the emitter. Most modern tubes have indirectly heated oxide-coated emitters.

In 1927, Albert Wallace Hull introduced the four-electrode vacuum tube, or tetrode. He placed an additional screen electrode between the collector and grid of a triode, where it provided an electrostatic shield and greatly improved the frequency range of the vacuum tube. The gain of the tube was increased by a factor of around 10 compared with the triode, and thus, it became possible to reduce the number of stages required for a given amplification factor.

In 1928, a fifth electrode—the suppressor—was added to form a pentode vacuum tube. The extra electrode was placed between the screen and collector to improve the performance of the vacuum tube at low anode voltages. This form of vacuum tube proved to have excellent characteristics over a wide frequency range but is no longer in general use for receiving purposes.

Applications and limitations

The middle decades of the 20th century saw vacuum tubes used as amplifiers and other electronic circuit components in devices for radio, television, telecommunications, radar, oscillators, and computing and many other applications. Their drawbacks are numerous, however. Delicate filaments and glass construction make vacuum tubes prone to damage by shock and vibration. Also, their physical bulk, the power demand of their heaters, and their rate of heat production make them unsuitable for portable battery operation. In addition, the tube heater has a relatively short life, and when it fails, the tube has to be replaced.

Semiconducting transistors perform well in many of the tasks of vacuum tubes, while suffering few of their drawbacks. Around 1960, transistors became available in commercial quantities and have replaced tubes in many fields, with the resulting possibility of miniaturization.

Vacuum tubes have not been made entirely redundant by semiconductors, however, and their continuing usefulness stems from their ability to handle heavier currents and higher voltages than can be managed by semiconductors. Such applications include the use of tetrodes for powerful transmitters and of triodes and tetrodes for particle-physics experiments, where they handle potential differences in excess of 100 kV.

SEE ALSO: DIODE • RADIO • TRANSISTOR • VACUUM

Valve, Mechanical

A valve is a device that controls the flow or pressure in a pipe or between the components of a machine. It does so by opening or closing—acting like a gate or a plug. Valves may be automatic—such as a valve operated by pressure against a spring behind it—or nonautomatic, such as a stopcock operated by turning a wheel. A mechanical valve with moving parts is required to provide adjustment to the flow control. It may vary infinitely between the open and closed positions, it may allow intermittent operation controlled by a timing device, or it may provide a simple on–off function.

Types of valves

Valves can be divided according to their function into pressure-control, flow-control, and fluidic logic valves. Pressure-control valves, normally either closed or open, are usually variable between the two extreme positions—according to flow rates and pressure differentials. A good example of this type would be a safety valve, which is held closed by a spring or a weight but will open if pressure—inside a steam boiler or a hydraulic mechanism, for example—exceeds a specified maximum. Another example would be

the needle valve, a tapered pin that moves up and down in a tapered seat to allow a larger or smaller flow. These valves are used in the radiator controls of domestic central heating systems.

Flow-control valves are single-input alternative-output devices that either divert or divide the flow. An example is a hinged plate in a pipe junction, which can allow flow from one input pipe to one or several outputs.

A fluidic logic valve is so called by analogy with the mathematical and philosophical discipline of logic. In its simplest form, it is a multi-input single-output valve that can invert a state of operation from flow to nonflow, or vice versa, as in a logical negation, or combine several states of input to one output, as in a logical conjunction or disjunction. A distinction must be made between fluid logic, in which switching systems are operated by the fluid flow itself, and fluid power, in which compressed air or hydraulic oil pressure supplied by pumps is used to do work.

Spool valves

In fluid-power designs, the logic function can be supplied by spool valves. The spool slides back and forth in a precisely machined cylindrical housing, covering and uncovering inlet and outlet ports as it goes. A spool valve controls the direction of flow of hydraulic oil under pressure to the various components of an automated machine tool, for example. The spool is fitted with neoprene O-rings to prevent leakage of oil past it and is usually operated by means of solenoid switches, which may in turn be operated by limit switches elsewhere on the machine, by a human operator at a control board, or by a computer program.

▼ In this pneumatic pipeline for moving bulk materials by capsule, air pressure builds up as the capsule approaches the valve (1) and opens it (2). A booster fan above then starts up to increase air pressure and close the valve (3).

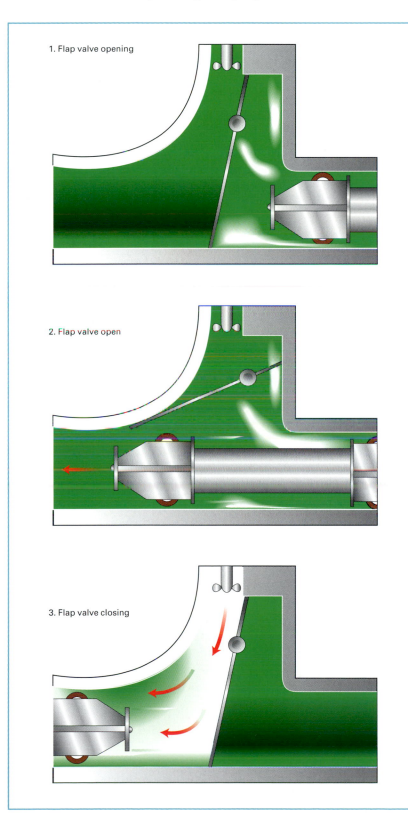

1. Flap valve opening

2. Flap valve open

3. Flap valve closing

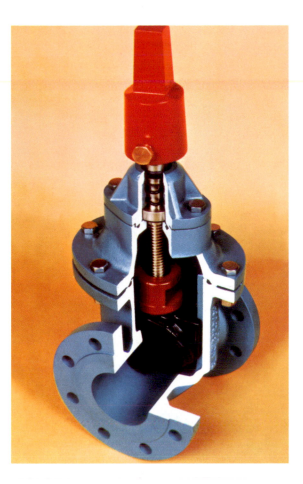

▲ A wedge gate valve for use in a water treatment plant. The gate slides up and down.

The function of these devices is impaired by dirt, so the spool and the body are sometimes cleaned by means of ultrasonics before assembly. A relay valve in a logic circuit is expected to perform 100 million cycles without failure.

The reliability and accuracy of such valves have been demonstrated by the construction of a pneumatic clock, which incorporates a spool valve less than 2 in. (2.5 cm) in length. The clock is operated by one pneumatic pulse per second, at high or low pressure, and keeping the clearance between body and spool at 0.000025 in. (about ⅛ micron), eliminates the necessity for seals. A combination of a spool valve and a needle valve is used in a pneumatic variable-delay timer. In this device, a miniature three-way spool valve is actuated by air pressure in a chamber supplied through an adjustable needle valve. When pressure in the chamber reaches a certain level—after a preset delay of up to 15 seconds—the spool moves to perform a snap-action switching function.

Other designs

Check valves, or nonreturn valves, are used in pumps and hydraulically operated machinery to prevent reversal of flow. The mechanical element may be a hinged flap or a ball fitting in a seat and operated by gravity or spring pressure. Forward flow can open the flap or move the ball, but on reversal of the flow, the valve is shut automatically. Lift valves are nonautomatic valves that have to be lifted vertically in and out of position, often by fitting them to a screw that is turned by a wheel or handle. The globe valve, so called because of the globular shape of its body, is used in plumbing to regulate flow around a 90-degree change of direction. The gate valve has a simple blade or gate as the control element; it is useful only for on–off operation—partial flow around the gate would result in turbulence. The stop valve is a round valve that fits in a round, tapered seal—one of the most common examples is the water faucet (fitted with a rubber or leather washer to prevent leakage in the closed position). The washer must be replaced when it wears, to prevent not only dripping but also damage to the relatively soft metal of the seat. By contrast, a stop valve for steam flow is precisely machined and lapped and intended to provide a tight seal, metal-to-metal. Stop valves in relatively small, low-pressure applications may be unbalanced, but for high-pressure applications, they must be balanced to allow equal flow around all sides of the valve and so equalize pressure on the stem and reduce the torque needed to operate the valve.

Another type of lift valve is the poppet valve, which is used in reciprocating machinery to allow intermittent flow in the appropriate part of the cycle. The intake and exhaust valves in an internal combustion engine are a common example. The valve and its seat are precision machined; the valves are hardened and ground. The valve has a stem fitted with a spring and is operated by timing gear driving a camshaft that pushes on the end of the stem against the spring pressure.

In designing valves for controlling flow or pressure, it is necessary to provide a passage area of definite size for the working medium. The area of the flow through the valve must be equal to that of the inlet, or a speed-up of flow will result. The same considerations apply in calculating the amount of lift for a lift valve; the area of the valve passage shut off by a poppet must be equal to the product of the poppet diameter and the lift.

Also finding application in reciprocating machinery is the slide valve. The sliding surfaces are machined to a precise fit and ground to be smooth and flat—the working medium (for example, steam) provides pressure from one direction, and springs provide it from the other. The valve slides back and forth, covering and uncovering ports—as in the valve gear of a steam locomotive, admitting steam to the cylinder at adjustable intervals.

Another sliding valve is the sleeve valve, a thin steel sleeve fitted between the cylinder and the piston in an internal combustion engine. It is moved in reciprocating and rotary oscillating motions.

The butterfly valve is a circular disk that rotates in a flow passage, operated by a lever. Butterfly valves are found in carburetors and in hot-air heating systems.

Mechanical heart valves come in two main types types; ball valves, such as the Starr-Edwards valve, and disk valves, which are available as either single leaflet disk valves, such as the Medtronic-Hall valve, or bileaflet disk valves, such as the St. Jude bileaflet valve, which is the most commonly used mechanical heart valve in the United States.

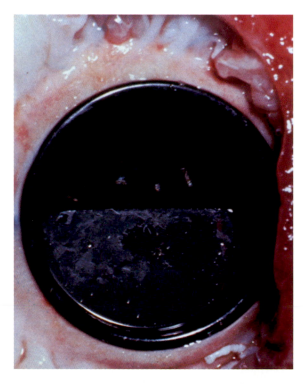

◀ A St. Jude bileaflet heart valve fully closed. First tested in 1976, it is so designed that only minimum pressure is needed to open it.

◀ Valve faces on car cylinder heads can become coated with carbon, here being scraped off.

SEE ALSO: CARBURETOR • FLUIDICS • HEATING AND VENTILATION SYSTEMS • HYDRAULICS

Vapor Pressure

A gas is referred to as a vapor when its temperature drops below a level called the critical point. Below this temperature, a gas may be liquefied by an increase in pressure. Above this temperature, however, a gas may not be liquefied no matter how much pressure is exerted. In the case of water, for example, the critical temperature is 705°F (374°C). The higher the temperature of a vapor, the greater is the pressure it exerts and the harder it must be compressed to change it into a liquid.

Molecules in a liquid have a certain amount of kinetic energy. This kinetic energy varies from molecule to molecule according to a distribution called the Maxwell-Boltzmann relationship. Some of the molecules at the surface of a liquid will have sufficient kinetic energy to escape from the attractive forces of other molecules and thus free themselves from the liquid to become a vapor. Some molecules will escape entirely, while others will return to the liquid. This process, known as evaporation, occurs continually on the surface of a liquid, so there is always some vapor in contact with the liquid. The same process is true of solids but to a lesser extent. The pressure exerted by this vapor, the vapor pressure, depends only on the temperature as long as there is some liquid present. Gas pressure is different—it depends on the volume of the gas as well as the temperature. In a gas, if the volume is increased, the pressure will decrease, but with a vapor, if the volume is increased, the pressure on the surface of the liquid decreases; thus more molecules are permitted to escape, and the vapor pressure consequently remains constant. In liquids where the intermolecular forces attracting the molecules to each other are low, it is easier for surface molecules to escape and become a vapor. Thus, liquids with lower intermolecular forces have higher vapor pressures.

Saturated and unsaturated vapor

When a gas below its critical temperature is reduced in volume, its pressure increases until it begins to condense into a liquid. From that point, the vapor pressure stays the same, and if the volume is further reduced, the pressure remains constant while more liquid condenses. This pressure is known as the saturated vapor pressure of the substance at that temperature and is the maximum pressure the vapor can have. The vapor pressure can be reduced if there is no liquid present, in which case the vapor is said to be unsaturated.

The saturated vapor pressure of water at room temperature is 0.02 atmosphere (about 0.2×10^5 Pa). If a vacuum pump is attached to a container holding water, the water will start to boil when the pressure falls to the saturated vapor pressure, because the liquid water turns rapidly to water vapor to keep the pressure at the saturated value. In general, the boiling point of a liquid is simply the temperature at which the saturated

◀ In this plant for producing liquid carbon dioxide, the pressure must be kept above five times atmospheric pressure, or the gas will condense to a solid (dry ice).

vapor pressure is equal to the external pressure of the atmosphere.

The amount of water vapor in the atmosphere can be measured by its vapor pressure, which ranges from the saturated value in still air in contact with water to practically zero in deserts. The relative humidity is the ratio of the actual vapor pressure to the saturated vapor pressure at that temperature and is measured by a hygrometer.

Clouds and dew

The dew on the grass in the morning is caused by the pressure of the water vapor in the air falling below its saturated value. Cold air can hold less water vapor than warm air, so near the ground, where it is coldest, the vapor condenses to form droplets of water. Clouds are formed by a similar process. Warm, moist air rises into cooler upper regions of the atmosphere. At this lower temperature, the moisture content is too great, and some of it condenses to form droplets. The British physicist Lord Kelvin showed that the saturated vapor pressure for small drops is greater than it is for large drops, because of the surface tension of the liquid. As a result, even when the water vapor pressure in clouds becomes greater than the theoretical saturated vapor pressure, it will not spontaneously form into small droplets.

▲ In the wake of an aircraft traveling at the speed of sound, a region of low pressure is produced that falls below the vapor pressure of gaseous water and causes the water to condense and form a cloud.

Water droplets therefore need nuclei of small dust particles or salt crystals on which to condense. The artificial production of clouds depends on spreading seeds of crystals, such as silver iodide, in regions of supersaturated water vapor—this method provides nuclei on which the droplets can condense.

A similar consideration lies behind the use of a cloud chamber in nuclear physics. High-energy particles pass through a chamber containing supersaturated vapor, and they disrupt the air molecules to give electrically charged ions. These ions are very efficient as nuclei for cloud formation, and the path of a particle is visible as a line of water droplets condensed on the ions.

Supersonic aircraft also produce clouds as they pass through the sound barrier. This phenomenon occurs because, as the aircraft reaches this speed, it produces a region of low pressure immediately in its wake. When this region of low pressure falls below the vapor pressure of gaseous water, the water condenses and forms a cloud.

The saturated vapor pressure of solids is much lower than that of liquids—the stronger chemical bonds prevent molecules from escaping readily from the surface. Solids, however, can sublime directly from the solid to the gaseous state, as can be seen when snow disappears without melting on a cold dry day. Solid carbon dioxide (dry ice) cannot exist as a liquid at atmospheric pressure, and it changes directly from solid to gas at −108°F (−78°C), the temperature at which the saturated vapor pressure is 1 atmosphere (the sublimation point).

FACT FILE

- In arid countries, farmers surround trees and vines with shallow, circular pits of stones that, at night, cool more swiftly than the earth around them. Because the saturated vapor content is too high for the air that has cooled above the stones, some of the vapor condenses, and thus dew forms.

- Cloud seeding provides condensation nuclei for water vapor. Scientists estimate that a single dry-ice pellet falling through a cloud two-thirds of a mile thick could cause 100,000 tons (90,700 tonnes) of snow to fall. This reaction would release heat equivalent to the Hiroshima atomic explosion.

- Fog, occurring when surface air is close to the dew point, provides earth moisture in tropical regions near the sea. In Tasmania, Australia, and the Hawaiian Islands, earth moisture from fog alone can be as high as 20 in. (0.5 m) per month.

SEE ALSO: AIR • GAS LAWS • HYGROMETER • METEOROLOGY • PRESSURE • SURFACE TENSION • WATER

Vault Construction

◄ The nave in Exeter Cathedral, England, showing the complex arrangement of ribbed vaults supporting the roof.

Since the principal reason for building is to enclose space, an important problem for the architect or builder has always been the construction of the roof. Wherever wood was abundant, it was always the easiest material to use; vaults of stone or brick evolved in countries where wood was scarce. Later they were felt to be desirable in well-wooded countries too because of their great strength, finer appearance, and better protection against fire. However, vaults in European countries are nearly always protected from above by wooden roofs covered usually with stone slates, tiles, lead, or copper.

The simplest kind of vault is a tunnel, or half-barrel, round-arched and borne on continuous lengths of wall. Vaults of this kind were constructed by the Assyrians and by the Romans—on an enormous scale in Rome itself, thanks to the presence locally of materials (a sandy earth known as pozzolana and lime) from which a very strong concrete could be produced. Roman vaults were usually coffered: coffers are sunken panels, square or polygonal and often in diminishing perspective, introduced not only for ornamental purposes but also to reduce weight.

Where two vaults intersect, their arched surfaces meet to form lines known as groins. The simple barrel vault was improved by combining it with a series of transverse vaults of equal widths; the result was a groined vault, which is the characteristic vault of Romanesque architecture. Its practical advantage was that the load was concentrated at the four corners of each bay; it thus allowed the insertion of larger windows and openings into the side aisles. As long as all the arches remained semicircular, the proportions were rigid—each bay could only be an exact square, and the resulting groins formed arches of a weak, elliptical shape.

Gothic vaults

The introduction of the pointed arch dealt with both of these disadvantages. If the apex of the vault is lifted to a point, it can be intersected at right angles by a narrower vault climbing to a sharper point. The resulting bay will be rectangular, and the intersection of the vaults can be made to produce a groin that is semicircular rather than elliptical. This basically simple discovery was exploited by the Gothic architects with infinite resourcefulness. Between 1100 and 1500 C.E., Gothic-style architecture was used in Europe in many large buildings, of which the cathedrals are the most famous.

Another innovation in vault design mainly associated with Gothic architecture is the appearance of ribs, which seem to strengthen the groins. It was believed that the whole weight of a Gothic vault was carried by the skeleton of ribs; this idea was proved to be an error in World War II, when at various places, ribs were destroyed without any subsequent collapse of the vault. The function of the ribs, in fact, is not structural but esthetic.

CONSTRUCTION OF MEDIEVAL VAULTS

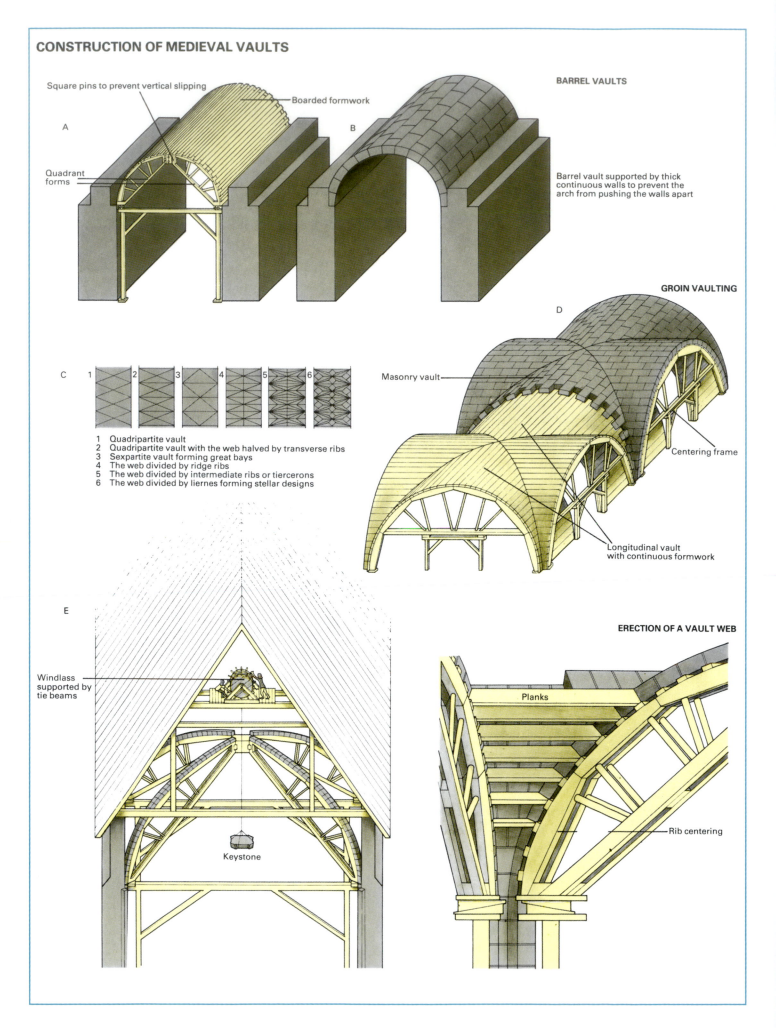

Square pins to prevent vertical slipping

Boarded formwork

BARREL VAULTS

A

B

Quadrant forms

Barrel vault supported by thick continuous walls to prevent the arch from pushing the walls apart

GROIN VAULTING

D

Masonry vault

Centering frame

C

1 Quadripartite vault
2 Quadripartite vault with the web halved by transverse ribs
3 Sexpartite vault forming great bays
4 The web divided by ridge ribs
5 The web divided by intermediate ribs or tiercerons
6 The web divided by liernes forming stellar designs

Longitudinal vault with continuous formwork

E

ERECTION OF A VAULT WEB

Windlass supported by tie beams

Planks

Rib centering

Keystone

▶ A plastic model of a cross section of a cathedral, which is used to analyze stresses in actual buildings. Weights are attached to the model, which is then heated so that it softens and deforms under load. Photographs taken though a polarizing filter reveal the stress areas.

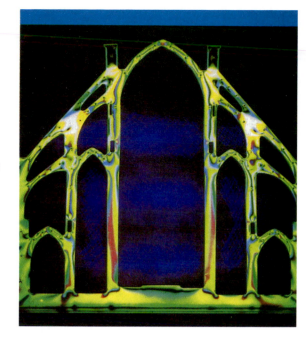

◀ The construction of medieval vaults showing a collapsible framework (A). The framework is removed, leaving the completed barrel vault (B). In (C), plan views of six types of vault are shown, the earliest first. Groin vaulting (D) is the intersection of two barrel vaults. In later vaults (E), the stones are hauled up from the ground below, and the space between the ribs is then bridged with planks (F).

As the Gothic period advanced vaults were constructed with ever-increasing skill. Such skill implied not only finer masoncraft but above all deeper understanding of how to counteract the thrusts that a vault exerts. Thrusts are twofold: downward, through the weight of the material itself, and outward in an oblique direction, through the pressure of the wedge-shaped blocks with which every stone vault is built. The downward thrust was a fairly simple matter—it was carried by the piers, which, as masoncraft improved, were able to become more and more slender. The outward thrust posed a much greater problem. The problem was solved by the development of buttresses and, as the churches grew loftier, of flying buttresses—even, at the boldest French cathedrals, in several tiers. The concentration of the whole thrust of each vault-bay at the four corners meant that the intervening sections of wall, so essential to the tunnel vault, now served no structural purpose. Hence the gradual removal of the walls and substitution of windows, until in the late Gothic period almost every church seemed to consist of more glass than wall.

Development of sexpartite vaults

The first vaults, whether groined or ribbed, were quadripartite—they comprised four compartments of equal size. In early Gothic vaults, an additional transverse rib (the one set at right angles to the axis of the portion of the building in question) was sometimes introduced. This rib divided the vault bay into six compartments (of unequal size) rather than four. This is known as a sexpartite vault and is mainly to be seen in French Gothic architecture but occurs also in England at Canterbury Cathedral.

Subsequent developments were all ornamental rather than structural. First came the tierceron vault. Tiercerons are pairs of ribs that have the same point of springing as the principal ribs but that meet at the ridge obliquely instead of being carried across from one side of the vault to the other in a continuous line. Such a vault is seen to perfection at Exeter Cathedral in England.

Lierne vaults did not appear before the 14th century. Liernes (from the French *lier*, "to tie") are short ribs that neither spring from the capitals nor, in many cases, rise to the central ridge; by crossing and recrossing the more functional ribs, it was possible, with liernes, to make patterns—stars, for example—of great decorative beauty.

Fan vaults

Still more original and ingenious was the fan vault, an English invention of the perpendicular period. It was never better used than in one of its earliest manifestations, the cloisters at Gloucester Cathedral, England. Its essential feature is the inverted half-conoid—a half-cone with concave sides. Each pair of half-conoids just touch at the centers of their curves. By comparison with the tierceron vault, from which it evolved, the fan vault was a step toward standardization. The ribs are not applied separately but are carved out of the surface of the solid block of stone; they are also all equidistant from one another, and usually their curvature is identical.

In fan vaulting it is the central spandrel that is the problem. Here the curvature is almost flat, and the spans are wide. To keep the distance from becoming dangerously large and therefore making the vault unsafe, the only thing to do was to slice off the sides of each fan rather than carrying them around the full 180 degrees. However, as can be seen at King's College Chapel, Cambridge, England, this does diminish the overall beauty of fan vaulting.

Pendant vaults

The final feat of late Gothic virtuosity was the pendant vault. There are both pendant liernes and pendant fans. Good examples of each can be seen in Oxford Cathedral, England, and in the Henry VII Chapel of Westminster Abbey, London, the vaulting of which is supported by hidden arches above the ceiling. These sophisticated vaults were achieved by elongating two of the voussoirs (wedge-shaped blocks of stone), of which each transverse arch is composed; the pressure of the others, properly counteracted by piers and buttresses, holds them in position. Each pendant is carved out of a single block of stone, which could be as much as 10 ft. (3 m) long. Not only

Construction methods

Vaults were built on a very strong temporary framework, known as centering, that consisted of timber framing in the form of the arches and that was the carpenter's responsibility. Once the centering had been built, the stonemason cut the stones to shape at ground level, numbered them, and winched them up as needed to the masons working high on the scaffolding above.

The centering was raised as work progressed, until the wedge-shaped arch stones, or voussoirs, were ready to be assembled on it using thick mortar joints. Finally, at the apex, the large keystone was dropped into place. Although the keystone acted to weigh the ribs against any tendency to rise, it was the shell characteristics of the web itself that gave the vault its strength. The compartments defined by these ribs were then filled in with the web. First, it was necessary to secure planks or lagging between the formwork to support the web. The mason stood on a platform below the vault and, working from the side, laid on one course of stones above the other, his masonry load being balanced by that of another mason working simultaneously on the

opposite side of the vault. Because of lack of space, the last few courses were laid by one mason. Sometimes the web stones rested on the back of the ribs, but another technique was to cut rebates into the rib so that the stones rested on them, separated by the rib stem, which projected upward between them.

was the pendant vault, in a girderless age, a feat of extraordinary architectural ingenuity, it was also a triumph of artistry.

▲ The ceiling of the vaulted Chapter House in Salisbury Cathedral, England.

◀ A vaulted passageway in Olympia, Greece, where games in honor of the god Zeus were held.

SEE ALSO: BRICK MANUFACTURE • BRIDGE • BUILDING TECHNIQUES • STAINED GLASS • SURVEYING • TENSILE STRUCTURE • WOODWORKING

Vending Machine

All vending machines consist of two basic parts: a system that identifies and totals the inserted coins or that identifies and processes other methods of payment, such as credit cards and prepayment cards, and a system for selecting and dispensing the product required.

Payment systems

The simplest coinage systems are those that require only one coin to operate the machine. They are commonly found in many of the smaller wall-mounted column type of candy machines. Larger vending machines generally have sophisticated totalizing coinage systems that are capable of accepting three, four, or even five different denominations of coins and adding them up to achieve the required product-selling price. Frequently, totalizing channels are also multi-price to enable the commodities offered to be priced differently and to give change for high-value coins when inserted.

All coinage systems have a method for checking the validity of the inserted coins before crediting them. The most common form of checking is mechanical, whereby the diameter, thickness, and weight of the coins are measured. Accepted coins then roll down an incline past the face of a magnet. The magnet causes eddy currents to be generated in the coin as it rolls by, the currents creating drag to slow the coin down. The magnitude of the eddy currents and the consequent drag will depend on the metallic properties of the coin. Coins leaving the end of the incline must travel at the right speed to be accepted. Coins of the wrong metallic composition will travel at the wrong speed and will be rejected.

Although the mechanical method for checking coins is still the most common, there is an increasing trend toward the use of electronic methods. Card-reader mechanisms have been developed to replace coin mechanisms. When cards are sold on a prepayment basis to give x value or y number of vends, the need for coin insertion every time the machine is used is eliminated. A visual LED display on the front of the machine will show the value of each purchase made and the remaining credit value of the card each time it is inserted in the machine.

By incorporating a memory chip in the coin- or card-mechanism circuitry, sales data can be retained within the machine for extraction and printout each time the machine is serviced.

Among other alternatives to the coin-operated machines are those with photoprocessors and

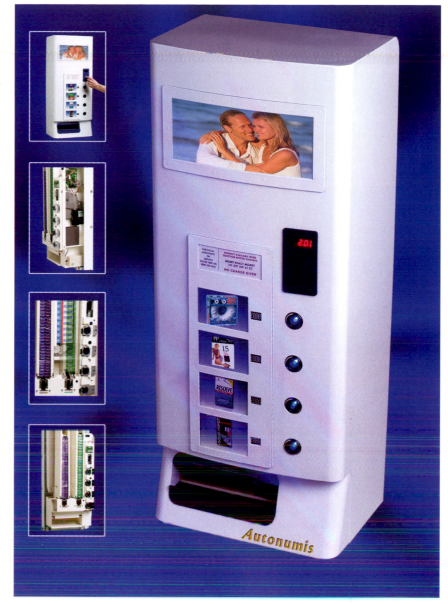

▲ This Autonumis vending machine can be used to dispense products ranging from suntan oil to toothbrushes. The left-hand inserts from top show payment being made, electronic validation of the coinage, insertion of the products into the machine, and the modular method of installation.

magnetic properties, able to accept bank notes and credit cards, and the sophisticated system that is activated by a holographically printed card.

Hot drinks

Hot-drinks machines form one of the largest sectors of the vending market. Instant ingredients are usually used to make coffee, tea, chocolate, and soup drinks, all of which can be dispensed by the same machine. These instant ingredients are often no different from those found in the home.

Nearly all cycles start with the dispensing of a cup into the cup station ready for the acceptance of a drink. The cups are stored in stacks in the dispenser mechanism, with the bottom cup being separated from the stack each time a drink is required. Vending cups are made from plastic or coated paper.

Cold water is taken from a normal water supply and is heated in a boiler inside the machine to a temperature of about 180°F (82°C). The final drink temperature will be about 165°F (74°C), suitable for immediate consumption. The mixing of drinks takes place in funnel-shaped mixing bowls. Hot water is injected at the top of the bowl, from where it swirls around and down to the outlet at the bottom. Measured amounts of the ingredients are dropped into the swirl of water, where they are dissolved to make the required drink before passing from the mixing bowl into the cup. Chocolate and soup drinks usually pass from the mixing bowl into a whipper chamber to ensure a better mix before passing into the cup.

For those who prefer conventional methods of producing drinks, machines using tea leaves or coffee grounds are available. The leaves or grounds are compressed in hot water to allow infusion to take place before dispensing.

Cold drinks

The coinage, selection, and cup-dispensing systems of cold-drinks machines are identical to those in hot-drinks machines. The ingredients are stored in the machine in the form of concentrated syrups, which on dispensing, are mixed with still or carbonated cold water.

Water is chilled by a refrigeration unit to a temperature of about 37 to 43°F (3–6°C). The cold water can then be mixed with syrup in the correct proportions to make a still drink. For carbonated drinks, the cold water must be passed first into a carbonator to allow carbon dioxide gas to be added.

In the carbonator, chilled water is injected under high pressure into a chamber filled with carbon dioxide (itself under pressure). The stream of water is broken up into fine droplets and absorbs the carbon dioxide to give carbonated water. A typical carbonation level for a fairly fizzy drink is 3.5 volumes of carbon dioxide for every volume of drink (at normal temperature and pressure). Other types of drink in the same machine usually require a lower carbonation level (orange would be at about 2.5 volumes), and this level is usually achieved by diluting the highly carbonated water with still water.

Other types of machines

Many drinks machines now combine both hot- and cold-drink selections and are programmed to use either their hot-water or chilled-water

◄ A drink-vending machine.
1) Cup-dispenser unit.
2) Water reservoir tank.
3) Ingredient container.
4) Ingredient container.
5) Water filter.
6) Beverage-selector mechanism.
7) Total-vends counter.
8) Drinks preset counter.
9) Display-sign light starters.
10) Cold-drinks counter.
11) Display-sign light chokes.
12) Display-sign lights hinged mounting.
13) Clear-view vend door.
14) Coin-selector mechanism.
15) Coin box.
16) Cooler unit water-filler plug.
17) Cooler unit.
18) Hot-water tank thermostat.
19) Grill.
20) Waste bucket.
21) Waste-bucket-overflow cut-off switch.

circuitry, according to the selection signaled by the push-button array on the front of the machine. With the incorporation of electronically controlled dispenser mechanisms, variations in the ingredients can be obtained to provide a high-, medium-, or low-density drink to suit the taste of the consumer. Such machines can provide up to 1,000 cupped drinks in 100 programmable permutations at one filling.

In-cup machines make use of disposable cups that are already loaded with dry ingredients before they are placed in the machine—but the capacity is limited to the number of preloaded cups that can be stacked in the machine at each filling.

Drinks dispensers make use of disposable bottles of dry ingredients that are upturned when placed in the machine to allow a measured volume of ingredient to fall to the cup at each pressing of a button.

Sachet machines make use of individual portion packs of dry ingredient sufficient to make one cup of beverage. Neither drinks dispenser nor sachet machines are fully automatic—manual assistance is required either to move the cup or to open the sachet before a finished drink can be obtained.

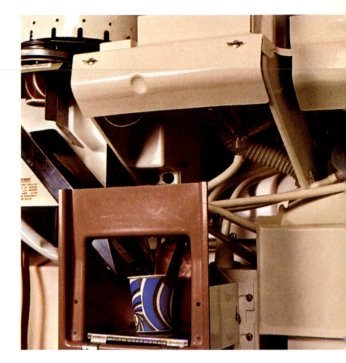

▶ A machine for vending drinks, with the cup dispenser and the various instant ingredient containers. Hot-drinks machines form one of the largest sectors of the vending market.

Carton, bottle, or can machines stock and sell a range of packaged soft or milk drinks. No mixing takes place within the machine, and the product-dispensing mechanism is accordingly simplified. Such machines contain cooling coils to permit their product to be vended at cooled temperatures.

Small items

Various systems are used for dispensing snacks and other small packaged goods.

In drawer-type column vendors, the products are held in a stack, with the bottom item being removed by a drawer mechanism. They are usually small, wall-mounted machines vending chewing gum, chocolate bars, and cigarettes. Alternatively, products may be loaded individually on shelves mounted in columns, as in a drop-shelf vendor. When a product is required, the lowest loaded shelf of the column drops to release it. Rotary conveyor vendors are similar to the drop-shelf merchandizers, except that products are lowered by conveyor to the dispensing point to reduce the drop on vending. For easily damaged items, there are drum vendors, in which the products are stored on shelves in a horizontal rotating drum and are removed by the customer opening a door on the front of the machine. In helix vendors, the products are stored in horizontal trays in a helix mechanism to drive them forward for dispensing. This type of machine has a large number of selections (usually 20 to 30), a large display area, and a high capacity.

FACT FILE

- *The first vending machine is thought to have been invented around the first century C.E. by the Greek mathematician Heron of Alexandria. This machine was placed in temples and dispensed holy water at the drop of a coin.*

- *Drinks manufacturers are currently considering making intelligent cold-drinks machines with heat sensors. These machines will increase the prices of drinks as the outside temperature increases and decrease them as the temperature goes down.*

- *The phone manufacturer Nokia has introduced a new payment concept for vending machine products. To purchase a drink, customers call a number listed on the vending machine; the drink is then dispensed, and the cost is charged to the customer's phone bill.*

- *Vending machines have been used to dispense products as diverse as Levi's jeans, flower arrangements, kangaroo jerky, and diving goggles.*

SEE ALSO: Automatic teller machine (atm) • Digital display • Soft-drink dispenser • Ticket machine

Veneer

A veneer is a thin layer of fine wood that is glued onto ordinary wood. Pieces of furniture and decorative wood paneling are often veneered to give them an expensive-looking finish.

To make veneers, logs are cut to length and then turned against a long knife blade that peels them into sheets the blade is adjustable for the thickness of veneer desired. The logs must be carefully chosen for quality because knots would spoil the veneer. The technique is much the same as that for making the plies of which plywood is made. A typical veneer thickness for a decorative table top would be 0.25 in. (6 mm); after sanding and finishing, the thickness is reduced to (0.16 in.) 4 mm. Veneers range in thickness from 0.25 in. (6 mm) to 0.11 in. (2.8 mm). The latter is termed a structural thickness and is unusual.

The veneers are sorted and graded for quality and trimmed as necessary to remove defects. Veneers for large pieces of furniture can be stitched together edge-to-edge by a machine. The careful matching of pieces to be joined is essential. The most commonly used adhesive for veneering is urea formaldehyde, a synthetic resin that requires a catalyst, usually ammonium chloride, to set it. In mass production of furniture, however, polyvinylacetate is more commonly used.

Veneer presses are used to ensure even adhesion. A vacuum press consists of a rubber sheet that covers the work; the air is pumped out from under the sheet, and atmospheric pressure does the pressing. A dome press works in the opposite way—a metal cover is placed over the work, and air under pressure is pumped into it. The use of male and female forms in the press allows veneers to conform to curved shapes. Edges of panels can be veneered by a lipping press, which is a combination of vertical and horizontal pressures with high-frequency curing.

Decorative veneers

Marquetry is the formation of intricate (often floral) patterns by inserting pieces of wood, shell, or ivory into the veneers. It is a very old craft, introduced into Europe in the 17th century. The ancient Persians and Egyptians decorated many pieces of their woodwork with inlay. The Egyptians, for instance, used tiles, ivory, gold, and precious stones to decorate chests, coffers, and other furniture of ritual importance.

Marqueters in Persia, India, and China created decorative pieces from inlay picture designs to complex techniques set into wood and tile mosaics on walls and furniture. Small inlay

▼ A factory worker handles a sheet of yellow birch veneer taken from a 500-year-old tree. The piece was cut using the industrial lathe to the left of the picture.

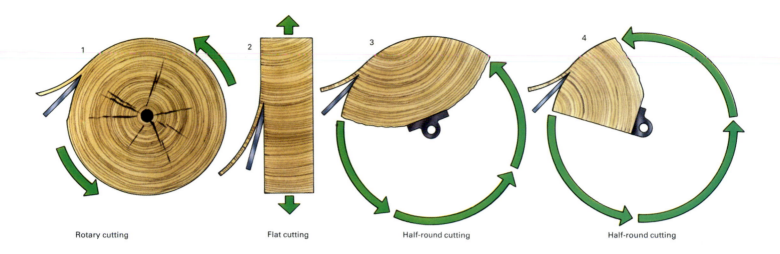

Rotary cutting   Flat cutting   Half-round cutting   Half-round cutting

designs were used to decorate jewelry boxes, chests, caskets, and tombs. Many buildings in ancient Egypt, Persia, and Rome were decorated with exotic mosaic tiles, inlay stones, and ceramics.

In Europe, complicated veneers in delicate patterns were used to decorate furniture and paneling. The patterns were cut in the veneer, and pieces of veneer made of a different wood were inserted or inlaid into it. Further designs were made with hot pokers and wood stains. Intarsia is an ambitious type of inlay work that was developed in 15th-century Italy—the earliest examples comprise pieces of veneer glued to a panel to make a picture, but later, a softwood panel was used as a ground covered with veneer that was then inlaid. Intricate views in perspective of buildings, religious subjects, and so forth were created in this way by such Italian artists as Filippino Lippi and Sandro Botticelli.

Marquetry and parquetry

Originally, the veneers were cut to shape with a fretsaw, but modern veneers are easier to cut and shape with a fine-pointed sharp knife. There are two main branches of marquetry, of which parquetry is the simpler form. In marquetry, most of the cutting is done freehand, and most of the shapes are complex. Parquetry, by contrast, is composed of geometric shapes cut with the aid of a straightedge. Virtually all parquetry designs are composed of a series of simple shapes—squares, triangles, rectangles, and diamonds.

Veneer decorations have largely declined in modern furniture because they require a lot of handwork, and production now relies on extensive use of machines. Also, hard-wearing plastic veneers—such as melamine laminate—are often used, especially for veneering countertops in kitchens, restaurants, and hospitals and on office furniture. Paper or cloth, printed with the desired pattern, forms the outer lamination that is

▲ Four ways to cut veneer. Flat cutting and half-round cutting produce the best grain patterns but are more expensive than rotary cutting, which is mainly used for producing large sheets of veneer.

impregnated with resin during production. Washable and more durable, such plastic veneers can be made in any size and with any color or pattern, including imitation wood grains.

▶ This chair is a fine example of the technique of marquetry, in which thin veneers of different colored woods are inlaid into the body of a piece of furniture to decorate it. Parquetry is a similar, but more geometric technique, used mainly for flooring.

 SEE ALSO: FORESTRY • LUMBER • WOOD COMPOSITE • WOODWORKING

Venturi Effect

The Venturi effect is the decrease in pressure that occurs when the flow rate of a fluid—a liquid or gas—increases through a constriction in a tube. It is directly related to the Bernoulli effect, which concerns the relationship between pressure and flow rate in more general circumstances.

When a volume of liquid or gas is at rest, the pressure at any point is the sum of any external pressure applied to the sample of fluid and the force per unit area arising from the weight of the fluid above that point. This pressure is therefore the same at all points in a horizontal plane within a given sample of fluid—a key principle of hydrostatics, the science of fluids at rest. When a fluid is in motion, the condition of constant pressure at a given height does not necessarily prevail, and the dynamic pressures of fluids in motion are governed by the laws of aerodynamics (for gases) and hydrodynamics (for liquids).

In 1791, the Italian physicist Giovanni Venturi started to examine the behavior of fluids flowing through constricted channels. He noted that the increases in flow rates caused by constrictions were accompanied by reductions in the pressure of the fluid. This phenomenon, known as the Venturi effect, can be demonstrated by holding two sheets of paper parallel to one another and blowing into the gap between them. The sheets form a constricted channel, and the increase in flow rate produces a reduction in pressure that causes the two sheets to move toward each other.

▲ This thrust chamber, seen here in a test rig, is a part of NASA's low-cost Fastrac rocket engine. By the Venturi effect, the increase in diameter from the throat of the chamber to the nozzle mouth helps build exhaust pressure to a maximum at the mouth.

The Venturi effect has since found many and diverse applications, ranging from the measurement of the flow rates of liquids to the production of aerosols of paint in air brushes.

Bernoulli effect

A theoretical explanation of the Venturi effect was postulated many years before Venturi's observations by the Swiss mathematician and physicist, Daniel Bernoulli. In 1738, Bernoulli established a connection between the pressure and flow rate of a fluid by applying the principle of conservation of energy to an idealized incompressible fluid of negligible viscosity and streamlined flow.

Bernoulli's theory can be understood by considering the motion of such a fluid in a horizontal pipe section. If there is a reduction in pressure from one end of the section of tube to the other—from p_1 to p_2, say—then the fluid will flow from the high pressure to the low pressure. For an interval of time in which the fluid advances through the tube by a distance d, work is done by the more fluid entering that section or by a piston in the tube, for example. According to basic mechanics, work is the product of force, F, and distance. The force is the product of the pressure and the cross section of the tube, A, so the work done on the fluid is p_1Ad. More conveniently, the work done per unit volume of fluid is p_1, since the volume of fluid that has flowed through the section is the product of the cross section and the distance moved through the tube, Ad.

At the other end of the section of tube, the fluid in the section under consideration does work on the fluid beyond the section or on a piston that is given by p_2Ad. Hence, the net work done on the fluid in the section, per unit volume of flow, is the difference: $p_1 - p_2$. The conservation of energy demands that this work done must end up as some other form of energy, and so it does: the result is an increase in kinetic energy.

If the velocity of the flow increases from v_1 to v_2 through the section, the increase in kinetic energy is $\frac{1}{2}mv_2^2 - \frac{1}{2}mv_1^2$, where m is the mass of fluid that has flowed. In terms of the energy change per unit volume of flow, which must be equal to the work done on the fluid, this expression becomes $\frac{1}{2}\rho(v_2^2 - v_1^2)$, where ρ is the density (mass per unit volume) of the fluid. Applying the conservation of energy gives the following:

$$p_1 - p_2 = \frac{1}{2}\rho(v_2^2 - v_1^2), \text{ or}$$

$$p_1 + \frac{1}{2}\rho v_1^2 = p_2 + \frac{1}{2}\rho v_2^2$$

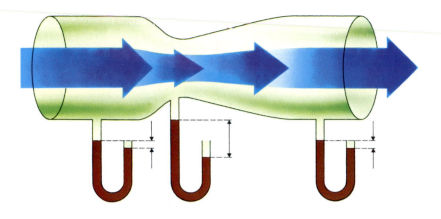

The second of these equations makes it clear that the sum of pressure and kinetic energy per unit volume must remain constant, the implication being that an increase in flow speed (and therefore kinetic energy) must be accompanied by a reduction in pressure, which is the basis of the Venturi effect.

The above description was formulated for a horizontal flow, but it is easily extended to more general cases if one change is made: include the contribution of potential energy to the total energy per unit volume. Since the change in potential energy for a mass m in moving from height h_1 to height h_2 is $mg(h_2 - h_1)$, where g is acceleration due to gravity, the change in potential energy per unit volume is $\rho g(h_2 - h_1)$, and the sum of pressure, kinetic energy per unit volume, and potential energy per unit volume must remain constant:

$$p + \tfrac{1}{2}\rho v^2 + \rho gh \text{ is constant.}$$

Bernoulli's statement of energy conservation is a good approximation for low-viscosity fluids such as air and water. It applies not only to flow through constricted channels—the Venturi effect—but also to the flow around aircraft wings, where the more rapid flow over the upper surface of an airfoil produces lift, and to the flow of air around sails and water around rudders of boats.

Applications

Many of the applications of the Venturi effect take advantage of its ability to create a partial vacuum without requiring a pump. Others use the pressure reduction caused by constricted flow to measure flow rates of liquids and gases.

Air brush and atomizer. Air brushes and atomizers are devices in which the Venturi effect produces reduced pressure in a stream of air. The reduced pressure draws liquid into the stream, where it breaks into droplets and forms an aerosol of paint or perfume, for example. Air from a pump or a hand-squeezed rubber ball passes

▲ A venturi is a tube that has a smoothly profiled throat, or constriction, partway along its length. Pressure drops as the flow rate increases through the constriction, as is shown by the variations in the manometer levels.

through a tube into which a nozzle protrudes. The nozzle serves to create a constriction and to help break the stream liquid into droplets.

Filter pump. The filter pump is a device that uses the Venturi effect to produce pressures as low as around $\tfrac{1}{5}$ atmospheric pressure. It is useful for drawing liquid through filters in Büchner funnels and for producing low pressures for vacuum distillation. A filter pump has a tapered nozzle through which water from a faucet streams downward into a wider cylindrical sleeve. The side arm in the sleeve admits air, and the lower end of the sleeve opens to a drain. The tapering of the nozzle forms a constriction in the path of the flowing water that creates a reduced pressure and so draws air from the side arm.

Flowmeter. A Venturi flowmeter consists of a tube that incorporates somewhere along its length a smoothly tapered constriction, or throat. The presence of this constriction causes the velocity of the fluid to increase. This is accompanied by a fall in static pressure that can be measured. The flow rate can thus be determined, since the pressure reduction depends on the square of the change in the flow velocity caused by the presence of the constriction. The meter is used for flow rate determination of liquids and gases.

ROTAMETER

A rotameter is a device that measures the flow rates of liquids and gases. It consists of a conical float that hovers on an upward flow of fluid within a tapered tube, its apex pointing downward. The position of the float is determined by the balance between the downward force of its weight and the upward forces created by the flow of fluid.

The float acts as a constriction in the tube, as can be seen if the unobstructed cross-sectional area is plotted against height. By the Venturi effect, the result is a decrease in pressure from the lower point of the float to its upper surface. The pressure difference creates a net upward force that makes the float hover. The tube tapers from a larger diameter at the top to a narrower diameter at the bottom, the float settles at a height where the upward force matches its weight. Greater flow rates correspond to higher equilibrium positions, so the flow rate can be read from graduations on the side of the tube. In liquids, this position must be corrected for the effects of buoyancy.

SEE ALSO: COMPRESSOR AND PUMP • CARBURETOR • FLOWMETER • HYDRODYNAMICS • VACUUM • VACUUM CLEANER • VISCOSITY

Vernier Scale

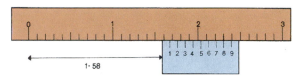

A vernier gauge, or caliper, is a device for providing more accurate measurements than can be achieved with a simple graduated scale. It is used on micrometers and precision instruments, such as lathes, and wherever else fine adjustments or precise control is required. The technique was invented by the French mathematician and military engineer Pierre Vernier in 1631.

A normal scale is limited in accuracy by the number of graduations (divisions) that can be set into the given space. For example, a scale measuring length may be graduated in inches and tenths of an inch. It would be difficult to set or read any smaller divisions, such as one-hundredth of an inch.

To overcome this limitation, an adjacent scale of slightly different size is used—this is the vernier scale. By using this scale in conjunction with the main scale mentioned above, measurements down to one-hundredth of an inch can be performed easily.

The vernier gauge depends for its operation on the difference between the smallest graduation on the main scale and that on the auxiliary (vernier) scale. For the sake of simplicity, this difference is chosen to be a convenient decimal number—for example, one-hundredth of an inch (0.01 in.). It is also normal practice to make the vernier scale that amount smaller than the main scale, although a larger scale can be used if the numbering sequence is reversed. This method is explained below.

◀ A vernier gauge on a microscope stage—each division is 0.9 of the main-scale divisions. The measurement indicated here is exactly 120, because it is the zero mark on the vernier that is aligned with the main-scale marking.

Consider a pointer set against the main scale, which indicates a measurement between 1.5 and 1.6 in., where finding the next decimal place is the object. It is found by aligning the zero mark on the vernier with the main scale measurement and determining which vernier graduation coincides with a graduation on the main scale. In this case, it is 8. The precise reading is therefore 1.58 in.

The reason why is as follows. Each vernier division is one-tenth smaller than the main scale division; ten vernier divisions correspond to nine main scale divisions (0.9 in.). In reverse: if the true reading is 1.51, there is 0.09 in. from the true reading to the next main scale division (1.6), and 0.09 in. corresponds to one division on the vernier scale.

Because the two scales are slightly different, only one mark on the vernier will correspond to a main scale division at any one time. Therefore, the result is unambiguous.

If the vernier scale divisions are made one-tenth larger than the main scale divisions, then ten vernier divisions correspond to 1.1 in., or one vernier division is 0.11 in. In this case, the vernier numbering sequence must be reversed.

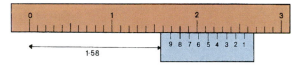

If the true reading is 1.59 in., then there is 0.11 in. to the 1.7 main scale marking. But 0.11 in. is one vernier division from the pointer. Because the vernier scale is numbered backward, this division corresponds to vernier division nine. Likewise, if the true reading is 1.58, then there is 0.22 in. to the 1.8 main scale marking. But 0.22 in. is two divisions along the vernier, and because of the reverse numbering, the vernier number corresponding to 1.8 on the main scale is 8.

The vernier scale can be used to make accurate angular as well as linear measurements.

SEE ALSO: BALANCE • MICROMETER

Veterinary Science and Medicine

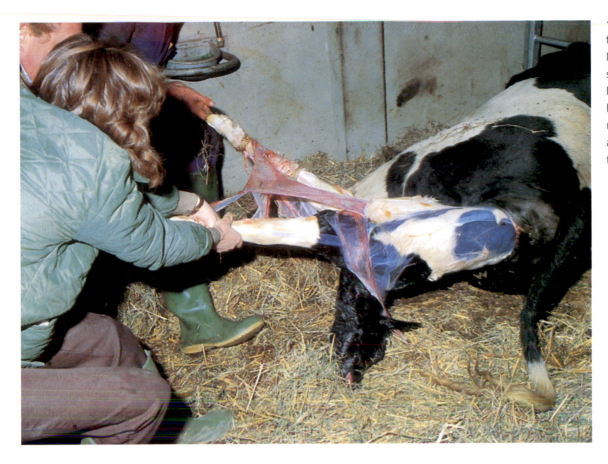

◀ A vet helps with the birth of a calf. Most animals give birth successfully without any kind of help, but as with humans, complications may occur, and some animals would die if they were left unaided.

Veterinary medicine has a long history dating back at least 4,000 years. There is evidence for its practice in ancient Egypt and Babylonia, where the main reason for its development was the treatment of domesticated farm animals. Despite its long history, the first college devoted to the study of veterinary medicine was not opened until 1762 in Lyon, France. Veterinary colleges were then established in other countries in Europe, and veterinary skills improved as scientific discoveries in human medicine enabled similar breakthroughs in the understanding and treatment of diseases in animals.

Veterinary medicine now uses technology every bit as sophisticated as that of human medicine. Veterinarians (vets, for short) have been quick to adopt the latest medical techniques, be they in surgery, pharmacology, or even neurology, and to apply them where appropriate in the two fields into which most veterinary work is now divided: that of small animals, such as domestic pets, and livestock in the farming industry.

Although vets still often carry out both small-animal and large-scale livestock work, there are growing differences between the two, and an increasing number of vets are specializing in one or the other. Vets working in small-animal practices spend most of their time caring for pets—from parakeets to boa constrictors but mainly cats and dogs. The animals are brought to the vets' offices, which are usually located in towns and cities. Vets working within the livestock farming industry, however, deal with a narrower range of animals, such as cows, pigs, and sheep, and travel to the farms to treat the animals. As the livestock industry in the United States, Europe, and Australia has become more intensive, economics has demanded the creation of smaller numbers of large units, often devoted to the rearing of one type of animal—and to ensure maximum profitability, it has been necessary to develop standardized systems of preventive medicine, requiring fewer but more highly specialized veterinary skills in turn.

Small-animal practice

The basis of every small-animal practice is the diagnosis and treatment of illnesses and injuries. In the United States, dogs and cats provide the bulk of the work—immunization against the common diseases of dogs and cats, such as canine distemper, infectious hepatitis, and leptospirosis, is one extremely important function.

Diagnosis of virus diseases and the development of methods of treatment have always been handicapped by the ultramicroscopic nature of

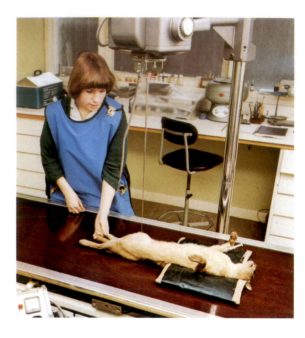

◄ A veterinarian positions an unconscious cat for an X-ray examination of a suspected broken limb.

the organisms. Consequently, accurate diagnosis has always depended to a great extent on serological tests, which reflect the animal's immune reaction to the disease. They have now reached a high level of sophistication and are combined as an enzyme-linked immunosorbent assay—commonly known as ELISA. The ELISA system uses immunoglobin linked to a fluorescent dye coupled with an enzyme.

Viruses can also be readily grown in cell cultures or in the embryos of hens' eggs. The virus particles are identified by staining the culture tissue with a special dye that is fluorescent under ultraviolet light. Electron microscopy is then used to magnify the particles, and the configuration of many viruses is now well recognized.

Eye diseases

It is not, however, necessary to use laboratory tests to diagnose all diseases. The abnormalities that occur in dogs' eyes, for instance, are a good

example. Here the veterinarian requires nothing more than a bright light, an ophthalmoscope, and a darkened room.

A number of specific eye diseases can be instantly recognized by direct examination by experienced people. Some of these abnormalities are especially prevalent in specific breeds—ectropion, for example, in which the eyelid is turned outward, is common in the bloodhound.

X rays not only are used to detect eye abnormalities, they also play an important part in many other aspects of small-animal work, for example, in the diagnosis of bone damage due to accidents. X rays are not always necessary at the diagnostic stage (it is often possible to determine the nature of a fracture by careful manual examination). However, treatments such as splinting by means of a metal pin within the bone and a plate screwed to its surface have to be checked by X-ray examination.

Some diseases of the bone in dogs are hereditary. One such is hip dysplasia—an abnormality in the development of the hip joint—which is prevalent among several breeds. The extent of the abnormality and the degree to which it affects an animal's activity and gait vary. The desirability or otherwise of breeding from an animal can be judged if the degree of abnormality is monitored by X-ray examination of the joint. In this way, a system of what is in effect genetic counseling has been built up in an effort to reduce the frequency of the condition in the breed.

Surgical work

Surgical work in general small-animal practice covers all the emergencies resulting from accidents. Bone fractures, which would be referred to a hospital for treatment in the case of humans, are dealt with as a routine matter by most veterinarians. If unusually complicated techniques are necessary, specialized help may be called in. With the right back-up facilities, extremely complicated and delicate work—such as immobilizing a jawbone with wire—can be undertaken.

The causes of low fertility in livestock are relatively well understood, but the problem has been less well researched in household pets, especially in cats and dogs. In bitches, the common causes of infertility are puberty delayed beyond the normal time of one year of age and, once it is reached, irregularities of the estrous cycle or abnormalities of the estrus itself. Investigation of the problem relies, apart from physical examination of the animal itself, on the use of smears from the cells of the vagina and bacteriological examination of vaginal discharge. The diagnosis of male infertility is based on examining specimens of semen.

▼ A thin flexible endoscope is used to locate a nasal blockage in a racehorse.

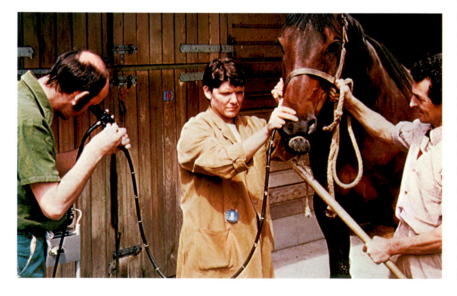

◀ A rhinoceros being loaded onto a truck ready for removal to new pasture as part of a wildlife conservation program in Africa. Below: The rhinoceros is sedated by a veterinarian before removal because of its size, weight, and aggressive disposition.

Routine surgery of the reproductive organs is well within the scope of all practices—the ovaro-hysterectomy (spaying) of cats and dogs and the caesarean section of bitches are normal tasks. The removal of neoplasms (tumors) and monitoring of their characteristics are almost daily occurrences. More complicated problems, such as surgery on the intervertebral disks or carbon-fiber strengthening of ligaments, are referred to specialists.

The scope of medical work is similarly wide-ranging, varying from the treatment of elderly dogs with heart disease to kittens with abnormalities of the kidneys. However, diagnosis is not always straightforward and often has to rely on laboratory aid. Among the most frequently encountered medical problems are those associated with diseases and abnormalities of the skin.

Treatment of skin diseases

Skin problems in cats and dogs may be due to ectoparasites, fungi, allergy, or bacterial infection. The specific cause may become obvious from superficial inspection, since fleas, ticks, and lice can be seen and instantly recognized. Harvest mites, which are small and cannot be detected with the naked eye, leave a characteristic orange-colored rash, which is easily diagnosed.

Such cases are quickly disposed of, although the vet has to bear in mind that several separate causes of skin disease may coexist.

Fungi—such as those that cause ringworm—may fluoresce under ultraviolet light and can be detected by exposing the animal to a suitable light source in a darkened room or else by examining its hair under the microscope. If the normal treatment is unsuccessful, the rather more complex method of fungal culture, which may require a specialized laboratory, must be tried.

In cases where pustular lesions occur, swabs are either examined in the vet's office or sent to a laboratory but in many cases, the tendency is to begin insecticide treatment to eliminate parasites immediately. This saves time and trouble and produces a cure in a high proportion of cases.

Farm animal veterinary work

The small-animal vet may play an important role, but even more important—from an economic point of view—is the role played by the vets that keep the world's livestock healthy; veterinary science is crucial wherever there is a well-developed, intensive livestock-farming industry.

The dairy cow is responsible for the major part of large-animal work in this branch of veterinary science, and a high proportion of bovine work is in turn provided by infertility. For example, artificial insemination may provide from 65 to 70 percent of bovine births in Western countries, and the vet must ensure that infectious diseases affecting fertility are not spread by the bull and that the bull provides adequate and normal sperm. Ensuring that cows conceive is another important function. Many of the diseases that affect fertility, for example, also depress estrus—the period when an animal is in heat—so that the cow may seem to be pregnant when it is not. It is important to detect this condition early on: as pregnancy diagnosis by clinical examination is possible only at about 50 days, valuable time can be saved. The examination of milk by the ELISA technique at 21 to 24 days for the presence of progesterone is another common detection method.

Controlled breeding programs

The size of the problem of infertility in cattle and the fact that financial loss is equated with loss of time have meant that some veterinarians maintain routine examination schedules. New drugs, especially the prostaglandins, are also being developed to control a cow's estrous cycle so that the breeding process can be more easily monitored.

An essential part of the breeding process is the initiation of lactation, which in itself brings its own problems in the form of mastitis—inflammation of the mammary gland. Again the affected cow requires immediate treatment because the milk cannot be used, and in some acute forms, the disease can be fatal. The treatment almost invariably depends on the use of antibiotics.

Calf diseases are also common in dairy herds; possibly as many as 10 percent of calves die in the neonatal stage, with great financial loss to the farmer. Calves depend for their protection against common infectious diseases on concentrated antibodies in their mother's milk, which they can absorb unchanged from the gut only during the first hours of life. When they do not get enough, disease arising from infection can be fatal. Again antibiotic treatment is prescribed and prevention advice given.

Helping to prevent such problems in the first place, however, is also an important part of the vet's job, and he or she can achieve this goal by advising the farmer on how to keep the environment as contamination free as possible.

Unlike cattle, sheep, whether raised for the production of wool or meat, are rarely of sufficient individual value to justify specific veterinary attention. Yet, as with other farm animals, keeping them healthy depends heavily on veterinary science.

Prevention of epidemics

Losses from epidemic diseases can be large. There are at least seven common infections that cause abortion in ewes; they sometimes produce a death rate of one in two lambs born. Parasites of the stomach, intestines, and liver occur frequently,

and all thrive in the conditions under which sheep are reared. In addition, deficiency diseases and diseases of management, such as pregnancy toxemia, demand the attention of the veterinarian. The value of the individual sheep is such that these disorders must be prevented rather than cured.

Vaccines, vermifuge (worming) drugs, and dietary supplements need to be prescribed. They are supplied by the veterinarian after samples, such as blood, placenta, feces, or carcasses, have been supplied to laboratories for diagnosis.

The pig industry in most developed countries is concentrated in the hands of a few large companies that have centralized production in a small number of large units. Profit margins are narrow, and as with sheep, successful husbandry depends on preventing disease rather than curing it. Veterinary advice comes from specialists who devote most of their time to pigs; they have found that the best way of preventing the wide range of diseases to which the animals are susceptible is by long-term planning of facilities and breeding programs.

Zoonoses

Zoonoses are human diseases that are transmitted from or to other vertebrate animals. Such diseases are a major cause of death in humans, especially in developing nations. Consequently the prevention of these diseases in animals is very important and is therefore the responsibility of veterinary science. In total, more than 150 zoonotic diseases are known, including rabies, herpes B, psittacosis, and tapeworms. The methods of transmission vary from bites and contact with feces to walking over infected ground, mosquito bites, and eating

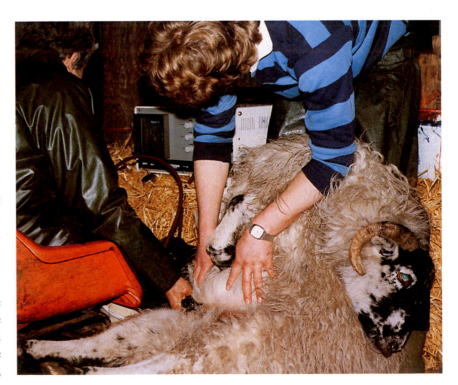

▼ The vet's traditional role in caring for farm animals has been augmented by modern techniques. Here, a pregnant ewe is undergoing ultrasound scanning to check for twins.

◄ A female border collie recovering from an operation during which a steel pin was inserted to help set a fractured femur (thigh bone). The site of the operation had to be shaved, but the coat will quickly grow back to hide the scar.

infected meat. Some diseases, such as tuberculosis in cattle, are prevented from infecting humans by a number of methods, including mass immunization of the cattle, quarantine, slaughter of infected animals, and environmental disinfection.

Bovine spongiform encephalopathy (BSE), a disease that effects cattle, causes erratic behavior and difficulty in coordination and ultimately leads to death. This disease was first discovered in cattle in England in 1986, and a program of eradication was instigated. In 1996, however, this disease was found to have been transmitted to humans via infected meat, causing a fatal human version of BSE called new-variant Creutzfeldt–Jakob disease (CJD). Data suggests BSE in cattle came about by using feeds derived from contaminated meat and bonemeal that contained a related disease mainly found in sheep, called scrapie.

Foot and mouth disease

Foot and mouth disease is an extremely contagious disease that effects cloven-footed animals, such as sheep and cattle, and in the severest forms causes death in up to 50 percent of infected animals. This disease causes a variety of symptoms in different animals but commonly causes blistering and rupturing of vesicles in and around the mouth, the nose, and the udders in females. Although the vesicles heal in about one or two weeks, the animal by this time has stopped eating solid food, with resulting weight loss, and may also be lame as a result of blistering around the hooves. This disease is endemic in Europe, Africa, Asia, and South America and is untreatable. Vaccines are available, but because of high costs and the fact that at least seven different strains of foot and mouth disease are known to exist, each

requiring a different vaccine, this technique of prevention is not widely used. In 2001, a major outbreak of this disease in the United Kingdom led to the culling of more than 1 million animals and severely damaged the U.K.'s livestock farming industry. In this instance, the task of the veterinary scientist was to assist government in the diagnosis and eradication of the disease.

Horse doctors

The veterinary profession was first involved with horses because they were of vital importance as a means of transportation. Horses still occupy much veterinary attention but mostly as sporting animals. The slightest ailment can affect a horse's performance and therefore its racing or show-jumping potential. Thus, the equine veterinarian will have the very latest diagnostic equipment and state-of-the-art operating and hospital facilities, with biometric equipment to monitor the performance of the equine athlete.

Genetic fingerprinting techniques enable each horse and its parentage to be precisely identified from a single blood sample. Any attempt to make a false claim for the breeding history of a horse or to pass off one horse as another can therefore be spotted easily.

Zoo veterinarians

Veterinary work in zoos has acquired a new dimension, as many wild animals are in danger of extinction. Much work in zoos is now devoted to preserving stocks of endangered species. Efforts to breed the panda from specimens in the world's zoos are an example of international cooperation in this field. Many captive-breeding programs aim to successfully return animals to the wild. The Californian Condor, for example, was on the brink of extinction but was saved by captive breeding, and a number of birds have now been returned to

► A wounded venomous puff adder benefiting from the highly specialized skills of a vet.

the wild. Many captive-bred animals, however, need to be taught skills to survive in the wild before they are released. In the Los Angeles Zoo, for example, which participates in more than 45 species-survival plans, tamarins are being trained to survive before they are released into their native Brazilian habitat. The interest in captive breeding has also led to increased knowledge of the behavior and diseases found in species, such as snakes, lizards, and frogs, that are not of economic importance or that are less commonly kept as pets. Scientists are also involved in the conservation of species in the wild. This exercise may involve sedating large or dangerous animals in order to treat them or move them to other locations for breeding or for their protection.

New developments

The role of veterinarians is constantly developing. Increasingly, they are called on to deal with behavioral problems, for example, cats that mess in the house or dogs that behave aggressively to people or to other dogs. Pet psychiatry has now

◄ A tranquilized Nepalese tigress is collared with a radio transmitter that will allow researchers to follow her movements and habits at all times.

become a recognized discipline, and psychological techniques are applied to train out a variety of undesirable behavior patterns.

Dogs and cats can suffer metabolic disorders, obesity, and diabetes, just like humans. Specially formulated diets have been devised to control many such disorders and to restore health and prolong the active life of a loved pet.

Study of some animal disease can be valuable in understanding and treating human conditions. When in the 1980s cats unaccountably started to die in Californian kennels, it was discovered that a virus very similar to the human immunodeficiency virus (HIV), responsible for AIDS, was the cause. This virus, called FIV, had its own similarities to one studied in Scotland in the 1960s, for which a successful vaccine was developed. While the source of the human AIDS virus remains a matter for controversy, it was found in 1992 that the members of the cat family that suffer from FIV diverged from other cats some two million years ago on the evolutionary tree. The implication is that at least one immunodeficiency virus has been around for a very long time.

Not all advances in veterinary science have been universally welcomed. Treatment of animals with the growth hormone somatotrophin can greatly enhance growth rates or, in cattle, increase milk yields without a corresponding increase in feed intakes. Although the hormone is available commercially, considerable controversy surrounds its use. Animal welfarists oppose its use, claiming it can create a health risk for the cow. Growth-promoting substances that economically improve meat quality are also available, but some, based on anabolic steroids, are banned in certain countries.

FACT FILE

- ■ Monitoring the health and welfare of a group of animals, such as a herd of cows, can be carried out automatically. An electronic device, consisting of a microchip connected to sensors and a radio transmitter, enables parameters such as blood pressure (a stress indicator) and temperature (an indicator of infection) to be recorded without having to handle the animals.

- ■ The multifunctional microchip measures about 0.16 in. by 1.18 in. (4 x 30 mm). It is inserted painlessly under the skin at the base of the ear and remains there during the animal's life. Data transmitted from each animal are picked up by an antenna and displayed on a computer screen. A code transmitted with the data identifies the animal from which it was obtained.

- ■ A smaller, simpler device, carrying only an identifying code and without a transmitter, is becoming used in dogs. It is inserted permanently under the skin. Any stray animal equipped in this way can be identified by reading the code with a special scanner. The owner can then be traced and notified that the dog is awaiting collection.

SEE ALSO: Agricultural science • Agriculture, intensive • Aquaculture • Fishing industry • Marine biology • Operating room • Surgery • Vaccine

Video Camera

A video camera is a device that converts a moving image into an electrical signal that—after suitable processing—can drive a television screen to recreate the original moving image. Video cameras differ from movie cameras in that their output is a stream of information that can be recorded on a magnetic tape or other storage medium, whereas the output from a movie camera is a reel of photosensitive film that must be developed before it can be viewed.

Video versus film

One of the main advantages of video cameras over film cameras is that a video recording allows instant replay of a scene after shooting. For this reason, film production teams use video recorders attached to the viewfinders of film cameras to monitor the output of each session of filming. The results on video help them decide whether repeat filming of a scene is needed.

The video format is also better suited to modern editing processes, where sequences of images can be blended and otherwise manipulated on computer before rerecording as a master video for transmission or for screening. In traditional film editing, strips of developed film had to be physically cut and spliced together or reshot through optical-effects devices, and the range of available effects was much more limited than with video. Furthermore, video recording media can be wiped and reused numerous times, whereas film stock can be used to film only once.

Video has the disadvantage of low resolution relative to film, because the photosensitive grains in film are smaller than the elements that make up the image-detecting systems of video cameras. Thus, video recording started to develop first in the television industry, while film remained the dominant medium for cinema—the inherent graininess of a video image is finer than the resolution of a television screen but becomes apparent when shown on a large screen. The development of high-resolution video cameras, hastened by the growth of high-definition television (HDTV), is helping video gain ground as an acceptable medium for moviemaking.

Video cameras have long been a favorite for making home movies, since the format requires no costly processing and the output can be played on standard video-cassette players. In recent years, the scope for more adventurous use of video in the home has been increased by the introduction of digital video cameras, whose output can be recorded on memory cards and transferred to personal computers. At the same time, increased processing power and sophisticated editing software have made it possible for the home movie enthusiast to produce professional-looking results on home equipment.

Lens systems

As with other types of cameras, the function of the lens system of a video camera is to focus an image on a focal plane. Hence, the construction

▲ This handheld video camera has a built-in microphone (above the lens), a motorized zoom system, and a detachable liquid-crystal viewfinder. Progressive miniaturization of video cameras has made them increasingly popular for amateur filmmakers and leisure users.

and features of lens systems for video cameras are essentially identical to those of other cameras. They include compound lenses that reduce aberrations and lens coatings that cut reflection.

The simplest video cameras have a single fixed lens with focusing and f-stop (aperture) adjustments. In some cameras, screw or bayonet mounts allow easy fitting of alternative lenses, such as wide-angle and telephoto units. Fixed-lens systems are becoming less commonplace, however, and most video cameras now come equipped with motorized zoom lenses that cater to a continuous range of focal lengths, from wide angle to telephoto. The zoom is operated by two buttons that control a motor to shift the focal length up or down between its limits. The amount of zoom is usually specified as the ratio between the maximum and minimum focal length, with a ratio of 6 x (or 6:1) being typical.

Focusing can be set manually or left to an automatic focus system that uses infrared or ultrasonic reflections from the objects in view. In either case, the zoom mechanism is designed to maintain a sharply focused image whenever the focal length changes. Lens hoods help reduce glare problems, and filter systems may be used for color correction or special effects. However, color balancing and special effects are more usually achieved by electronic processing.

Viewfinder

A simple camera with a single fixed lens can use a direct optical viewfinder, but more elaborate arrangements are needed where interchangeable or zoom lenses are used. Some cameras have through-the-lens viewing systems that use a beam splitter behind the lens system to divide the incom-

▶ The dark square within the metal frame is an array of charge-coupled devices, or CCDs. The array occupies the focal plane of the lens system, and a charge collects on each element of the array in response to the intensity of light that falls on it. The video signal is produced by reading the charge on each element.

▼ Filming with video cameras allows camera operators to see the result of their efforts more immediately than with movie cameras— images can be output to a television screen for instant playback. The smaller size of these cameras also makes them useful for location work and capturing the more spontaneous moments that may arise during filming, as is often the case in wildlife programs.

ing light between the video optics and an optical viewfinder. This system ensures that the image in the viewfinder is exactly what is being recorded. Apart from a preview of the video recording, viewfinders typically include light indicators, such as LEDs (light-emitting diodes), that warn when battery or tape (or memory) reserves are low or if there is insufficient light for recording.

Electronic viewfinders combine the output of the video camera with warning information in a miniature television display. The fact that the same display can be used for instant playback of recorded material helps ensure that there have been no problems in recording the video signal.

Early electronic viewfinders used miniature cathode-ray tubes to display monochrome images, and the necessary depth of the tubes made them bulky. Modern cameras have flat-screen LCD (liquid crystal display) viewfinders that provide clear images and are much less bulky than their cathode-ray counterparts.

Image detection

There is an image detector at the heart of any video camera; its function is to convert the optical image into an electronic signal for processing and subsequent recording. Older video cameras used bulky image-intensifying tubes to convert images into signals. They have now been replaced by arrays of charge-coupled devices (CCDs), which are much more compact and reliable than image tubes. They in turn are being replaced by CMOS (complementary metal-oxide-semiconductor) devices for some applications.

The smallest element of any electronic image is called a pixel (from "picture element"). An image that consists of 1,000 rows of 1,000 pixels each has 1 million pixels, and the greater the number of pixels, the better is the definition and resolution of a video image. The recording of each single pixel in an image requires devices that can encode the brightness and color of the corresponding part of the image as projected onto a detector array by the lens system.

In some early cameras, color was encoded by splitting the beam from the lens into three and passing one beam each through red, green, and blue filters into three separate detector tubes. The requirement for three bulky image-intensifying tubes made this an inconvenient arrangement. An alternative technique for some industrial applications, such as equipment inspection via fiber optics, allowed a color image to be obtained from a single monochromatic camera. Such cameras had integral fiber-optic lighting systems. In operation, the color of the light supplied by the fiber optics switched rapidly between the primary colors, and a synchronized processing system separated the monochrome brightness images corresponding to each color. These images would then recombine with the appropriate color information to give the final picture.

In modern cameras, a single detector array has a triplet of CCDs for each pixel. Each CCD in a given triplet is filtered for one of the three primary colors, so the three color images can be recorded simultaneously by a single detector.

Solid-state detectors

The basis of the operation of charge-coupled devices is the interaction of photons of light with photodiodes. For each row of CCDs in a detector array, the equivalent of a film frame starts with a charging period, called integration, in which photons cause charge to accumulate in the CCDs. The amount of charge that accumulates in a given CCD is dictated by the number of photons that fall on it in the integration period. At the end of integration, a change in a control voltage causes the charges to drain off at one end of the row.

Charge from the CCDs closest to the output arrive first, followed by the charge from each successive CCD along the row. The charges form a current whose strength varies in proportion with the variation of light along the row during the integration period. When the control voltage changes again, that row of CCDs starts the next integration period, and charges from the next row of CCDs continue the signal. The output from an array of CCDs is therefore an analog signal that, coupled with an appropriate scanning signal, could reproduce the image on a television screen that had the same number and arrangement of pixels as are in the detector array.

CCDs are sensitive to a wide range of light intensities but are limited by the amount of charge each CCD can hold. In high-intensity lighting, the CCDs can reach their maximum charge level and start spilling charge into their neighbors, the charge causing a distortion, or bloom.

▲ The introduction of portable video cameras for television work greatly increased the scope for location recordings of drama and documentary programs, as well as for news broadcasting.

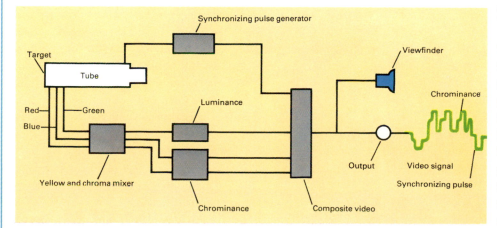

Diagram labels: Synchronizing pulse generator · Target · Tube · Viewfinder · Chrominance · Red · Green · Blue · Luminance · Yellow and chroma mixer · Output · Video signal · Synchronizing pulse · Chrominance · Composite video

SIGNAL PROCESSING

The retrieval of image information from the pixels of a detector array or tube is started by a synchronization (sync) pulse. The signal from the detector is then color balanced and separated into luminance and chrominance signals. They are then recombined with the sync pulse to form a composite video signal that drives the viewfinder and can be recorded on tape or stored on a memory card as compressed data.

The signal that passes from an array of CCDs is digitized by an analog-to-digital converter (ADC). In digital form, the video signal is easier to manipulate and more robust against interference than an analog signal.

Although conventional CCDs are based on composite structures of metal, silicon oxide, and semiconductor, the term *CMOS detector* refers to a slightly different arrangement, in which each photodiode has associated transistors that amplify its output and feed it through dedicated conducting wires to a contact at the edge of the chip. CMOS detector arrays have the advantages that they use less power than CCDs, thus, they are better for portable, battery-operated applications. Also they can be manufactured on the same production lines as other integrated circuits, so costs are low when compared with CCDs. The disadvantage is that proportionately less space on the array is occupied by photodiodes, and more is given over to transistors, so CMOSs are less light-sensitive than CCDs.

Sound

Video recordings are almost always accompanied by soundtracks recorded simultaneously with the video recording. For convenience, most video cameras include a directional condenser microphone, fixed to the casing of the camera, that records sounds originating close to the line of sight. This system is usually satisfactory for close-range filming, but telephoto shots require greater exclusion of ambient sounds near the camera in favor of sounds originating around the shot. In such circumstances, a more strongly directional microphone, such as a rifle microphone, can be connected through a socket.

Camcorders

Whereas a basic video camera simply produces an output signal that can be fed to other equipment, such as a separate video recorder or a microwave transmitter for electronic news gathering (ENG), a camcorder has an integral recording device.

Early camcorders recorded on standard magnetic video tape in Betamax or VHS formats. They are gradually being superseded by cameras that record in compressed digital data formats on interchangeable memory cards. One of the advantages of a memory card is that it is smaller than a video cassette and hence more suitable for incorporation into handheld cameras. This compactness has made camcorders popular for home use. The other main advantage is that the recording format is more appropriate for downloading onto computers, where it can be edited or used to produce short clips for inclusion in websites.

WEBCAM

The ability of the Internet to convey visual information in digital form led to the development of the webcam, an image-detecting device intermediate between a low-resolution digital camera and a video camera. A webcam uses charge-coupled devices to produce still digital images that are refreshed, or updated, on a frequent basis. It then passes this data signal to a computer—usually straight through a cable connection but sometimes through a radio link to a base station that is itself connected to the computer.

The refresh frequency is often much lower than the frame rate of a true video camera, and moving images are at best jerky. However, the low refresh rate has the advantage of generating information at a slower rate than would be required for real-time video and is therefore more appropriate for the data transfer rates of most Internet connections. Webcams are put to various uses—from providing a stream of images to accompany the voice signal in an Internet-protocol (IP) telephone call to providing website images of famous monuments, streets, and beaches that vary throughout the day.

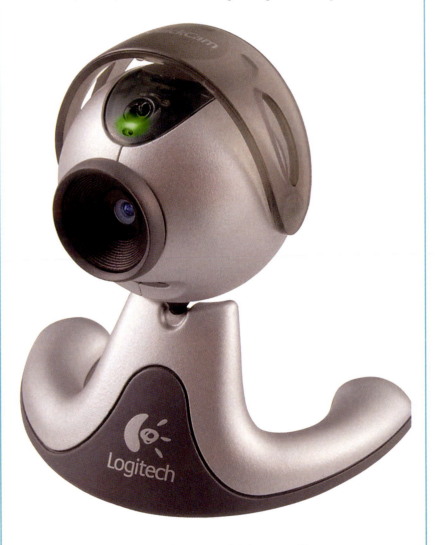

▲ Webcams have become part of many people's home or office computer system. Although there is a slight time delay between frames, users can see each other online, giving a more personalized feeling to computer communications.

SEE ALSO: CAMERA, DIGITAL • CHARGE-COUPLED DEVICE • IMAGE INTENSIFIER • LENS • MOVIE CAMERA • MOVIE PRODUCTION

Index

Page numbers in **bold** refer to main articles; those in *italics* refer to picture captions.